Contracts

William H. Eldridge

PRENTICE HALL PARALEGAL SERIES

Prentice Hall
Upper Saddle River, New Jersey 07458

Library of Congress Cataloging-in-Publication Data

Eldridge, William H.
 Contracts / William H. Eldridge.
  p. cm.
 Includes index.
 ISBN 0-13-565961-2
 1. Contracts—United States. 2. Legal assistants—United States—
Handbooks, manuals, etc. I. Title.
KF801.Z9E5 1998
346.7302—dc21   97-1783
                CIP

Acquisitions Editor: Elizabeth Sugg
Director of Production and Manufacturing: Bruce Johnson
Managing Editor: Mary Carnis
Editorial/Production Supervision: Inkwell Publishing Services
Manufacturing Buyer: Edward O'Dougherty

© 1998 by Prentice-Hall, Inc.
A Division of Simon & Schuster
Upper Saddle River, New Jersey 07458

Printed in the United States of America

10 9 8 7 6 5 4 3 2 1

ISBN 0-13-565961-2

PRENTICE-HALL INTERNATIONAL (UK) LIMITED, *London*
PRENTICE-HALL OF AUSTRALIA PTY. LIMITED, *Sydney*
PRENTICE-HALL CANADA INC., *Toronto*
PRENTICE-HALL HISPANOAMERICANA, S.A., *Mexico*
PRENTICE-HALL OF INDIA PRIVATE LIMITED, *New Delhi*
PRENTICE-HALL OF JAPAN, INC., *Tokyo*
PRENTICE-HALL OF SOUTHEAST ASIA PTE. LTD., *Singapore*
EDITORA PRENTICE-HALL DO BRASIL, LTDA., *Rio de Janeiro*

Contents

3
Contracts Requiring a Writing   23

4
The Doctrine of Consideration   35

5
Legal Capacity   45

6
Contracts and Third Parties   63

7
Legality of Contracts   75

8
Ending the Contract and Remedies   91

9
Sale of Goods (UCC)   111

10
Performance, Termination, and Breach (UCC)   125

11
Uniform Commercial Code (Title, Risk of Loss, Warranties)   139

Preface

This book is designed to provide a college and paralegal student with an understanding of the basic principles of contract law. It is written in a simple and understandable manner. Contracts provide the foundation of all law. Reading this edition will allow the student to understand the basic building blocks of the law.

Acknowledgments

The author and editors would like to extend special thanks to these experts for their input:

        Karen Holmes, Maria College and Mildred Elley Business School
        Carol Ann Palso, Bergen Community College
        Robert Loomis, Spokane Community College
        Gail M. Krebs, Commonwealth College

William H. Eldridge
Kean College

1 *Introduction to Contracts*

Students will learn that contracts are agreements between two or more persons that the law will enforce. Conversely, certain agreements that the parties may have thought would be binding will not be enforced by the courts. Students will learn to distinguish between the two. Students will learn the elements necessary for the creation of a legally enforceable contract. These elements include the legal capacity of the parties, a lawful purpose, consideration (an exchange of values or significant detriments), promises to do certain acts, and execution in proper form.

Students will learn how contracts are created. Contracts are created by the acceptance by one party of an offer made by the other party. The contract may be formed by an exchange of promises (bilateral contract) or by the performance of one act in exchange for the promise to perform another act (unilateral contract).

Students will learn the importance of carefully defining the terms of the contract. At common law, the parties had to have a precise agreement on all major terms in order for there to be a legally binding contract.

This is called a "meeting of the minds" and is one of the essential elements of a contract.

Students will learn how to classify contracts. Contracts can be classified in various ways. These classifications help lawyers identify contracts and form the basis for legal analysis. They relate to the ways in which offers are made and accepted, the manner in which the agreement was reached, the legal capacity of the parties, and the status of the contract with respect to its completion.

ESTABLISHING THE CONTRACT

Student Skill: Attorneys are responsible for drafting contracts. Paralegals can assist attorneys in developing legal contracts that protect clients.

An important part of the legal environment of business is the establishment of contractual relationships between individuals or organizations. A contract establishes the responsibilities of each party to the business relationship and the basic purposes underlying their duties.

Because contracts form the basis for much of the law relating to business transactions, the study of contracts is perhaps the most important part of the preparation for a career as a paralegal. It is extremely useful for paralegals to know enough about contracts to assist attorneys with whom they work in the preparation of contracts that will benefit their clients.

A contract is an agreement, normally relating to business matters, that the law will enforce. The common or judge-made law of contracts requires that an enforceable contract be definite as to all the major terms. This is sometimes called a meeting of the minds.

The common law also requires that certain additional elements exist with respect to the contract. These include consideration (an exchange of values), legal capacity on the part of the parties, a lawful purpose, and execution in proper form (some contracts must be put into writing).

Typically, contracts contain the names of the parties involved, a description of the subject matter of the agreement, and other important terms such as price, quantity, and the delivery date. The common law, which is derived from centuries of judges' decisions, governs the sale of real estate and the provision of services. The importance of contracts is that they require the parties to perform their obligations. This provides a needed element of certainty in our economy.

<u>**Working at the Law Office**</u>

Contracts form the basis for all business and many personal transactions. The paralegal must be as knowledgeable as possible about all aspects of contracts. A paralegal may be asked to draft all or part of a contract under the supervision of an attorney. The paralegal may find contract provisions in cases, in form books, or in this text. One should check each of these sources to develop appropriate contractual provisions. A good knowledge of contracts will make a paralegal a valuable addition to a law office.

CLASSIFYING CONTRACTS BY TYPE OF OFFER

*Student Skill: **Understanding contracts is an important part of a paralegal's duties.***

An offeror is the party making an offer. An offeree receives the offer. A *bilateral* offer by one party asks the other party to exchange one promise for another promise.

> <u>Example</u> Alan offers to drive Ollie James to the airport for a one-year period for $3,000. If Ollie James accepts the offer, they have created a one-year bilateral contract which will bind them both immediately upon the acceptance. Both parties must perform their portion of the contract. If one of them does not, he will be liable to the other.
> <u>Example</u> John offers to sell a special knife to Lorena for $300. If she accepts, the two parties have a binding bilateral contract. Both parties have exchanged promises. The promises are a sufficient exchange of values to create a binding contract.
> <u>Example</u> Donaldson offers to sell Roberts Whiteacre for $100,000 with a closing date of November 5th. On October 15th, Roberts accepts the offer. They have a binding bilateral contract as of October 15th.

A *unilateral* offer asks the offeree to perform a specific act prior to the offeror performing a promised action of her own.

> <u>Example</u> Mary places an advertisement in the local paper offering a $200 reward for the return of her dog, Fluffy. Sally finds the dog and brings it to Mary. She has now completed the act requested and is entitled to receive the reward. At the time of the exchange of the money and the dog, the parties have completed a unilateral contract.

Real estate brokers regularly engage in unilateral contracts. They promise to find a "ready, willing, and able" buyer for the owner of the real estate.

When the broker finds a person who has the necessary financial resources and is willing to purchase the real estate, she has completed her portion of the unilateral brokerage contract. She is now entitled to her commission and may recover for breach of the contract if it is not paid. This is true even if the owner does not sell the real estate.

> EXAMPLE   Mary signs a brokerage contract with Jones to help him sell Blackacre. Mary finds Smith, who has adequate financial resources and is willing to purchase the land. Jones decides not to sell Blackacre after deciding to build a house on it. Despite his decision, Jones will owe Mary the agreed-upon brokerage commission. She performed her duties and is entitled to be paid under the unilateral contract.

CLASSIFICATION BY HOW CONTRACTS WERE MADE

Another way to classify contracts is by the manner in which they are reached. This classification allows individuals to identify contracts in a useful manner similar to a physician's classification of parts of the body. One method of reaching a contract is through negotiation between the parties. When the terms of the agreement have been explicitly agreed upon by the parties, they have created an *express* contract, either oral or written.

> EXAMPLE   Harry and Harriet discuss the sale and purchase of Blackacre for 12 months. During this period, they negotiate about the price, the exact description of the land, the inclusion of various items on the land, and the closing date for the transfer. Harry and Harriet have created an *express* contract because the major terms have been explicitly defined.
>
> EXAMPLE   Hanson agrees to serve as Chauncey's butler for $300 per week. He agrees to work 40 hours each week and to have two afternoons off every week. Hanson and Chauncey have agreed to an *express* oral contract because they have explicitly agreed to the major terms in the contract.

An *implied* contract is one in which the agreement must be inferred from the conduct of the parties rather than from the words of the parties. The court must find that the conduct of the parties was intended to create a legally binding contract. This is a much more difficult situation to show than in the case of an explicit contract.

> EXAMPLE Bill walks into the local barber shop and sits down in the chair. Donald cuts his hair in accord with the picture on the wall. Neither party says a word to each other. However, the conduct of each party indicates that they intended to create a contract, and the court will rule that the parties have created an *implied* contract.
>
> EXAMPLE Donaldson is sitting on the front porch of his house when he observes a gardener entering the property. The gardener plants a number of trees and flowering bushes on Donaldson's property. Donaldson sits on the porch and does nothing. A reasonable person would have said or done something about the gardener's actions. By doing nothing, Donaldson has created an *implied* contract.

The concept of *implied* contract recognizes that while the parties did not agree to an express contract, it is clear that they did reach an agreement and it should be enforced. One or both parties are stopped from denying the contract because of the acceptance of benefits received.

While the courts will find implied contracts, one may not create a contract by simply engaging in particular acts without some actions on the part of another. If one's negligence resulted in conferring a benefit there will be no implied contract.

> EXAMPLE Johnson is supposed to pave a sidewalk at 101 Rose Street. Instead, he paves the sidewalk at 101 Tulip Street when the owners are not at home. There is no implied contract, and Johnson may not collect any money. There was no conduct on the part of the homeowner that would create a contract. Therefore, no implied contract could exist.

In the above example, there would have been an implied contract if the homeowner had seen the paving being performed. The act of watching the work being accomplished would have been sufficient to create an implied contract.

A *quasi* contract is a contract that the courts will impose in order to do justice or to prevent a person from being unjustly enriched.

> EXAMPLE Nicole suffers a major cut and collapses on the street unconscious. Dr. Lee walks by, stops, and renders appropriate medical treatment. After Nicole recovers, Dr. Lee sends her a bill for the treatment provided. Under the theory of quasi contracts, Dr. Lee would be entitled to receive his fee. A medical doctor is entitled to receive reasonable compensation for medical services rendered. It would be unjust for him not to receive his fee. In addition, Nicole would be unjustly enriched if she did

not pay the fee. She received the medical treatment and should pay Dr. Lee's fee.

The theory of quasi contract does not permit one to recover for the consequences of one's own negligence. If Dr. Lee had performed negligently, he could not recover. For example, if he had operated on the wrong leg, he could not recover any money from the patient for the operation.

CLASSIFICATION BY VALIDITY OF CONTRACT

Student Skill: The paralegal will understand which contracts are valid and the reasons they are valid.

A valid contract is one that possesses all of the elements necessary for an enforceable, binding contract. There are no legal problems associated with either the agreement or the parties to the contract.

> EXAMPLE   Barbara, a 33-year-old woman, buys a new automobile from Blast Motors for $20,000. The written contract provides that the automobile will be delivered on October 1. This is an example of a valid contract because there appear to be no problems with the contract, and the parties both appear to be of legal age and to possess contractual capacity.

A *void* contract is one that is unlawful on its face and will not be enforceable from its inception.

> EXAMPLE   Sampson agrees to murder his business law instructor for $39.97. Because this agreement violates the law, it is void from its inception. Regardless of the parties' intentions, the contract is not legally enforceable.

Contracts that provide for gambling or gambling operations are also void. Similarly, contracts that violate public policy would be unlawful and void.

> EXAMPLE   Sally arranges for a lottery on the World Series and collects $777. The winner of the lottery will not be able to collect the pool of money. This contract is not legally enforceable. The courts will not permit one to benefit from an illegal contract.

A *voidable* contract is between a valid and a void contract. It is a contract that may appear valid, but there is some problem that would allow one party to render the contract void. Often, this problem relates to the capacity of one or more of the parties.

If a person is a minor, or lacks contractual capacity, that person may rescind the contract. The courts have always held that people must have the capacity to understand the nature of the agreement to be bound by the contract.

> EXAMPLE Tom Thumb is a minor who buys a luxury sports car. Because he is a minor, the contract may be voided by Tom. This is an example of a voidable contract because it may be rescinded at any time by one of the parties.

A minor may enter any contract he wants. However, a minor will only be bound by contracts that are for necessities of life. These include relatively minor items such as reasonable food, clothing, and shelter. A minor may rescind any contract that is not for these necessities. This is what makes the contract voidable.

> EXAMPLE Hanson is a 33-year-old man who suffers bouts of severe clinical depression. During one of these periods he purchased a very expensive watch. He was unaware of the nature of the transaction at the time he bought the watch. It appears that Hanson lacked contractual capacity at the moment he purchased the watch. This would make the purchase a voidable contract because Hanson may rescind the agreement as he regains his capacity.

Normally, an adult is presumed to have adequate contractual capacity. However, if he has been ruled insane by a court, any contracts agreed upon by this person will be void from their inception. If the person suffers from temporary insanity, a mental defect, or intoxication, the contract will be voidable.

CLASSIFICATION BY EXTENT OF COMPLETION OF CONTRACT

Student Skill: The paralegal will understand how contracts are completed.

If a contract has been fully completed, it is said to have been executed.

> EXAMPLE Johnson has a contract to build a new home on Hanson's land. When he has fully completed the house in accordance with the contract's specifications, the contract will be regarded as executed.

A contract is regarded as being executory until it is completed.

> EXAMPLE In the above example, the contract would be regarded as executory until the house is completed in accordance with all the contract's specifications.

This classification is useful because it permits people to identify certain contracts at various stages. For example, a trustee in a bankruptcy action has the legal power to cancel all executory contracts. This means that the trustee may cancel all leases between the bankrupt and landlords or tenants and any other contracts that have not yet been fully performed.

SOURCES OF CONTRACT LAW

One major source of contract law is the thousands of cases that have been decided by judges in England and the United States. These cases are known as precedents because they provide guidance to future courts with respect to the law as it applies to specific fact situations.

These cases also offer guidance to lawyers when writing contracts or offering advice to clients. One of the reasons written contracts seem so long to nonlawyers is that attorneys have learned to draft them with a view to many possible future events. Lawyers have become aware of the many possibilities that must be considered when protecting the client.

The other major source of contract law is the Uniform Commercial Code (UCC), which applies to the sale of goods. Goods are movable, tangible items that are commonly sold in the marketplace. The UCC was drafted to be more flexible than the common law. In this way, it more adequately reflects the rapidly changing marketplace.

The UCC was drafted in a way that helps foster the completion of contracts by providing gap-filling provisions. These sections can be used to fill in any terms left out by the parties. At common law, a missing important term means that there was no contract. Under the UCC, a contract might still exist. As a result, it is important to first determine which law applies.

> EXAMPLE Hopkins purchases a new house. The purchase also includes all of the furniture inside of the house. The land and the house would be re-

garded as real estate. The furniture is tangible and movable. As a result, the pieces of furniture would be regarded as goods. However, the crux of the contract is for the sale of the house. As a result, the contract would be governed by the common law of contracts.

EXAMPLE Fudrammer goes to the local computer store and purchases a brand new computer. The purchase also includes a provision for the servicing of the computer. Services are governed by common law. However, the most important part of this contract is the purchase of the computer. This is a tangible, movable item and is controlled by the Uniform Commercial Code.

Because the law under the UCC is different from the common law, one may have different results depending on which is applied. One should look at the facts to determine the most important purpose for the purchase. This is the *predominant purpose rule*. If the predominant purpose is to acquire goods, the UCC applies. Otherwise, apply common law.

QUESTIONS

1. What is an offer?
2. Define a contract.
3. What is an acceptance?
4. When is a contract created?
5. How must an offer be accepted?
6. What is the purpose of classifying contracts?
7. Name some types of contracts whose classification is based on the type of offer.
8. Name some types of contracts based on the method of creating the contract.
9. Name some types of contracts based on whether the contract is valid.
10. Name some contracts based on whether the contract has been completed.
11. What is contractual capacity?
12. What are the elements of a valid contract?
13. What is the difference between a bilateral and a unilateral offer?
14. How is a contract formed in the case of a bilateral offer?

15. How is a unilateral offer accepted?
16. What is the difference between an explicit and an implied contract?
17. How is each type of contract formed?
18. What is a quasi contract?
19. What is an unjust enrichment?
20. Identify some unlawful contracts.

PROBLEMS

1. Smits offers to sell Jones Blackacre for $100,000. If Jones replies that he will buy Blackacre for $99,000, what is Smits' responsibility to Jones?
2. Sandy puts an advertisement in the paper asking for the return of her lost pig, Porky. If Sally reads about the reward, how may she form a contract? What type of contract is this?
3. Sammy agrees to kill his contracts instructor for $300. What type of contract is this? If Sammy performs his contractual obligations, may he collect his fee? Why or why not? What type of contract is this?
4. Dolly organizes a party and wagering pool around the college basketball championships. She collects $600. When the pool's winner asks for the money, Dolly refuses. Is she obligated to make the payment? What type of contract is this?
5. Michael Mason is supposed to fix the front walk at 101 Elm Street. Instead, he goes to 101 Maple Street. While he is fixing the walk, Mrs. Smith watches him, but says nothing. May Mason recover for fixing the walk? What type of contract would this be?
6. Alan Attorney, your boss, has asked you to look at a contract for the sale of real estate. What law applies to the contract?
7. Alice Attorney, your boss, asks you to review a contract for your client to give a concert at a local establishment. What law applies to this contract?
8. Danson has a contract to sell ten television sets to Jones. What law applies to this transaction?

2 *Offer and Acceptance*

Students will learn how a contract is formed. Students will understand that an offer is the willingness to create a contract between the offeror and offeree.

Students will learn that an offeror has the legal capacity to control the offer's terms, and the method and the time of acceptance by the other party.

Students will learn that an acceptance is the offeree's expression of a desire to create a contract in accordance with the offeror's terms.

Students will learn that at common law, the acceptance must be an exact replica of the offer. An attempt to change any of the material terms is a counteroffer and may be treated as a rejection of the offer.

Students will learn that a party may revoke the offer at any time prior to the other party's acceptance. A revocation or rejection of the offer is effective when received.

Students will learn that an acceptance is effective when it is dispatched. This is sometimes called the "mailbox rule" because the acceptance becomes effective when placed into the mailbox.

MAKING THE OFFER

Student Skill: Students will learn how a contract is formed.

An offer is the indication by one person that he is willing to create a contract with another. The offeror may control all the terms of the offer as well as the method and timing of the acceptance. As a result, the offeror bears most of the risk if some problem occurs in the process relating to the completion of the offer and acceptance. The offeree is a person to whom the offer has been communicated. That person may accept the offer.

At common law, there must be an exact agreement on all of the material terms relating to the contract. If one of these terms is missing or left out of the agreement, there is no enforceable contract and the discussions will have been meaningless.

> EXAMPLE The parties to an agreement reach a complete understanding as to all the terms except the date for its performance. They do not have a binding contract at common law. If the agreement relates to real estate or the provision of services, it will not be legally enforceable.

A *bilateral* offer is one that requests the offeree to make a promise in return for another promise. If the offeree accepts the offer, there is a legally enforceable contract from the moment of acceptance.

> EXAMPLE Donaldson offers to sell Blackacre to Johnson for $100,000 with a closing date of October 10th. If Johnson says that he will accept the offer, the parties have a contract immediately. If either party withdraws from the agreement by not performing, the other party may bring an action for breach of contract and recover money damages.

As noted in the previous chapter, a *unilateral* offer requests the other party to perform an act in exchange for a promise by the offeror. The offer is phrased in a different manner than a bilateral offer.

> EXAMPLE Conover asks Jones to find a buyer for his antique automobile, which he wants to sell for $100,000. He further states that he will pay him a commission of 6 percent when this is accomplished. Jones does find a buyer willing to purchase the automobile at this price. Jones has now completed the requested act and Conover has the obligation to pay the commission promised to him.

COMMUNICATING THE OFFER

Student Skill: Students will learn how an offer is communicated between an offeror and offeree.

An offer must also be reasonably communicated from one party to another in order to be effective. If a party does not adequately inform the other party of the material terms of the offer, there will not be a contract.

Material terms normally include the names of the parties, the subject matter, price, quantity, delivery dates, and other terms normally associated with such an offer. The offer must also be phrased in such a way that it can be accepted unconditionally. That is, the offeree could create the contract simply by stating, "yes."

> EXAMPLE Mary loses her dog, Spot. She places a notice in the local newspaper that offers a reward for its return. Sally does not read about the reward, but finds Spot and returns the dog to Mary. Sally is not entitled to the reward because the offer was not communicated to her. There must be a deliberate meeting of the minds in order for there to be a legally enforceable contract. This is the fundamental premise underlying the law of contracts.
>
> EXAMPLE Bob says to Bill that he would like to buy his house. Bill says, "Sure, why not?" There is no legally enforceable contract in this case. Bob's comments are not sufficient to create an offer that could form the basis of a legally binding contract. The usual terms such as price, closing date, and land description are not included in his comment.

Some statements that may look like offers and acceptances have been held not to be such because they were not sufficiently definite. If a statement was made in jest, it cannot constitute an offer. If statements are clearly preliminary negotiations, they will not be regarded as legally binding offers and acceptances.

Some court decisions that held that advertisements were merely negotiations allowed some stores to adopt "bait and switch" tactics in which they advertised items at low prices. When customers came in, the items were not in stock or customers were steered to more expensive items. Most states have now passed laws that prohibit this type of activity.

An offeror may control the terms of the offer and the method and timing of acceptance. Not only is this helpful to the offeror, it protects him from possible liability. If there is a problem later, the risk is normally on the offeror. If the offeror controls all of the aspects of the process, she can reduce this risk.

> EXAMPLE Smith sends an offer for bids on a particular project to various contractors. He notes that bids must be mailed and delivered no later than October 15, 199X. If he receives bids later than October 15th, he may reject them.

Because the offeror may control the terms of the offer, he will also have the terms held against him if they are vague or ambiguous. This issue often arises with printed contracts such as leases or sales agreements. In these cases, ambiguous terms or clauses will be interpreted in a manner against the person who drafted or provided the form.

> EXAMPLE Dotson moves into an apartment building owned by Wilson. When Dotson began his tenancy, Wilson gave him a lease that stated that the rent was due "at the end of each month." It is unclear whether this phrase means the rent should be paid at the end of the month in which Dotson lived in the building or should be prepaid for the following month. In this case, the clause will be construed against Wilson and in Dotson's favor.

HOLDING AN OFFER OPEN

Student Skill: Students will learn the legal characteristics of an offer held open for an offeree.

An option is an offer that the offeror agrees to hold open for a period of time. At common law, an option is revocable at any time prior to its acceptance by the offeree unless the offeree has given the offeror something of value.

> EXAMPLE Smith tells Thomson that he will sell him Greenacre for $200,000. Thomson asks for time to think about it. Smith states that he will hold the offer open for ten days. Thomson says, "Thanks." Smith may revoke this offer at any time prior to Thomson's acceptance of the offer. Smith has received nothing of value in exchange for his promise to keep the offer open.

The above example strikes some people as unfair. However, it is clearly based on contract law stating that there must be an exchange of values for an agreement to be binding. Almost anything given by the offeree to the offeror will be considered sufficient.

The offeror must give to the offeree some notice of the revocation. The offeror could accomplish this by directly informing the offeree of the revocation or by doing so in a constructive manner. In the above example, Smith could have told Thomson of the revocation or let him know by selling the house to another.

The right to revoke an offer has been maintained under the Uniform Commercial Code, but has been altered. The UCC provides that a merchant, someone who regularly deals in goods, will be bound by an offer put into writing for a period of up to three months. This recognizes that a merchant should be held to a high standard in dealing with customers and should not be able to revoke an offer simply because he received nothing of value for making it.

LENGTH OF OFFER

Student Skill: Students will learn the law with respect to the length of time that an offer will be held open.

The offeror may control the length of time that the offeree has to accept the offer. As noted, it can be very useful for the offeror to do this. The offeror may also control the method of reply by the offeree.

If no time is specified in the offer, the offeree has a reasonable time in which to reply. In these cases, "reasonable" is one of those terms that are difficult to define. It will depend on all the circumstances surrounding the offer and its subject matter.

> EXAMPLE Franklin offers to send 100 cartons to milk to Grant, 50 miles away, for a certain price. Because of the rapid perishability of milk, Grant should know that he has a very limited time in which to reply. If the subject matter was iron, the time would be longer.

Events such as the death or insanity of the offeror or offeree will terminate the offer. The destruction of the subject matter, intervening illegality, or other circumstances that would cause a reasonable person to know that the offer should be terminated will also end the offer.

EXCEPTIONAL TYPES OF OFFERS

Student Skill: Students will learn about unusual contractual offers such as auctions.

At an auction, people make bids on items that are placed on sale. Each bid is an offer that may or may not be accepted by the person who puts the items up for sale. At an auction held "without reserve," the property owner must accept the highest bid made at the auction. The owner may set a floor below which a bid may not be made. This establishes a minimum price for the property.

An auction "with reserve" allows the owner to reject all bids. Because this may not seem fair to the highest bidder, notice that the auction is being held "with reserve" must be given to all bidders attending.

A reward is a unilateral offer that the offeror makes either to a specific person or to a broader segment of the population. One may place the reward in the form of an advertisement in a newspaper, or in some other publication of general circulation.

> EXAMPLE Joe places an advertisement in an entertainment-oriented magazine asking for a copy of Elvis Presley's original Sun recording of *That's All Right Mama*. Joe offers a reward of $1,000. Pat reads the advertisement and brings the record to Joe. Pat is now entitled to the reward.

A person must have known of the reward in order to claim it. In the above example, if Pat had not known of the advertisement, she would not be entitled to the reward. An offer must be communicated in order to be effective.

REJECTING OR REVOKING THE OFFER

Student Skill: The student will learn other methods for terminating an offer.

A person may hear or read about an offer and reject it. Once a person has rejected the offer, it is too late to change one's mind. If an offeree rejects an offer, the offeror may simply walk away and act as if the transaction never took place.

A rejection of an offer is effective when received. As a result, a person could reject an offer and change his mind before the offeror received the rejection.

EXAMPLE Don receives an offer from Mary. He sends a rejection by mail to Mary. He later changes his mind. He may still call her and accept the offer because his rejection had not been received by her.

A counteroffer is a type of rejection. The offeree attempts to change the terms of the offer by making a counteroffer. Under common law, this is not permitted. The offeror may listen to the counteroffer and accept it. The offeror may also listen to the counteroffer and simply walk away.

EXAMPLE Mike offers to sell Sam Greenacre for $90,000 with a closing date of October 15. Sam states that he is willing to buy the property, but wants a closing date of October 30. Mike may walk away from Sam without a reply and without legal liability.

At common law, the judges placed enormous importance on a precise meeting of the minds. As a result, a counteroffer that deviated from the offer in any respect could not form the basis of a binding legal agreement.

The requirement for a precise meeting of the minds has been relaxed with respect to the sale of goods under the Uniform Commercial Code. The Code permits changes in the terms by the offeree. These changes will become part of the contract unless objected to by an offeror who is a merchant seller.

An offeror may revoke the offer at any time prior to the offeree accepting it and forming a contract. The offeror may revoke unless he has received something of value from the offeree. This is because there must be an exchange of values in any agreement between parties.

A revocation is effective when it is received by the offeree. If the offeree has already accepted the offer, there is a binding contract and the revocation is too late.

EXAMPLE Donald offers to sell Purpleacre to Harry for $80,000. Donald then changes his mind and sends Harry a revocation through the mail. Harry receives Donald's mailed offer on June 1. On June 2, Harry sends an acceptance to Donald. On June 3, Harry receives Donald's revocation. The revocation has no effect. There was a contract on June 3 when Harry mailed his acceptance.

ACCEPTANCE

Student Skill: The student will learn how an offer is legally accepted.

Acceptance is the indication by the offeree that she is willing to create a contract in accordance with the terms of the offer. It is important to note that a binding contract exists at the precise moment that the acceptance is dispatched unless the offeror specified otherwise. From this moment, both parties must perform their part of the contract.

The contract could result from the offeree's acceptance of the original offer, or the offeror's acceptance of a counteroffer from the offeree. If there has been no legally effective acceptance, there has been no binding contract and neither party has any remedies. At common law, this means that the communications between the parties had no legal significance.

> EXAMPLE Dan sent an offer to Dolly that stated that he would sell her Orangeacre for $80,000. The offer noted that the purchase price also included $5,000 worth of furnishings that were in the house. Dolly wires back her acceptance that she will purchase the house for $75,000 without the furnishings. Dan may ignore the acceptance and sell the house to someone else because Dolly made a counteroffer.
>
> EXAMPLE Same facts as above, except that Dolly wires back an acceptance that conforms with the offer. Her wire states, "Yes, I accept." Dan and Dolly have a contract as of the date of her wire.

A revocation sent by Dan and received by Dolly after her acceptance wire will be ineffective. An acceptance is effective when mailed, but a revocation is not effective until received. The parties now have a binding contract. If either party breaches the contract, the other will have a remedy for damages.

SILENCE

Student Skill: The student will learn when silence constitutes acceptance.

Generally, acceptance must be an affirmative act. One may not compel another party to accept an offer through silence. That is, one may not send an offer to another party and then argue there has been acceptance because the other party did not reply.

Silence will constitute acceptance if the parties have previously agreed that silence will be construed as acceptance or if they have established a pattern of allowing silence to constitute acceptance.

> EXAMPLE Frank joins the Pizza of the Day Club. The club's contract provides that members will have accepted the pizza unless they return it when delivered. In this case, the parties have agreed that silence will be acceptance. As a result, if Frank does not return the pizza, his silence will be construed as acceptance.
>
> EXAMPLE Frank has Chinese food delivered every day. The delivery person leaves the food at the door and Frank sends him a check for the amount due. In this case, the two parties have established a pattern of conduct such that silence will constitute acceptance. Frank will be held liable if he takes the Chinese food without paying for it because his silence will constitute acceptance.

WORKING AT THE LAW OFFICE

A paralegal can prove very valuable to a law office by understanding whether a contract has been created. In a perfect world, the parties would be able to work out disputes involving their business agreements. However, this is often not what occurs. A paralegal who knows the finer points of contract law can be of great assistance to the supervising attorney by protecting the client's interests.

PARALEGAL'S "THINGS TO DO"

Student Skill: Students will learn the fundamentals of drafting a contract.

1. Check to see if the offer contains the necessary legal elements. These include:

reasonable communication of its terms.

an intent to create a binding contract.

terms are defined with reasonable definity. The average person can understand the offer's key terms.

the offer states consideration for the other party.

the offer asks for consideration from the other party.

2. Check to see if the consideration expressed by the offer is legally binding. The consideration:

> is related to the present or the future.
>
> may not be based on a preexisting obligation. The consideration may not relate to something one is already legally or contractually obligated to do.
>
> may not be based on merely a "moral" basis.
>
> must be legally sufficient.

3. The offer and acceptance must be mirror images of each other under the common law. The paralegal should look at both the offer and acceptance to ensure:

> The acceptance conforms exactly with the offer's requirements regarding the method and time for the acceptance to reach the offeror.
>
> If the offer does not contain a specific method and time, the offeree has a reasonable time in which to accept the offer. The acceptance is effective as soon as it is sent.
>
> The acceptance should not attempt to change any of the terms of the offer. If it does, it will be regarded as a counteroffer. Then its effect is to terminate the offer and there is no contract.
>
> The offer and acceptance should specify the terms usually associated with contracts of such a type. For example, construction contracts usually contain specific provisions that relate to the assignment of the various tasks associated with the contract. In addition, the contract may require the services of an expert such as an engineer or an architect who may be required to inspect the performance of the parties doing the construction.

4. The paralegal should check to ensure that the interests of clients are adequately protected. People are more likely to perform the contract if they have some stake in the outcome. If they have been adequately protected, they are less likely to violate the terms of the contract. Ways of protecting the client include:

> determining the real goals and interests of the client.
>
> determining the solutions to the client's problems and to obtaining the client's interests and goals.
>
> drafting the contracts or other documents that will achieve the goals of the client.

preparing the documents in a manner that avoids difficulties in the future.

5. If the client has already begun the contract, the paralegal should examine:

Is the contract in the best interests of the client?

If it is not, can the contract be modified to better meet the client's needs?

May the client discontinue the contract without breaching the contract?

If the client may not discontinue the contract, what are the obligations under the current contract and what would be the consequences if the contractual obligations were not performed?

QUESTIONS

1. What is an offer?
2. What are the ingredients of a legally enforceable offer?
3. How may an offeror control the timing and method of the acceptance by the offeree?
4. How may the offeree accept an offer?
5. When is the acceptance effective?
6. What is the mailbox rule?
7. What is a bilateral offer?
8. What does a bilateral offer request in return?
9. What is a unilateral offer?
10. What does a unilateral offer request in return?
11. What is a counteroffer?
12. What is the result of a counteroffer?
13. How long will an offer remain open if it is not specified in the offer?
14. When may an offer be revoked?
15. If an offer has been legally accepted, may it be revoked a second later?
16. What is the underlying rationale for the decision in question 15?
17. May silence legally constitute acceptance?
18. What is the rationale for the results in question 17?

PROBLEMS

1. Hudson offers to be Bellamy's butler for $700 per week. Bellamy states that he would be willing to hire Hudson at $100 per day. Later Hudson brings suit to enforce their contract. Will Hudson be able to enforce their agreement?

2. Jackson sends Franklin an offer to sell him Blackacre for $100,000. The offer states that it will be held open until April 10th. Franklin sends his acceptance to Jackson on April 9th. However, it does not reach him until April 11th. Do the two parties have a contract?

3. When there is a mix-up with respect to an offer and an acceptance, as a general rule should the offeror or offeree bear the risk of loss? Who is in the best position to prevent the loss? Why?

4. Patty puts an advertisement in the paper that asks for the return of her lost cat, Fluffy. The advertisement offers a reward of $100. If Sally finds Fluffy without reading of the reward, may she recover the $100? What are the reasons for this result? Do you agree with the result?

5. Donna offers to sell Betty four tables for $2,000. Betty replies that she will buy two tables for $1,000. Donna says nothing, but sells the four tables to Joan for $2,000. Betty brings an action against Donna. May she recover any damages?

6. Harry offers to sell Barry Greenacre for $100,000. Barry rejects the offer, but one minute later changes his mind and tries to accept the offer. Harry refused to let him to do so. Barry later brings a legal action against Harry. Will he recover?

7. Alan goes to an auction that was advertised as being held "without reserve." Alan is the only bidder on an antique table. He bids $10, but the bid is refused. Will Alan recover if he brings a lawsuit?

3 *Contracts Requiring a Writing*

SKILLS STUDENTS WILL LEARN

Students will learn which contracts require a writing in order to be legally enforceable, and will also learn the extent of the writing required.

Students will learn that the legislation passed by the English Parliament and United States legislatures states that certain contracts are not enforceable by the courts unless there is some written evidence of the contract.

Students will learn that the various statutes of fraud are rules of evidence that are interpreted by the courts. These judicial bodies have found numerous exceptions that allow oral contracts to be enforced.

Students will learn that the major exception to the requirement that certain types of contracts must be evidenced by a writing is the substantial performance exemption, which states that contracts that have already been substantially performed will be enforced even if they have not been placed into writing. This means that the statute of frauds applies primarily to contracts not yet performed.

Students will learn that written contracts should include the names of the parties, their signatures, a description of the subject matter, the quantity, the consideration, and other terms usually associated with a similar contract.

Students will learn that the parol evidence rule states that if a contract has been put into writing, oral evidence to contradict the written terms will not be admitted except in certain circumstances.

STATUTE OF FRAUDS

Student Skill: Students will learn the requirements for writings regarding certain types of contracts.

The statute of frauds was passed by the English Parliament in order to prevent people from falsely swearing that certain types of contracts exist. This modified the traditional common law that oral contracts were as binding as written agreements.

After United States independence, nearly every state legislature adopted similar state statutes requiring that specific types of contracts would not be enforced unless they were put into writing. These include the following:

the sale of any interest in real estate;

a contract that, on its terms, cannot be performed within one year;

the promise to answer for the debt or default of another;

a promise to personally pay the debt of an estate;

contracts relating to marriage;

a contract for the sale of goods (tangible, movable items) of $500 or more (Uniform Commercial Code);

a contract for the sale of securities.

WORKING AT THE LAW OFFICE

Knowledge of the statute of frauds can prove critical in a law office. Parties may believe they have a binding agreement. However, suppose that there is no written evidence of a contract. A paralegal could become an instant hero by recognizing whether the agreement is legally enforceable or not legally enforceable. The answer could be critical to the client's interests.

CONTRACTS FOR THE SALE OF REAL ESTATE

Land has always been important in societies because it is the one resource that cannot increase. In addition, one can utilize land to grow crops or mine for ore. Ownership of land also formed the basis of alliances and social prestige. As a result, the temptation to lie in order to acquire land has always been substantial.

The passage of the statute of frauds was an attempt to reduce the likelihood that a person would lie in order to claim that a contract existed for the sale of land. A written contract for the sale of land should contain a description of the property, the names of the parties, the date for the completion of the transaction, and the signatures of the parties. There must be some writing to evidence the sale of any interest in land or real estate. This includes life estates and other interests such as easements.

A major exception to the requirement for some writing is when the parties have already performed a substantial portion of their duties under the contract.

> EXAMPLE   Franklin orally agrees to buy Brownacre from Jefferson for $89,000. He sends a check to Jefferson who deposits it into his account. This is substantial performance on the part of Jefferson.

By accepting the check and depositing it, Jefferson has provided evidence that this oral contract existed. By sending the check, Franklin has also agreed that a contract existed. Therefore, the courts will hold that the contract is binding, although it was not put into writing.

The substantial performance exemption means that the statute of frauds applies to executory contracts. That is, the statute will not prevent the contract from being enforced even though it was not put into writing. This result promotes justice because the parties clearly intended that there be a contract.

CONTRACTS THAT CANNOT BE PERFORMED WITHIN ONE YEAR

The statute of frauds also recognizes that long-term contracts will bind the parties for extensive periods of time, and that memories tend to fade as time passes. Therefore, the statute requires that contracts that, on their terms, cannot be performed within one year be put into writing.

A lifetime contract could be performed within one year. Therefore, it need not be placed into writing. However, a three-year contract could not be performed within one year, and must be placed into writing in order to be enforceable.

The substantial performance exception also applies to this type of contract. If the terms of the contract have already been performed, the lack of a writing will not render it void.

> EXAMPLE Jones and Franks have a five-year employment contract. Jones worked two years and three months for Franks when there was a dispute about the oral agreement. Although the contract was for more than one year, it will be enforceable because the two parties maintained a working relationship for more than two years.

CONTRACTS TO ANSWER FOR THE DEBTS OR DEFAULT OF ANOTHER

It would not be difficult to claim that a person made a promise to pay someone's debt. As a result, the statute of frauds requires that such promises be placed into writing.

> EXAMPLE Sally claims that Mary promised to pay Martin's debt if Martin did not. Sally must have some written evidence to show that Mary had actually made this promise. If she does not, the promise will not be enforceable.

This provision of the statute is one of the reasons that a cosignor of a loan must place the promise to pay into writing. Similarly, a surety or guarantor's promise to pay the loan must also be placed into writing.

The courts have ruled that the substantial performance exception applies to these promises. If the promise has already been carried out, the lack of a writing will not affect it.

In addition, some courts have ruled that if the promise to pay another's debt was made to benefit the promisor, the promise does not have to be placed into writing.

> EXAMPLE Tom hires a new head of marketing, Pat, for his firm. He brings her to New York from Chicago. He tells the moving company that he will pay Pat's moving costs if she does not.

In this case, Tom's promise also benefits him because a happy employee is a better employee. The promise will be enforceable although it is not in writing. The promise helped the promisor and the statute does not prevent its enforcement.

PROMISES RELATING TO MARRIAGE

Marriages were often the source of military alliances in England and a way of cementing social alliances in the United States. Prominent families in both countries have utilized marriages to build on positions of power and influence. As a result, the drafters of the various statutes of frauds believed that contracts relating to marriage should be placed into writing.

Marriages are also important to society because they often result in children who become society's burden if the parents do not assume their responsibility for them. Furthermore, some individuals still exchange property or decide how property will be divided when they are married. These agreements must be placed into writing.

> EXAMPLE Harry and Mary decide to get married. As part of their discussions, they agree that they will each keep their property before marriage and that Mary will only be entitled to 30 percent of the property acquired during the marriage.

The statute of frauds requires that these discussions be in writing in order to be enforceable. If they were not put into writing, the parties would divide the property in accord with state law.

These agreements must be drafted carefully with a view toward the provisions of the applicable state law, the potential results of a divorce for the family, and the interests of the parties.

PROMISES TO PAY OBLIGATIONS OF AN ESTATE

An estate is the amount of assets a person has when she dies. Upon that person's death, someone becomes responsible for administering that person's estate. If the deceased appointed an executor, the executor must act in accordance with the provisions in the will. If the deceased died without a will, the court-appointed administrator must distribute the estate in accordance with applicable state law.

A person might claim that an executor or administrator promised to pay an obligation of the estate from one's own funds. Unless that promise is in writing, it is not enforceable.

> EXAMPLE Mary states that Joe Jr., who is the executor of Joe Sr.'s estate, had agreed to pay one of the estate's obligations out of his own funds. Unless Mary has this promise in writing, it will not be enforceable.

This provision of the statute of frauds prevents various people from claiming that administrators or executors promised to make payments relating to obligations of the estate from their own funds unless these promises are in writing.

OTHER STATUTE OF FRAUDS REQUIREMENTS

The laws of various states have imposed additional requirements for written contracts. The Uniform Commercial Code, which has been adopted by nearly every state, requires that contracts for the sale of securities and for goods of $500 or more must be placed into writing.

Securities, such as stocks and bonds, form the foundation of a free enterprise economy. As a result, it is essential that contracts for their sale be in writing.

Goods are tangible, movable items such as television sets, refrigerators, and furniture. Contracts for the sale of goods of $500 or more must be in writing.

> EXAMPLE   Sally agrees to sell her automobile to Mary for $3,000. This agreement must be in writing in order to be legally enforceable.

The usual exception relating to the substantial performance of the contract also applies to these statute of frauds provisions. In addition, contracts for the sale of goods that are specially made for the buyer will be enforced even though they are not in writing.

SUFFICIENCY OF THE WRITING

Student Skill: Students will learn how much writing is required to satisfy the statute of frauds.

The writing necessary to satisfy the statute of frauds does not need to be a lengthy document. It should contain the names of the parties, a reasonable description of the subject matter, the quantity of items, the consideration given by the parties, the signatures of the parties, and other terms.

Under the Uniform Commercial Code, the parties need to identify themselves, the subject matter of the contract, and the quantity of the goods. The UCC provides gap fillers and other contractual terms are provided by provisions in the code. For example, the price can be determined by looking out into the marketplace to determine the prevailing market price for goods of a similar kind and quality. The date of delivery is a reasonable time for delivery unless otherwise stated.

PAROL EVIDENCE RULE

Student Skill: Students will learn how the writing will be interpreted in court.

The parol evidence rule provides that oral evidence will not be admitted to contradict the terms of a written contract except under certain circumstances. These exceptions include the following:

> The terms of the written contract are vague or are subject to different meanings. Oral evidence will be admitted to supply the missing term or to clarify ambiguities.

> The courts will allow oral evidence if it goes to show lack of true consent to the agreement. For example, evidence of fraud, duress, or mistake would be admitted.

PARALEGAL'S "THINGS TO DO"

Student Skill: Students will learn the fundamentals regarding placing a contract into writing.

1. The paralegal should check the proposed agreement to determine if the statute of frauds will require that the contract be in writing. The following agreements must normally be written:

> contracts for the sale of interests in real estate;

> contracts that cannot be completed within one year;

> contracts for the sale of goods of $500 or more;

> contracts to answer (pay) for the debt of another;

> contracts in consideration of marriage;

> contracts to pay for the debt of an estate from the personal funds of the executor.

2.   The paralegal should check to ensure that the appropriate terms are included in the writing:

> A contract for the sale of land should include a reasonable description of the property, the names and signatures of the parties, the price of the land, the date for closing the transaction between the parties, a description of any fixtures or other property that are to be included in the sale, and any conditions that relate to the completion of the transaction.

> A contract for the sale of goods must include the quantity or amount of goods that are to be sold.

> A contract that cannot be completed within one year ought to include the duties of each party and the dates of completion.

> Service contracts should be as explicit as possible with respect to the nature of the duties.

> Contracts to answer for the debt of another must be in writing. This includes agreements in which one agrees to be a surety or consignor on a loan agreement. Given the rather unusual nature of an agreement to pay another's debts, the reasons for such a promise could add clarity to the agreement if they were included in the writing.

> Contracts relating to marriages should be drafted extremely carefully with the help of an expert in matrimonial law. They should normally include any agreement relating to the division of assets that were acquired during the marriage.

3.   The paralegal should be aware of the exceptions to the statute of frauds if the agreement was not placed into writing. These include:

> A partial performance exemption covers all of the contractual situations but is especially important in cases involving the sale of real estate. The exception provides that if all or significant parts of the contractual duties have been performed, the contract will not be unenforceable because it was not placed into writing.

> The reason for the above exception is that evidence of the parties performing the contract substitutes for the evidence of the contract provided by the writing.

> The cases involving agreements to answer for the debt of another have resulted in two exceptions worth noting. First, if the promise was made to the creditor, it must be in writing, but if the promise was

made to the debtor, it need not be in writing. Second, if the promise also benefited the promisor it need not have been placed into writing.

It is important for the paralegal to recognize these exceptions because the client may be able to enforce the contract. Courts want to do justice and are likely to find a contract if there is sufficient evidence to support it.

4. There are a number of other issues of which the paralegal should be aware.

> The promisor may have made a promise on which the promisee relied. In this case, the promise may be enforceable because the promisor should have known that the promisee would rely on it.

> One might also consider bringing an action for restitution if the oral promise is unenforceable. An action for restitution is designed to recover benefits conferred in order to prevent unjust enrichment.

5. The parol evidence rule provides that if the agreement has been placed into writing, oral evidence that contradicts the written terms will not be admitted.

> The paralegal should review any written agreements or letters between the parties.

> While oral evidence is not normally admissible, the paralegal should also look at possible exceptions to the rule. These include:

>> Evidence that the agreement was the result of fraud, duress, or some other issue involving lack of genuine consent will be admitted.

>> Terms that are unclear or ambiguous may be clarified by oral evidence or other writings.

>> The paralegal should also check to determine if any terms were left out of the agreement. If they were, oral evidence may be introduced to clarify the missing terms.

>> The paralegal should also recognize that the parol evidence rule adds additional importance to making the written agreement as clear as possible. However, it is also the paralegal's responsibility to recognize the exceptions to the rule in order to best represent the interests of the client.

QUESTIONS

1. What is the statute of frauds?
2. What is the purpose of the statute of frauds?
3. Why is it proper to call the statute of frauds a rule of evidence?
4. What types of contracts fall under the statute of frauds?
5. Would a lifetime guarantee or contract fall under the statute of frauds?
6. Would a three-year contract fall under the statute of frauds?
7. What is the sale of an interest in land?
8. Name some interests in land.
9. What are some exceptions to the statute of frauds?
10. What are the reasons for these exceptions?
11. What is the parol evidence rule?
12. What is the reason for the parol evidence rule?
13. What are some exceptions to the parol evidence rule?
14. What are the reasons for the exceptions to the parol evidence rule?
15. How do the statute of frauds and parol evidence rule affect oral and written contracts?

PROBLEMS

1. Hanson agrees to a 3-year oral employment contract with XYZ Corporation for $100,000 per year. He works for XYZ for 15 months. At that time, XYZ Corporation decides to reduce expenses and terminates Hanson's employment. Hanson seeks to recover for the remaining portion of the contract. However, XYZ Corporation cites the statute of frauds. Will Hanson prevail in his lawsuit?

2. The R.R. Realty Company orally agrees to sell Brownacre to Jones for $200,000. Jones mails the check to R.R. Realty and moves onto the land. He remains on the land for 20 days before R.R. Realty tells Jones that the contract was not enforceable because it was not in writing. If Jones brings an action to enforce the contract, will he recover? Will the statute of frauds prevent recovery by Jones? If you were the attorney advising Jones, what would you tell him?

3. Dotson hires Sampson to manage his new store on Main Street. He orally promises Mammouth Moving Company that he will pay Sampson's moving expenses if Sampson does not. When Mammouth brings an action to recover the moving expenses, Dotson argues that the promise was oral and not enforceable. Is Dotson correct?

4. Sally orally agrees to marry Sam and to accept only 40 percent of the income incurred during the marriage. After the marriage dissolves, Sally argues that the premarital agreement was not valid because it was not in writing. Is Sally obligated to abide by the oral agreement with Sam? If you were the attorney advising Sam, what would you tell him?

5. Dorothy, who is a 97-year-old woman, signs a contract to sell all of her assets to her nurse for $1,000. Later, Dorothy seeks to show that she had discussions with the nurse to sell her the assets for $100,000 and that the written agreement was the result of duress. The nurse argues that the oral evidence should not be admitted because of the parol evidence rule. Is the nurse correct? If you were advising Dorothy, what would you tell her?

6. Mary and Mike agree to a written contract for the sale of Blackacre. The contract notes that some of the furniture will be included in the agreement. The parties had also agreed on the sale of a large piano located in the living room for $3,000. However, the parties neglected to include the sale in the contract. Mike later seeks to introduce oral evidence of the sale. Will it be admissible?

7. You are a paralegal working in a large law firm. You notice that many real estate agreements drafted by your firm do not mention whether personal property is included in the sale of the real estate. The managing partner of the firm asks for your advice. What do you tell her?

4 *The Doctrine of Consideration*

Students will learn that for a contract to be legally enforceable, both sides must provide consideration. That is, both parties must give something of value or incur a substantial detriment.

Students will learn that the consideration must be one of present value. Past consideration or existing obligations are not sufficient to constitute new consideration. An exception would be if there are substantial unforeseen difficulties with a party performing his obligations.

Students will learn that moral consideration given by doing a good deed is not legally adequate consideration.

DEFINING CONSIDERATION

Student Skill: Students will learn what constitutes consideration.

Consideration is a legally required element of an enforceable contract. Both parties to the contract must give up something of value or incur a substantial detriment if the agreement is to be legally binding.

> EXAMPLE Uncle Bill promises to give his niece, Katie, a new bicycle on her birthday. She promises him nothing in return. Bill has simply made a gratuitous promise. Katie has provided no consideration and Uncle Bill's promise is not legally enforceable.
>
> EXAMPLE Sally agrees to sell Blackacre to Terry for $100,000. Terry agrees to the purchase of Blackacre and to a closing date of November 1st. Both parties have now given adequate consideration. Sally has a buyer for Blackacre and Terry knows that she will be able to acquire a piece of real estate.
>
> EXAMPLE Jason hits John on the head with an ax. John brings a lawsuit to recover for his injuries. Jason agrees to pay John $80,000 and John agrees to drop the lawsuit. In this case, Jason has given consideration in the amount of $80,000 and John has given consideration by incurring a substantial detriment: He dropped his lawsuit.

PURPOSE OF CONSIDERATION

Student Skill: Students will learn the legal purpose of requiring consideration for contracts to be enforceable.

The purpose of the requirement for consideration is to separate those serious agreements that the law will enforce from social arrangements that the courts do not want to enforce.

The courts are backlogged with all types of civil and criminal cases. If they began to accept social arrangements such as dates or gifts, the courts would be even more clogged than they are now. As a result, the major cases would become lost in a sea of minor agreements.

The consideration required by the courts does not need to be substantial, but it must be legally sufficient. There must be some exchange of things of value. Promises to perform certain acts can be things of value. If there is no exchange of items of value, there must be an exchange of substantial detriments.

In some rare instances, the courts have set aside contracts because one side gave so little consideration in return for what the other party gave. In these cases, one party often was able to take advantage of a vastly superior bargaining position.

> EXAMPLE Knotts is an old man in need of constant nursing care. His nurse continually urges him to deed his house to her. One day, he deeds the house to her for $1,000. This contract would be set aside because the unequal levels of consideration would shock the conscience of the court.

DOCTRINE OF PROMISSORY ESTOPPEL

The doctrine of promissory estoppel states that a promisor's promise will be enforced regardless of whether there was consideration if the promisor knew or should have known that the promisee would rely on that promise to his detriment. This prevents someone from making a promise and then walking away from it if the promisee would be injured.

> EXAMPLE Smits tells Johnson that he will name her head of his company if she is willing to move from New York to Los Angeles. Johnson makes the move at considerable expense to herself. The promise by Smits will be enforced regardless of whether she gave him any consideration. He knew or should have known that she would rely on his promise to her detriment.

The doctrine of promissory estoppel does not require that the promisor know to a certainty that the promisee will rely on the promise. Rather, it will be sufficient that the promisee act as a reasonable person would do in relying on the promise to her detriment.

PREEXISTING OBLIGATIONS

Student Skill: Students will learn the reasons that consideration must be based on present value.

Consideration may not be something one was already obligated to perform. If the obligation is legal or contractual, it cannot form the basis for new consideration.

EXAMPLE Frank has an obligation to do the gardening at Joe's house for $2,000 per year. Halfway through the year, he tells Joe that the cost of labor has gone up and that he wants an additional $1,000 to complete the work. Joe agrees to pay him the additional $1,000. When the year ends, Joe must only pay him the original $2,000. Frank has given Joe nothing additional of value for Joe's promise to pay him the additional $1,000. He was already obligated to do the gardening. This preexisting obligation is not sufficient to constitute new consideration.

EXAMPLE Sam sees a person, Mary, stuck in a snowbank along the side of the road. After Sam pulls Mary out of the snowbank, she says that she will pay him $100 for his actions. If Mary does not pay Sam the $100, he will have no legal remedy. He had already performed the action when Mary made her promise, and it cannot constitute consideration for Mary's promise.

These results seem to be unfair to some people. However, they are based on the idea that each party must give something to the other in return for that person's promise. The consideration cannot be based on past acts.

An exception to this doctrine is when the parties encounter unforeseen difficulties. These are externally caused problems that were not reasonably foreseeable at the time the contract was agreed upon.

EXAMPLE Jones contracts to build a new deck on the side of Bill's house. Halfway through the job, Jones encounters some unusual rock formations that neither party could have foreseen when the contract was created. This would be an unforeseen difficulty. Bill agrees to pay Jones an additional $1,000 for finishing the job. Because of the unforeseen difficulty, Bill would be liable for the additional $1,000. In this case, the unforeseen difficulty would substitute for additional consideration.

However, it should be noted that mere changes in circumstances will not be sufficient to constitute unforeseen difficulties. For example, a simple rise in prices or a change in the cost of materials or labor will not be an unforeseen difficulty. Changes in the cost of materials and labor occur frequently. One should expect to encounter changes in circumstances. These changes are part of the reason that one agrees to contracts. The contract provides a degree of certainty in a changing world. One expects that the other party will perform even if some circumstances change.

EXAMPLE Jones has a contract with Smith to paint his house. The cost of materials and labor goes up. This is not an unforeseen difficulty. Cost increases in materials and labor are to be expected.

> EXAMPLE Sam has a contract with Don to provide pizzas for all of Dan's 1,100 pizzerias. He claims that the cost of pizza dough and cheese has gone up by 20 percent over the past year. He claims that these unforeseen difficulties entitle him to more money. He is incorrect. He could have reasonably foreseen these circumstances.

EXCEPTIONS TO THE CONSIDERATION DOCTRINE

Student Skill: Students will learn the exceptions to the requirement for consideration.

Contracts will not be enforced as a general rule unless both parties have given up something of value. However, there are certain contracts that will be enforced even if one cannot specifically find consideration.

A requirements contract is one in which one party agrees to supply everything that the other party needs of a specific item. The other party agrees to sell him all of his requirements of the item. A requirements contract does not specifically state that there is some exchange of values or detriments.

However, the courts have found consideration in the implied covenants of reasonableness and good faith that exist in contracts generally.

> EXAMPLE Smith has a contract to supply all of Jones' requirements for widgets. In year one, Jones needs 2,500 widgets and Smith gears up to produce a similar amount in year two. However, Jones has found a cheaper supplier and tells Smith that he has no requirements and that Smith had provided no consideration for their contract. Smith will be able to recover under the contract based on the implied covenants of good faith and reasonableness.

After Jones had ordered 2,500 widgets, Smith had the right to expect that Jones would order a similar amount the following year. It is a breach of their implied covenant of good faith and reasonableness not to order a similar amount in year two. Smith should be able to recover his lost profits based on 2,500 widgets.

An outputs contract provides that a person will buy the entire output of a supplier. A requirements contract essentially states, "I will buy all I need from you and an outputs contract states, "I will buy all you make."

EXAMPLE Harry has an outputs contract with Olga's outsized ox yokes. Olga's ox yokes have become collectors' items in many stores throughout the country and Harry is able to sell them at a profit. In year one, Olga makes and Harry takes 100 ox yokes. In year two, Olga tells Harry that "The yoke's on you because I've sold them all to Barry." What remedy does Harry have?

Based on the implied covenants of good faith and reasonableness, Olga must provide a reasonable number of ox yokes to Harry. The law provides that parties must act in good faith. Olga's refusal to sell any ox yokes to Harry was not reasonable.

There are certain contracts that do not require consideration in order to be valid. Contributions to charities or other institutions that promote the general welfare are designed to help society. In these cases, the courts have found consideration in the general benefit to the public.

EXAMPLE Hanson promises to give $1,000 to the Dandruff Association of America. His promise is enforceable although the Association gave him nothing of value.

PARALEGAL'S "THINGS TO DO"

Student Skill: Students will learn how to conform with the contractual requirement for consideration.

1. The doctrine of consideration requires that each party either give up something of value or incur a substantial detriment in order for the law to enforce a contract. If there is no consideration, there is no legally enforceable contract.

> The paralegal should see if the promise is real or illusory. An exchange of real promises will constitute a sufficient consideration to create a legally binding contract.

> Illusory promises cannot create a contract because they omit essential terms that a court could use to find a contract and to form a remedy.

2. A bilateral promise is one that offers a promise as consideration for another promise.

> The paralegal should know that a legally enforceable contract exists at the moment that the two promises are exchanged. Some people be-

lieve that the parties can change their minds before performance. This is not true.

The promises normally must contain the terms that set forth the contractual obligations of each party. This permits the court to enforce the agreement and to find remedies for nonperformance by the parties.

3. A unilateral promise asks the other party to perform a specific act first. After that, the promisor agrees to perform her action.

> The paralegal should know that the performance of the act is consideration.

> The paralegal should know that one must perform his promise after the promisee performed the requested act.

> The promises of each party must be phrased carefully to ensure that each of them knows when to perform and precisely what they are supposed to be doing in order to satisfy their obligations.

4. Consideration must be legally sufficient in order for there to be a binding contract. Normally, the courts do not look at the adequacy of consideration, but there must be some exchange of either values or detriments.

> The paralegal should ensure that the contract specifically mentions the consideration provided by each party.

5. Consideration may not be based on preexisting obligations or prior duties.

> The paralegal should check to ensure that each of the parties' duties relates to some act that will occur after the exchange of promises.

> The promises of each party must result in an agreement to perform some action in the future that does not relate to a prior duty.

6. The paralegal should check to determine whether the contract is one that falls under the common law or the Uniform Commercial Code. The requirements for consideration are different under common law.

> Contracts for the sale of real estate or services are governed by common law.

> Contracts for the sale of goods are controlled by the Uniform Commercial Code.

7. The paralegal should also research the laws of the state to determine if:

> statutes exist that alter or eliminate the need for consideration.

court decisions have altered traditional legal doctrines relating to consideration by supplying missing terms or by interpreting the contract
in such a way as to find consideration.

8. The paralegal should also look into the doctrine of promissory estoppel to
see if it will substitute for consideration. The doctrine will apply if:

the promisor made a promise to another;

the promisor either knew or should have known that the promisee
would rely on the promise;

the promisee relied on the promise to his detriment;

the promisee suffered an injury as a result.

QUESTIONS

1. What is consideration?
2. What is the role of consideration with respect to contracts?
3. Why is consideration necessary in the formation of a legally enforce-
    able contract?
4. Will a promise unsupported by consideration from the other party be
    enforceable?
5. What is an outputs contract?
6. What is a requirements contract?
7. Name some exceptions to the legal doctrine requiring consideration in
    order for a contract to be valid?
8. Can moral actions constitute consideration?
9. Do you agree with the result in question 8?
10. Why are preexisting obligations normally not satisfactory considera-
    tions?
11. What is the major exception to the preexisting obligation rule?
12. What is the consideration in an outputs contract or a requirements
    contract?
13. Explain the doctrine of promissory estoppel.

PROBLEMS

1. Joe receives a job offer from MTX Corporation. He moves his family from New Jersey to California. When he arrives, the company informs him that because of corporate downsizing there is no job for him. When he brings an action to obtain damages for the failure of MTX to give him a job, the corporation states that he has provided no consideration. Is the corporation correct?

2. Harry agrees to build a new office building for ZBR Corporation. During the construction, he encounters an unusual rock formation under the ground. Harry asks for more money to complete the construction. ZBR agrees to provide the additional consideration. However, it later refuses to pay the additional consideration and argues that Harry was already obligated to complete the building and is not entitled to the additional consideration. Who will prevail?

3. Uncle Bill promises to give his nephew, Robert, an expensive watch for his birthday. Later, Uncle Bill suffers some financial reversals and is unable to give Robert the watch. If Robert brings a lawsuit, will he be able to recover? If yes, why? If no, what could Robert have done to increase his chances for recovery?

4. Harry has a contract to build a new office building for Bert at a price of $1,000,000. Halfway through the job, Harry realizes that he is going to lose money. He goes to Bert and asks for an additional $250,000. When Harry finishes the construction job, Bert pays him only $1,000,000. Harry brings suit for the additional $250,000. Will he recover the additional money?

5. Sally agrees to give $100 to Knowledge College, her alma mater, because of her affection for that great center of learning. Later, she changes her mind and refuses to pay. The college brings a suit to collect the $100. Sally argues that she received no consideration for her pledge of $100 and need not pay. Is she correct?

6. Jackson has a contract to buy all of the output of widgets made by Johnson. In year number one, Johnson produces 2,000 widgets and Jackson purchases them all. Johnson decides that he has a foolproof way of making additional profits and produces 5,000 widgets. When Jackson objects, Johnson tells him that there is nothing he can do because he is obligated to buy all of Johnson's output. Who will prevail in a lawsuit between the two?

7. Carter has a contract to buy all of his requirements of widgets from Germond. Later, Carter finds a supplier who will deliver the widgets for a lower price. He argues that there is no legally binding contract because Germond has provided no consideration. Who will prevail in a lawsuit between Carter and Germond? Can you find consideration in this contract? Where?

5 *Legal Capacity*

Students will learn that the legal capacity to a contract is one of the elements necessary to a legally binding contract.

Students will learn that in order to have legal capacity one must be an adult and have the ability to understand the nature of the agreement and its essential terms.

Students will learn that a minor is presumed not to have legal capacity to enter contracts except for basic necessities of life relating to food, shelter, clothing, and other reasonable expenses. The age of consent for majority is 18.

Students will learn that there are other grounds such as insanity, mistake, duress, and fraud that go to the actual consent of the parties and could be used as reasons to terminate the contract.

CAPACITY OF PARTIES

Student Skill: Students will understand the nature of the requirement that the parties have capacity to enter a contract.

The parties to the contract must have legal capacity in order for the contract to be valid. If they do not, the contract will be voidable by at least one of the parties. This is based on a fundamental concept of contract law that the parties must reach informed consent. That is, the parties must understand the nature and the terms of the contract they are entering.

MINORS

Someone below the age of majority (normally age 18) is presumed not to have legal capacity to enter a contract. As a result, the law is especially sensitive to the need to protect minors from the consequences of their own actions.

A minor will be allowed to withdraw from contracts into which she entered before reaching age 18.

> EXAMPLE Mary, age 17, buys a new fur coat from Fred's Furriers. She wears the coat for several months, but decides to return it. She may do so even though she has caused a significant amount of depreciation to the coat.

The law is intended to protect minors even though they have received benefits under the contract. The adult other party will be the one who bears the loss.

> EXAMPLE Steve, age 16, buys a video game from Harold, an adult. One day Steve becomes enraged at the results of the game and smashes it to bits. He will be allowed to return it to Harold and receive full purchase price in return. Again, the burden is placed on the adult if some problem occurs.

Businesspeople should understand that they deal with minors at their own risk. They can reduce the risk of contracting with minors by dealing with adults instead. That is, the contract should be placed in an adult's name rather than the minor's.

A major exception relates to necessities of life that are acquired by minors. Unless a minor could be held legally liable for purchasing certain items, a minor could never buy food, clothing, transportation, or shelter.

Items that would be considered necessities of life would include:

- a hamburger at a local fast-food chain,
- a reasonably inexpensive item of clothing,
- a train ticket to attend school,
- a ticket to go to the movies.

Items that would clearly not constitute necessities of life include:

- a television set,
- an expensive automobile,
- a luxury stereo center,
- a trip on a cruise ship.

It is difficult to determine when an item will be classified as a necessity of life. A younger minor should have very few needs. As a person gets older, her needs increase and she should be held to higher levels of purchases.

RATIFICATION OF CONTRACTS

When a minor reaches age 18, he has the choice of either affirming or rejecting any contracts he may have made during his minority. The minor may disaffirm the contract by notifying the other party that she wants to reject the contract.

Conversely, the minor may affirm in a number of ways. First, the minor may wait beyond a reasonable time in which to reject the contract. If the new adult does so, it will be too late to reject the contract.

> EXAMPLE Fred agrees to a contract with Jones to supply him with new videocassettes every day beginning at age 17. When he reaches age 18, he continues to accept the videocassettes for an additional seven months. This is beyond a reasonable time after reaching adulthood. Fred will be bound by the contract. He has affirmed the contract by waiting beyond a reasonable time.

> EXAMPLE Don agreed to a contract when he was 17. At age 18, he is serving in the United States Army at a foreign military base. As a result, he will be given an additional period of time in which to disaffirm the contract. A reasonable time will not begin until Don has returned to the United States. Don must then make a decision about whether he wants to affirm or reject the contract.

One may also ratify the contract by explicitly informing the other party either orally or in writing that one wishes the contract to continue. The minor is now an adult and will be bound by affirmations of the contract.

A third way for the new adult to ratify the contract is to continue accepting the benefits under the contract.

> EXAMPLE Sally contracts to receive a bottle of hairspray every day from Rent a Bottle of Hairspray Company at age 17. She continues to receive the hairspray every day for eight months after reaching age 18. Sally has continued to accept the benefits under the contract, and will be bound for the remainder of the contract.

A fourth way for the former minor to be bound on the contract is to alter the subject matter of the contract in some manner.

> EXAMPLE Herb buys a car from John at age 17. At age 18 and one week, Herb takes out the rear suspension and lifts up the rear end by 18 inches. He has altered the subject matter of the contract and will be bound by it.

MINORS WHO MISREPRESENT AGE

If the minor represents that he is an adult in order to convince the other party to create a contract, the minor has committed fraud. In this case, either party may rescind the contract.

Generally, both parties can cancel the contract and must attempt to restore the position of the other party. This means that the minor must attempt to return as much of the property as possible. In other words, both parties should try to place each other in the positions they were in before the contract.

However, the majority rule is that the minor must only return what he can. That is, the minor may return damaged or depreciated property without liability for the loss. Again, the burden is placed on the adult. He should be especially careful to validate the minor's identification. If the minor misleads the adult, the adult will bear the risk of any loss that results.

OTHER PERSONS LACKING CAPACITY

A person who has been judged insane will obviously be lacking capacity. Any contract agreed to by such a person will be void from its inception. The insane person does not have to take action to void the contract.

A person who lacks contractual capacity because of a mental defect or because he was intoxicated may rescind or void the contract. An adult is presumed to have contractual capacity unless he can demonstrate to the contrary.

A person will have contractual capacity unless he can demonstrate that he could not understand the contract or its essential terms. If the contract is ruled invalid, the person must pay for what was received and return the subject matter of the contract.

MISTAKES

Student Skill: Students will learn which mistakes will allow one or both parties to excuse the performance under the contract.

If one or both of the parties made a mistake before they entered the contract, the courts are on the horns of a dilemma. One one hand, the courts would be reluctant to enforce contracts based on mistakes. On the other hand, the courts would be reluctant to overturn contracts merely because there was a mistake.

A mistake goes to the essential nature of whether the parties actually rendered an agreement. However, if courts were regularly to set aside contracts simply because there was a mistake, it would undercut the certainty of all contracts. This would have a detrimental impact on the law and the economy.

As a result, the law has attempted to strike a balance between material mistakes and those that should not be grounds for setting aside the contract. This can be a difficult line to walk, but it does represent a balance between these two competing interests.

A *bilateral* mistake is a mistake about a material fact made by both parties. In this case, either party may rescind (cancel) the contract upon learning of the mistake.

EXAMPLE Fred and Sue agree on the sale and purchase of a special diamond necklace for $10,000. They later discover that the necklace was not diamond. If the necklace later turns out to be rhinestones, the buyer will want to rescind the contract. If it turns out that the necklace was emeralds, the seller will want to rescind (cancel) the contract. In either case, either of the parties may rescind the contract because of the mutual mistake.

Unilateral mistakes are not normally grounds for rescinding the contract. However, if the other party knew or should have known of the mistake, the party who made the mistake may rescind the contract.

> EXAMPLE Dorothy solicits bids on the construction of a new boathouse. She receives the following five bids:
>
> > Steve, $33,000; Mary, $32,500; Frank, $32,000; Sally, $31,800; Pat, $21,800.
>
> Dorothy should recognize that Pat may have made a mistake. A reasonable person would ask Pat before merely accepting her bid. If Dorothy simply accepts the bid, Pat will be able to rescind the contract. Dorothy knew or should have known of Pat's unilateral mistake. The law will not permit her to profit from Pat's unilateral mistake in this instance.

However, a person will not be able to cancel a contract just because they made a mistake. One is expected to exercise a degree of self-help and good judgment. One will not be able to use routine changes in circumstance as grounds for rescinding the contract.

> EXAMPLE Charley opens a video store near a local college. He expects that the college will be a source of customers for his store. However, the college closes three months after Charley opens his store. He may not use this as an excuse for not performing contracts related to his video store. Other parties to contracts cannot be expected to bear the responsibility for his misfortune.
>
> EXAMPLE Hanson opens a pizza supply company. He agrees to supply pizza dough to Dominic's Pizzeria for a set price every day. The price of flour rises sharply, which makes Hanson's pizza dough contract unprofitable. He may not rescind his contract with Dominic's because of the increase in the price of flour.

FRAUD AND INNOCENT MISREPRESENTATION

Student Skill: Students will learn the elements of fraud and innocent misrepresentation.

A contract may be rescinded on the grounds of fraud, which relates to the consent of the parties. Fraud consists of the following elements:

There is a misstatement about a material fact.

Either the deliberate intent to deceive the other party or a reckless disregard of the truth exists.

There is knowledge that the other party would rely on the misstatement.

The other party does rely on the misstatement and suffers a loss as a result of the reliance.

> EXAMPLE Donna has a glass ring. She tells Irma that the ring is a diamond and sells it to her for $3,000. Later, Irma has the ring valued and discovers it is worth only $100. Donna has committed fraud and Irma is entitled to rescind the contract. This was a deliberate misrepresentation and Irma relied on it to her detriment.
>
> EXAMPLE Daphne has a glass ring. She does not know what stone is in the ring. Her friend, Gertrude, asks if the ring is a diamond. Daphne says "If that's what you think it is, I guess it is." This statement is in reckless disregard of the truth. If she sells the ring to Gertrude on that basis, she will be held liable for fraud.

One remedy for fraud is to rescind the contract and to restore the parties to their original positions. Some jurisdictions also allow the injured party to recover three times the damages suffered by the injured party. This is designed to punish the person who commits fraud because of the wrongful nature of the conduct.

Fraud must include a misstatement about a material fact. For example, statements about the number of miles a car was driven relate to a fact. Statements about the quality of the subject matter would normally fall into the category of sales talk or mere sales puffery.

> EXAMPLE Smith tells Johnson that his automobile is "a real beauty" and that Johnson "will have no trouble with it." If Johnson buys the car, he may not bring an action for fraud. These statements constitute mere sales talk and not misstatements about material facts.

While these statements of opinion would not constitute fraud, deliberately misleading statements of opinion by recognized experts such as architects, accountants, attorneys, or physicians could constitute fraud.

> EXAMPLE Angie is a customer at 19th National Bank. She has a question about retirement planning and asks the chief teller where she should place her money. The chief teller tells Angie that she should place all her

deposits in long-term accounts at 3 percent interest at the local branch. Because Angie may have perceived the teller as an expert, this could constitute fraud.

Silence by a person is normally not considered fraud. However, concealing information that one has the duty to disclose may constitute fraud. For example, certain individuals have the legal obligation to inform others about all the facts related to certain transactions. If they do not, the contract can be rescinded.

> EXAMPLE   Rose is the administrator of Willy's estate. She wants to purchase a particular piece of property from the estate. She must inform the beneficiaries of all the details regarding the purchase. If she is in a position to earn a profit from the purchase, she must disclose this fact to everyone else. Fiduciaries are supposed to work on behalf of their clients (customers) and not themselves.

Innocent misrepresentation is informing the other party of a material fact in an incorrect manner. An innocent misrepresentation would not be fraud.

> EXAMPLE   Jagger tells Richards that his property is zoned for commercial use. As a result, Richards purchases the property to build a restaurant. This was innocent misrepresentation by Jagger, who read the zoning map incorrectly and gave wrong information to Richards.

The difference between a mistake and innocent misrepresentation is that innocent misrepresentation implies a specific incorrect statement given by one party to another. The difference between it and fraud is that while the statement was false, it was not intentionally false. The proper legal remedy is to allow the other party to rescind the contract.

WORKING AT THE LAW OFFICE

People often have a difficult time understanding how mistakes affect a contract. Some believe that mistakes always excuse performance. They fail to understand the need for certainty as it relates to contractual obligations. Conversely, the courts do not want to bind parties when there is not a genuine meeting of the minds. A paralegal who understands the law relating to capacity and genuine consent will be a valuable asset to a law office.

COVENANTS NOT TO COMPETE

Student Skill: Students will learn the purpose of covenants not to compete and how they should be drafted.

A covenant not to compete is a clause that states that one party may not compete with another within some geographical area and for some period of time. Such clauses are not favored by the courts because they limit competition. However, these clauses will be upheld as long as they are reasonable in terms of geographical area, scope, and time.

> EXAMPLE Mom sells her diner to Joe for $100,000. There is a covenant in their contract that provides that Mom may not open a competing diner within 100 miles for a period of 10 years. This covenant not to compete is clearly too broad and therefore will not be legally enforceable. A clause that will be enforced would limit competition for a shorter period of time and within a narrower distance.
>
> EXAMPLE Bill goes to work for 2BX Corporation. When he assumes his new position, he is given a form stating that new employees agree not to open a competing business or join a competing business for 20 years. This is clearly too broad and will not be upheld by the courts. A more reasonable clause would have forbidden one from competing for a year. This is what is necessary to protect the employer from unfair competition in the future.

Covenants not to compete must also be part of a larger agreement. That is, one may not merely agree to covenants not to compete without some other purpose.

The covenant not to compete should be large enough in scope to protect the business interests of the party to whom it is given. Generally, courts will give greater latitude to covenants not to compete that relate to the sale of a business. The rationale is that a person who buys a business has the right to expect that the former owner will not compete with him.

An employer also has the right to expect that employees will not use their contacts or knowledge gained during their employment to form competing businesses or to pursue their customers. Conversely, society benefits from robust competition that permits individuals to use their knowledge to benefit customers and society.

This is an area in which the courts need to strike a balance between fair protection of a person's business and the right of another person to earn a living. Generally, courts will also be more likely to uphold covenants not to compete when they relate to current customers of the employer as opposed to new customers.

> EXAMPLE Joe goes to work for MNO Corporation. He signs an agreement that forbids him from contacting existing or potential customers of MNO Corporation if Joe should stop working for MNO Corporation. While the clause preventing him from contacting current customers is valid, the clause that prohibits him from contacting potential customers is too broad and too speculative. A person needs to be able to earn a living in a field that utilizes his skills.

While covenants not to compete have their limitations, they also have their uses. A person drafting an agreement for the purchase of a business should be particularly mindful of the usefulness of such clauses. It is important to protect this new owner of a business against situations in which a previous owner would unfairly compete with the new owner. However, one must draft it carefully or it will be struck down and have no effect.

DURESS

Student Skill: Students will learn the different types and elements of duress.

Duress is the improper use of force to compel the other party to form a contract. The duress could be either physical or economic.

> EXAMPLE Jack is told by the local loan shark to sign a loan agreement at 30 percent interest or he will have his legs broken. This is duress on the part of the loan shark. Jack will be able to rescind the contract.

The above example is an extreme instance of duress. However, duress could also take more subtle forms.

> EXAMPLE Bob is the supervisor of a large number of low-skilled workers at a plant near the Mexican border. Many of the workers are illegal immigrants. Bob asks each of the new workers to sign an agreement in which they agree to pay him ten percent of their salary. This is a form of economic duress. The workers could have these contracts rescinded.

In certain areas of the United States, agreements such as the one described in the above example are relatively common. Individuals are brought into this country and made to work as indentured servants. A good legal team might be able to have these agreements set aside on the grounds of duress.

Another form of duress is to take advantage of a person's weakened economic situation in order to benefit oneself. While it is permissible to be a tough negotiator, there are certain actions that will shock the sensibilities of the courts and amount to duress.

> EXAMPLE Simpson knows that Johnson has a problem making payments at the end of each month and needs cash during these periods. As a result, Simpson calls up Johnson and tells him that he will pay him cash for certain products and prior debts, but only if he receives substantial discounts. This is a mild form of economic duress. Simpson is taking advantage of Johnson's weakened economic position.
>
> EXAMPLE Marla is a nurse employed by Frank. She is currently earning $400 per week. When Frank suffers a heart attack, he is near death for several days. During this period, Marla asks for and receives a raise of $300 per week. Marla has taken advantage of her position and of Frank's poor health. Her raise should be set aside on the grounds of economic duress.

IMPOSSIBILITY OF PERFORMANCE

Student Skill: The student will learn what constitutes the common law doctrine of impossibility, which excuses one's obligation to perform.

There are certain changes in circumstances that will make it very difficult for one or both parties to perform their contractual obligations. In these situations, the court again finds itself in a difficult situation. If it compels the parties to perform, the courts can create unjust situations that do not make economic sense. Conversely, a legal policy that too quickly excuses performance will reduce the certainty of performance associated with contracts.

The ability to rely on the party's willingness to perform contracts is one of their major benefits. If the law permits people to ignore their contractual obligations, people will become reluctant to enter into contracts at all.

The law provides that a person's performance will be excused if it becomes impossible to perform one's duties. Courts have held "impossibility" to be a very difficult condition to meet. The change in circumstances must be caused by external reasons and be reasonably unforeseeable. That is, the parties could not have reasonably expected the situation to occur.

EXAMPLE Sam and Sally agree to the sale of Blackacre from Sam to Sally for $150,000 on March 1st. Sally had expected to receive a major portion of the purchase price from an inheritance from her aunt. Unfortunately, Sally only receives $1,000 from her aunt and does not have the purchase price to give Sam. She asks to be excused from the contract on the grounds of impossibility. She argues that these events were externally caused and unforeseeable. Sally will not prevail. It is still possible for her to perform the contract. She can obtain the purchase price from another source. These are not the types of circumstances that rise to the level of impossibility.

EXAMPLE Sandy agrees to ship 1,000 widgets to Phil. However, a fire a Sandy's place of business makes the shipment exceedingly difficult. Sandy claims she should be excused on the grounds of impossibility. Fires are foreseeable events. Unless the entire subject matter of the contract was destroyed, Sandy is not excused from performing the contract.

EXAMPLE Frank has a contract to provide certain services at Molly's house. However, two weeks of very bad weather makes it difficult to travel the roads between Frank's residence and Molly's. Frank asks to be excused from the contract on the grounds of impossibility. Bad weather, even long periods of bad weather, is foreseeable. This does not rise to the level of impossibility.

EXAMPLE Jim's workers go on strike. He asks to be released from his contract with Jill. Strikes are caused by internal rather than external factors. In addition, strikes are foreseeable events. Strikes happen regularly. A strike is not grounds for excusing performance. One can find other ways of performing the contract.

EXAMPLE A hurricane hits the town of East Overshoe for the first time in history. It wipes out Frank's place of business. As a result, Frank cannot perform several of his contracts. This would be an example of true impossibility because the circumstances were external and unforeseeable.

COMMERCIAL IMPRACTICABILITY

As one can observe from the preceding examples, the common law standard of impossibility is very difficult to meet. The drafters of the Uniform Commercial Code believed that the standard was too high. As a result, the standard for excusing for performance under the UCC is commercial impracticability.

While this is still a high standard, it is less onerous than the common law standard of impossibility. The drafters of the code indicated that they wanted to excuse performance when the circumstances made it clear that continuing performance no longer made economic sense.

However, even in contracts for the sale of goods under the UCC, the change in circumstances must still be external and reasonably unforeseeable. There must be some event that changes the positions of the parties since the time the contract was created.

A change in governmental regulations might cause commercial impracticability. For example, the government might impose certain price controls on goods which would make it very difficult to perform the contract.

In this case, the party could argue it was commercially impractical to perform the contract. The nonperforming party could then allocate the items among his existing customers and negotiate different prices in a manner that would be fairest in light of the changed circumstances.

A flood could wipe out a significant portion of one party's crop that was the subject matter of the contract. In this case, the party could then allocate the remaining portion of the crops to current customers. This would permit each party to obtain some benefit from the situation.

DUTY TO DISCLOSE

Generally, one has little duty to disclose facts that are not known to the other party. Contracts are based on the premise that two knowledgeable adults will reach an agreement that is fair to both sides. This means that each party is expected to do her own research and analysis of the situation.

However, there are instances when a party does have the duty to disclose material facts. A material fact is one that is important enough that a party might change her mind about entering the contract. Many jurisdictions have enacted consumer protection laws that require the seller not to engage in dishonest activities. This places greater burdens on a seller to disclose material facts to the buyer.

If the party knows of a defect that is unknown to the other party, he must disclose it to the other party. This is called a latent defect. The purpose of requiring a person to disclose a latent defect is that failure to disclose could prove dangerous to the other party.

> EXAMPLE Newfeld sells his house to Jones. Newfeld knows that his house is infested with termites. He does not tell Jones of this latent defect. This was improper. Newfeld had a duty to disclose the latent defect to Jones. The infestation of termites in the house could prove dangerous to Jones and others. This defect was about a material fact. Jones may rescind the contract.

FIDUCIARIES

Student Skill: Students will understand the nature of a fiduciary and her special obligations.

A party who serves in a fiduciary capacity has a duty to disclose all facts to the other party. Fiduciary capacity means that one party is in a special position of trust which requires the fiduciary always to act in the interest of the other party. Fiduciaries include guardians, executors, and trustees. Because of the nature of their position, the fiduciary must always act on behalf of the other party. This means that there is an affirmative duty to disclose all pertinent facts.

> EXAMPLE Hank is the trustee for a trust that names Sally as a beneficiary. The trust contains real property that Hank wishes to purchase. Hank is aware that someone else is interested in acquiring the real estate for a shopping center. He must disclose this fact to all parties involved in the trust before the purchase.

PARALEGAL'S "THINGS TO DO"

Student Skill: The student will be able to determine all of the elements relating to the capacity of a party to a contract.

1. One of the duties of a paralegal is to protect her supervising attorney's client. This is especially true if the client is someone who is a member of a protected group of people, such as a minor or others who are incapable of protecting themselves.
2. If one of the parties is a minor:

> The paralegal should be aware that adults should not enter into contracts with minors because they bear the risk if problems should later develop.

> The paralegal should check the agreement to determine if it is for necessities of life. If it is, the contract will be binding. However, most contracts for a minor's necessities tend to include rather small amounts.

> A contract that is not for necessities may be carried out by the minor if he wishes. Conversely, the minor may disaffirm the contract at any time prior to reaching age 18.

If the minor disaffirms the contract, the minor must return whatever property he can. However, in most states, he need only return what he can, and need not give the adult money to place her in the same position as she was before the contract. All the risk is on the adult.

The minor client should be advised to take some action upon reaching age 18. The minor may explicitly affirm the contract, in which case the new adult will be bound on the contract for its term. The minor may also reject the contract by explicitly informing the other party of her desire to do so.

The minor will also have ratified the contract if she waits beyond a reasonable time to disaffirm the contract. A reasonable time is what is considered reasonable in light of all the circumstances.

The minor will also have ratified the contract if she alters the property, resells it, or otherwise acts as if she were the owner.

3. The paralegal should also check to determine if any of the parties might be lacking contractual capacity. Contractual capacity is defined as the ability to understand the nature of the contract and its essential terms. Adults are presumed to have contractual capacity unless it can be shown otherwise.

If a person has already been judged insane, he does not have contractual capacity.

A person claiming lack of contractual capacity has the burden of showing it through clear and convincing evidence.

One can use excessive alcohol or drug use as evidence of lack of contractual capacity. However, it is not, by itself, evidence of lack of capacity.

4. The paralegal also ought to check to determine if the parties may have made a mistake that would excuse performance. When drafting the contract, the paralegal should exercise caution in order to help the parties avoid mistakes.

If both parties made a mistake about a material fact, either one may rescind the contract.

If one party made a mistake about a material fact, she may be excused from performance if the other party knew or should have known about the mistake.

5. Covenants against competition should be drafted carefully if they are necessary to protect the interest of your client. They must be reasonable with ref-

erence to time and geographical area. They may take the form of one of the following, among others.

A covenant against using information obtained in an employer's business to further one's own interest is quite common and is often required when a new employee begins work at a company.

While such clauses are binding, they must be drafted carefully. There is a need to protect the employer. However, the clause must not be so restrictive as to limit the employee's ability to earn a living in the future. Courts will not reform these clauses. As a result, if they are unreasonable, they will be struck down entirely.

The courts have generally permitted greater freedom in restricting a previous owner's ability to compete with the new owner of a business. The reason is that the new owner does not expect the prior owner to deprive him of customers through direct competition.

The covenant not to compete must still be drafted so that it is reasonable in terms of geographical area and time. Overly restrictive covenants will be struck down as having no effect.

QUESTIONS

1. What is contractual capacity?
2. Which minor's contracts will be enforced by the courts?
3. What is a necessity of life?
4. Name some necessities of life for minors.
5. How may a minor affirm a contract upon reaching age 18?
6. Will a mistake excuse the performance of the parties to a contract?
7. What is a bilateral mistake?
8. What is a unilateral mistake?
9. What are the consequences of bilateral and unilateral mistakes?
10. What are the parties' responsibilities with respect to disclosing unknown defects?
11. What are the special responsibilities of a fiduciary with respect to contracts?
12. What is fraud?
13. What is misrepresentation?

14. What are remedies for fraud?

15. What are the remedies for innocent misrepresentation?

16. What is a covenant not to compete?

17. What are the major considerations with respect to a covenant not to compete?

18. How would you draft a covenant not to compete?

PROBLEMS

1. Joe has agreed to a written contract with Mary. Later, he wants to be relieved from his contractual duties on the grounds that he lacked contractual capacity. He argues that he had been drinking on the day that he signed the contract. Will this be sufficient to excuse his performance under the contract? If not, what would be sufficient to excuse performance?

2. Johnson and Samuels agree to the purchase and sale of a table that both believed to be an antique of a particular type. Later, they discover that the table is different than they had believed. Who will be able to rescind the contract?

3. Sampson agrees to build a home for Franklin on Blackacre. Sampson is not aware that Franklin has an engineering report that indicates that there is an unusual rock formation below the surface of Blackacre. Sampson later discovers this rock formation and brings an action to have the contract rescinded. Will he prevail?

4. Hawthorne, age 15, purchases a new leather coat and wears it for several months. Unfortunately, the coat catches on fire at a local barbecue. Hawthorne attempts to return the coat to the seller. Will he be able to do so? Should he be able to do so?

5. Smith runs a business that has a significant number of trade secrets. He wants you to draft a clause in his new employees' contracts that states that none of them may work for a competing firm for their lifetimes. Do you draft this contract for Smith? Do you have any different suggestions for him? How might they be placed into words?

6. Jones is about to purchase a furniture store from Fred. He wants to draft a contract that would prohibit Fred from ever opening another furniture store within the same state. Is this a good idea? What should he do?

7. Donald has a contract to deliver one dozen silver bracelets to Smith. He sends the bracelets but fails to notice that they are silver-plated rather than silver. Smith wants to cancel the contract. What grounds should he state in the request?

8. Johnson goes to Cal's car lot. He notices the odometer reading of 50,000 miles on the car he buys. He asks Cal if it is correct. Cal does not know if the reading is correct, but tells Johnson that it is. Johnson later discovers that the car had actually been driven 100,000 miles. Johnson would like to rescind the contract. He should bring what type of action?

6 *Contracts and Third Parties*

Students will learn to recognize that only third parties who the original two parties intended to benefit from the contract may bring an action to enforce it.

Students will learn that this prevents people who have only a slight interest from enforcing the contract. Third parties who may enforce the contract are called third party beneficiaries. Those who may not enforce the contract are called incidental beneficiaries.

Students will learn how the original two parties may alter the contract through assignments, delegations, or novations.

Students will learn that an assignment transfers one party's rights and obligations under the contract to another. A delegation shifts one of the party's duties to another. A novation is an agreement by the original two parties to substitute a third party for one of the original parties.

BENEFICIARIES OF CONTRACTS

A contract is an agreement between two parties that the law will enforce. Generally, people other than the original parties have no legal right to enforce. If third parties could enforce the contract, the courts would be flooded with various claims from people who might receive some small benefit if the contract was enforced.

However, the law will allow third parties to enforce the contract if the original two parties clearly intended that the third party would benefit under the contract. This person is called a third party beneficiary.

A third party beneficiary might include someone who is named in an insurance policy.

> EXAMPLE   Bob takes out a life insurance policy with XYZ Insurance Company. He names his daughter, Mary, as the beneficiary of his policy in the event of his death.

It is clear from the insurance contract that the parties intended that the named beneficiary should be able to enforce the policy. As a result, Mary will be able to bring a legal action to collect the benefits under the contract.

Another third party beneficiary who would be able to enforce the contract would be a creditor who the parties clearly intended to benefit.

> EXAMPLE   Jones takes out a loan with 19th National Bank. He gives the bank a security interest in some of his property. Jones later sells the property to Smith. As part of the sales agreement, Smith also agrees to repay Jones' loan to the bank. Clearly, the agreement between Jones and Smith was intended to benefit the bank. The bank is a creditor beneficiary and could enforce their contract.

Conversely, people who may only benefit from the contract in an incidental manner will not be able to enforce the contract.

> EXAMPLE   Sam lives next door to Joe who contracts with Al's Aluminum Siding to have aluminum placed on all four sides on his house. If this job is done, it will substantially improve the appearance of Joe's house. As a result, the value of Sam's house will also increase. Although Sam would benefit under the contract between Al and Joe, he was not intended to benefit by the two parties. Therefore, Sam could not bring an action to enforce the contract.

A member of the general public would not be regarded as a third party beneficiary even if the person would have benefited from the contract.

> EXAMPLE Franklin has a contract to operate a toll gate for the city of Middleberg. After one week, Franklin goes on strike. He leaves the gate in the down position, which prevents motorists from using the road. Bill brings an action to recover damages for the breach of contract between Franklin and Middleberg. He argues that he was unable to get to work because the toll bridge was down. Bill is merely a member of the general public. There was no specific intention to allow him to benefit from the contract. Therefore, he may not recover.

This last example strikes some people as unfair. However, it would be enormously expensive to allow members of the general public to recover in these cases. First, the court costs would be huge. Second, large amounts of money would have to be spent defending and resolving these lawsuits. As a result, the costs of governmental improvements would become prohibitive and they might not be made.

A person drafting a contract might want to specifically state if there are third parties who the original parties would want to be able to enforce the contract. The drafter might also note certain classes of people who would not be able to enforce the contract.

TRANSFER OF CONTRACTUAL DUTIES (ASSIGNMENT OF CONTRACT)

Student Skill: Students will learn the process of assigning contractual rights and the duties of each party to an assignment.

Parties to contracts may transfer their duties and rights under the contract to other parties. This transfer is called an assignment. Parties may generally assign their contracts to other individuals. The ability to transfer these contractual rights and obligations is important to our system of free enterprise and is essential in the construction and other industries.

Parties may prohibit the assignment of contractual duties and rights in their contract. This may be important if the parties want to ensure that only they will be involved with the contract.

Personal service contracts may not be assigned without the consent of the other party. This is because of the uniquely personal nature of certain services.

> EXAMPLE Simpson acts as Jone's chauffeur. He may not assign this contract to someone else. This would be unfair to Jones. Conversely, Jones may not assign the contract to someone else. This would be unfair to

Simpson. The prohibition against assignments of personal service contracts ensures that each of the parties receives what they bargained for in the original agreement.

An assignment that would materially increase the burdens of the other party is also prohibited. This might occur when the assignee of the contract is located in a different area of the country.

> EXAMPLE Samuels has a contract to ship generators to Al in Atlanta. Al assigns the contract to Charlie in Chicago. The assignment of the contract would impose additional shipping costs on Samuels. This would be an unfair burden to place on him. Therefore, the assignment of the contractual duties would be prohibited because it would materially increase the burdens of the other party.

Because assignments are essential to the United States economy, the exceptions noted above will not prevent assignments of contracts involving some minor degree of individualized work or change in performance.

> EXAMPLE ATX Corporation has a contract to build a major new office building. ATX Corporation subcontracts (assigns) plumbing, carpentry, and masonry work. While these subcontracts might result in slightly different levels of performance and burdens for the other party, these subcontracts are permissible. If prime contractors were unable to assign (subcontract) their contractual obligations, many contracts could not be performed at all.

NOTIFYING OTHERS OF ASSIGNMENT

The person who receives the assignment (assignee) must notify the other party to the contract of the assignment. The purpose of the notice is to ensure that there are no problems relating to performance now that there is a new party involved with the performance of the contract.

> EXAMPLE John and Joe have a contract in which John agrees to deliver ten cartons of widgets to Joe. Joe assigns the contract to Jill. In order to prevent John from delivering the widgets to the wrong person, Jill should inform him of the assignment. If Jill neglects to notify John, she will have no remedy against him if John delivers the widgets to Joe. This properly places the legal burden on the assignee to ensure that the contract's provisions are performed smoothly.

LIABILITIES OF PARTIES

An assignment does not relieve the parties of their liabilities under the contract. The person to whom the contractual rights and obligations are transferred (the assignee) becomes primarily obligated to complete the contract. However, the assignor remains secondarily liable on the contract. That is, the assignor will be liable to complete the contract if the assignee does not.

> <u>EXAMPLE</u> Burke and Barone have a contract in which Burke is to send Barone a large generator. Burke assigns the contract to Dawson. Barone neither objects nor consents to the assignment. Dawson must now perform the contract and deliver the generator to Barone. If Dawson does not perform the contract, Burke is liable to do so. Therefore, Burke must send the generator to Barone. If Dawson had delivered the generator to Barone, he would now have the right to receive payment from her. If Burke delivers the generator to Barone, she is entitled to the payment.

Assignments are extremely important in the construction and other industries. It is important for persons involved in these industries to understand the various liabilities of the parties. In addition, a person drafting a contract should understand the liabilities involved in an assignment.

DELEGATION OF DUTIES

Under the law of contracts, a person may also delegate her duties under the contract without delegating the benefits of the contract. Rules governing situations when delegations will be permitted are similar to those relating to assignments.

Delegations are not permitted if the contract prohibits delegations. They are also not permitted if the contract provides for personal services or the delegation would materially increase the burdens of the other party. However, unlike an assignment, the delegator retains her rights under the contract.

> <u>EXAMPLE</u> Dean has a contract to supply Lewis with 1,000 pies. He delegates his duties to Crystal. Lewis neither objects nor consents to the delegation. Crystal now has the obligation to ship the pies to Lewis. After he ships the pies to Lewis, he is entitled to receive payment from Dean, who has the right to collect from Lewis.

This example illustrates the major difference between an assignment and a delegation. In an assignment, all the rights and obligations are transferred to the assignee from the assignor. In a delegation, only the obligations are transferred. The rights under the contract remain with the delegator.

Because a new person (the delegatee) is now involved in the providing of duties, the other party may object to the delegation if the delegation was forbidden by the contract or involves personal services.

> EXAMPLE   Hanson agrees to provide interior decorating services for one year to Lois. Hanson attempts to delegate these duties to Johnson. Lois may object to Hanson's attempted delegation to Johnson.

SUBSTITUTING PARTIES (NOVATION)

The original parties to the contract may agree to substitute one party for another. This is called a novation. The new party then takes over both the responsibilities and rights of the original party.

> EXAMPLE   Mary has a contract to deliver 1,000 wicker chairs to Natalie. Later, both parties agree to substitute Olga for Mary. Olga now has the responsibility to deliver the chairs and the right to receive the purchase price when she does.

The difference between a novation and an assignment or a delegation is that the original party no longer has any rights or responsibilities under the contract. As a result, the remaining party should take special care that the new party is responsible and will carry out the contract.

ACCORD AND SATISFACTION

The parties to the contract may want to change the nature of the performance. A contract is simply an agreement between two parties and they may do what they want with the level of performance. An accord and satisfaction is an agreement among the parties to change their obligations. Their new duties substitute for the old and form the basis for determining the parties' obligations.

> EXAMPLE   Herb agrees to sell Greenacre to Frank for $100,000 with a delivery date of November 1st. On October 23rd, Herb asks Frank if he could sell him Blueacre instead of Greenacre for the same price. If Frank agrees

to the substitution, the two parties have agreed to an accord and satisfaction. Herb should now sell Blueacre to Frank on November 1st for $100,000.

THIRD PARTY INTERFERENCE

A person may not interfere with the contractual rights of others, and will be liable for tortious interference with a contract if she does. The party bringing the action may recover if he can show the following events:

A valid contract existed.

The interfering party knew of the contract.

The interfering party intentionally and unjustifiably asked a party to breach the contract.

The party breached the contract and the breach resulted in an injury to the other party.

This may not be an easy case to prove. Parties have the right to discuss engaging in contractual relationships in a free market economy and parties may breach contracts without criminal penalties.

There are a number of remedies that the courts may impose. Money damages can be awarded to compensate individuals for losses. The court could also grant injunctive relief to stop the conduct. An injunction is a court order that demands that someone cease certain forms of conduct.

> EXAMPLE Slam Dunk Dawson is a star player for the North Maine Lobsters basketball team. He has a 3-year contract with the Lobsters. A representative of the Vermont Valiants, a competing basketball team, contacts Slam Dunk to persuade him to breach the contract and to play for the Valiants. The Lobsters may go to court and obtain an injunction that would prohibit the Valiants from inducing Slam Dunk to breach his contract with them.

If Slam Dunk had stopped playing for the Lobsters, they could also obtain legal relief. They could not obtain a court order of specific performance that would compel Slam Dunk to play for them. Orders of specific performance will not be granted to complete performance of services. However, a court order preventing Slam Dunk from playing for someone else is appropriate.

This puts Slam Dunk in the position of either playing for the Lobsters or not playing at all.

PARALEGAL'S "THINGS TO DO"

Student Skill: The student will be able to write a contract to protect the interest of third parties.

1. The paralegal should review the discussions of all the parties to determine if there is a legally enforceable agreement. Without a binding contract, none of the original or third parties have any rights or remedies.

> The paralegal should check to see if the original parties intend to create a contract that would benefit a third party.

> The paralegal should determine if the original parties want to include references to the third party in the contract. In this case, the drafter should specifically indicate the reason that the third party should be able to benefit under the contract.

> The beneficiary may be a donee beneficiary. This is someone the parties have designated as a beneficiary. For example, someone named as a beneficiary under an insurance contract would be a donee beneficiary entitled to enforce the contract.

> A creditor beneficiary is likely to be someone who has an interest in the property because it is a way of securing her loan to the borrower (creditor beneficiary). Often, the creditor beneficiary has an agreement that provides that he will be able to enforce the loan agreement against other parties. The paralegal should determine who may acquire the property.

2. The duties and obligations of the parties may have been transferred to another party.

> There may have been an assignment of the contractual duties and rights. In this case, the new party to the contract must perform the responsibilities of the original party.

> The assignor remains liable to perform the duties under the contract if the assignee does not.

> If the assignee does perform the contractual duties, she is entitled to receive the benefits under the contract.

One of the original parties may also delegate the duties under the contract to another party. In this case, the person delegating the duties still retains the benefits under the contract. The drafter of any contractual provisions relating to assignments or delegations should recognize the legal consequences of the substitutions.

If the drafter wants different results, she should include these in the original or any subsequent contracts.

3. Unless indicated, contractual duties may be assigned or delegated except in the case of personal service contracts.

The contract may prohibit the assignment or delegation of duties. If one or both of the parties do not want assignments or delegations, such a clause should be included in the contract. The law will recognize and honor such a prohibition.

The drafter may also want to indicate who may not enforce the contract. For example, certain contractual duties may involve the public. The contract's drafter could specifically forbid general members of the public from enforcing the contract by indicating that it is not the parties' intention to permit them to do so.

4. After the contract has been agreed to, a number of issues may occur related to third party contractual interests. The paralegal should review the conduct of the parties to determine how the rights of the original or third parties may have been affected by changes in circumstances.

The parties may have taken actions that affect the ability of the original parties to perform their contractual obligations. One should also check to determine whether the rights of third parties may have been affected.

If the duties have been performed or if certain conditions have occurred, the third parties' contractual rights may become effective. If the paralegal represents a third party, she should determine if the third party is entitled to the performance of the contract. The third party may have to take specific action to enforce these rights. For example, while most insurance companies pay claims promptly, others may have to be pursued more vigorously.

If contractual duties have been delegated, the delegator remains liable on the contact until the delegatee performs the delegator's contractual obligations. At that time, the delegator should obtain the performance of the other party. If this involves payment of money, the delegator should collect it and send it to the delegatee.

Under an assignment, the assignor also remains liable to perform his original duties until the assignee performs them. However, the assignee also has the right to collect any payment from the other party.

The paralegal should make sure that a client delegatee or client assignee notifies the other party of the change in relationship. This will protect the client and help ensure that the relationship goes as smoothly as possible.

The relationships are different in a novation. In this case, the parties have agreed to replace one party with a completely different party. The paralegal should consider drawing up an entirely new contract. This would help avoid any difficulties at a later date.

5. The paralegal may also want to periodically review the agreements and positions of the parties to the agreement. These tend to change over time and the parties' positions should be reviewed frequently in light of changing circumstances. The various parties should have their duties and rights reviewed on a regular basis.

6. The paralegal should also determine if there has been interference with the contract. This will be shown if the following elements can be proved:

a valid contract,

knowledge of the contract,

intentional interference with the contract,

a breach of the contract,

resulting in injury to one of the parties.

QUESTIONS

1. What is a third party interest?
2. What is the difference between a third party beneficiary and an incidental beneficiary?
3. How does one distinguish between the two?
4. What is an incidental beneficiary?
5. What is a third party beneficiary?

6. What is an assignment?

7. What is a delegation?

8. What is a novation?

9. What is an accord and satisfaction?

10. What constitutes interference with a contract?

11. Which duties to a contract may be assigned?

12. Which duties to a contract may not be assigned?

13. What are the legal differences between an assignment and a delegation?

14. Explain the purpose of notification with respect to an assignment and a delegation.

PROBLEMS

1. Your supervising attorney's client has a contract with ZNB Corporation. She would like to assign the contract to Sarah. She is not certain how to proceed. What do you do? What do you say to your boss?

2. Jones works for the Rocky Mountain Roughriders football team as a chiropractor. He would like to delegate these duties to Hanson. May he do so?

3. Sam operates a ferry boat between New Duke and New Earl. He works for the Duke and Earl Authority. One week he decides to stop working. As a result, Tom Thomspon is unable to go to work in New Duke City. Tom brings suit against Sam because he was unable to get to work. Will he recover?

4. Jim is a waiter for a restaurant in the town of New Blatz. All the waiters in New Blatz go on strike. Several of the waiters' customers bring an action to recover damages from them as a result of the waiters' strike. Can the customers recover. Why or why not? What are the consequences of each result to the parties and to the larger society?

5. Sally has a contract with the Tiny Tots Nursery School to teach 3- and 4-year-olds. She agrees to delegate her duties to Bert, but the school objects. The school's contracts with the teachers contains no reference to assignments or delegations. How should this matter be decided?

6. Irene owes a debt to Harriet, who assigns it to Jane. Irene pays the debt to Harriet, who then skips town. How should Jane handle similar transactions in the future?

7. Jill and Jim have a written contract for Jill to deliver 100 widgets to Jim. They would like to substitute Jack for Jim. How should they handle this?

8. Frank has a written contract to buy a rare dime from Joe. They later discuss the matter. Both parties would like to substitute a rare nickel as the subject matter of the contract. May they do so? What is the best method?

9. Stuart and Judy have a contract for Stuart to supply Jill with 100 cases of nail polish. They later agree to substitute hair coloring liquid. Still later, Stuart runs out of hair coloring liquid and sends Judy the nail polish instead. Does Judy have any remedies?

7 *Legality of Contracts*

SKILLS STUDENTS WILL LEARN

Students will learn that legality of the subject matter is one of the elements necessary to an enforceable contract and that contracts that violate the law or public policy will not be enforced by the courts.

Students will learn that contracts that restrain trade or violate public policy are likely to be held unlawful. This will include contracts that violate antitrust laws and may include contracts of individuals not to compete with an employer or with a business.

LEGALITY OF CONTRACTS

One of the elements of a legally enforceable contract is that it be for a legal purpose. The provisions of a contract must not violate statutes of the legislature, administrative regulations, or public policy announced by the courts. Contractual provisions contrary to criminal laws will not be enforced.

However, in some cases, one must examine the intent of the law to determine if the purpose of the law has been violated by the contract's terms. This is particularly true with respect to licensing laws that regulate various occupations and professions.

LICENSING STATUTES

Licensing statutes are designed to regulate various professions and to require a certain minimum level of competence. Physicians, lawyers, and accountants are examples of such professions. A person who performs professional services without having satisfied the requirements necessary to become a member of that profession is committing an unlawful act. As a result, she may not enforce any contract she has to provide these services.

> EXAMPLE Williams spent many hours watching various trials on television. He decides to begin defending people without the benefit of law school. He decides that he has seen enough trials on television to do a good job. Williams opens a small office and begins defending a number of people in municipal and county courts. Although he does an adequate job, his "clients" do not owe him any fee. Williams is not entitled to enforce any contracts agreed upon with his clients. He is also liable to be sent to jail for practicing law without a license.

A person who has not complied with licensing statutes cannot enforce contracts on which they are based. However, the law draws a distinction between licensing statutes that are designed to ensure competent professionals and those that are merely revenue-raising measures. If the statute violated is only designed to raise governmental revenues, the contract will still be enforceable.

> EXAMPLE Betty goes to the local beautician and has her hair cut. She notes that the beauty shop does not have a license. She refuses to pay for her haircut and manicure. Betty is wrong. The license for the beauty shop is predominantly a revenue-raising device. The failure of the beauty shop to obtain a license will not prevent it from collecting its fees.

ANTICOMPETITIVE PROVISIONS

Student Skill: Students will understand which contractual provisions will be permissible and which will not.

Contracts that are in restraint of trade violate the federal Sherman and Clayton Antitrust Acts. These laws were designed to prevent large organizations

from engaging in certain conduct that created economic monopolies or resulted in restraint of trade. Other contractual provisions may also violate common
law prohibiting restraint of trade.

In business, an agreement not to compete with another's business is
called a covenant not to compete. Such covenants are valid only if part of a
larger agreement and reasonably limited in terms of time and geographical
scope.

While such covenants have a useful purpose to the extent that they protect
a business from unfair competition, they also serve to limit competition. The
courts seek to find a balance between these two competing interests in determining the covenant's validity.

The law states that the covenant not to compete must be reasonable in
order to be enforceable. That is, it should be broad enough to protect the business or employer, but not so broad as to excessively limit the other's ability to
earn a living.

> EXAMPLE Albert goes to work for XBG Corporation. They ask him to sign
> a covenant not to compete in a similar industry on the East Coast for a pe-
> riod of ten years. This clause is clearly too broad and will not be enforce-
> able.
> EXAMPLE Molly works as a waitress for the Tomain Diner. The manager
> of the diner asks all of his employees to agree to a covenant not to com-
> pete with the diner. The covenant states that employees shall not work
> for any other eating establishment within the city of Bigberg for three
> years. This clause is not enforceable. It overly restricts Molly's ability to
> earn a living.
> EXAMPLE Bob buys a store from Joe. The contract contains a clause that
> Bob will not open a competing business within five miles of the store for
> two years. This clause would appear to be reasonable given the nature of
> the transactions and the necessity to protect Joe's interest.

The last example illustrates the point that the courts are more likely to extend greater protection to the new owners of businesses than to employers. A
person who sells a business is aware that a person buying a business does not
expect the previous owner to compete with her. As a result, the protections
given to the new owner can be broader than those protections given to an employer.

Drafters of contracts should be aware that courts will seldom reform or
rewrite the covenants for the parties. If the covenant is too broad, it will be
struck down and will have no effect. Drafters should write the provision in a
manner that will protect the intended party, but not be so broad as to be unlawful.

ANTITRUST LAWS

Some contractual provisions violate antitrust laws and are unlawful on their face. It is illegal to agree to contracts that deliberately limit competition regardless of the intentions of the parties.

> EXAMPLE   The four heads of the largest corporations that manufacture widgets meet. They decide that they all could make more money if they simply divided up the national widget market. They decide that each company should take a section of the country. One takes the East, another the West, the third takes the South, and the fourth takes the North. This is unlawful on its face and will be struck down. Not only will this clause not be enforced, these individuals could be sent to jail for their conduct.

> EXAMPLE   Sally and Bob work in the same industry, but for different companies. One day, they are talking about a mutual product on which they are working. They decide that the product would be of higher quality and safer if they could keep the price at a certain level. Sally and Bob agree to hold the price of the product at a certain level. Although they may have good intentions, their conduct is unlawful. It is illegal to fix prices under any circumstances.

As noted in the above examples, conduct such as price fixing or the dividing up of markets is unlawful regardless of the reason. Certain other contractual provisions may also be unlawful unless the provision is drafted correctly. Resale price maintenance agreements are those that require a person not to sell a product below a particular price. Such a clause is unlawful.

> EXAMPLE   ZNT Corporation makes flidgies. It requires all of its retailers to sign contracts stating that none of them will sell flidgies for below $1 per unit.

This contract would be unlawful under the Sherman Antitrust Act. This is true regardless of the intent of the parties.

However, one does not violate the Sherman Act if one simply suggests certain retail prices. This would be permissible as long as the retailers are allowed to sell the items for whatever price they wish.

> EXAMPLE   TZB Corporation sells Blidgie golf carts. It places stickers on the carts with a suggested retail price. But the retailers are allowed to sell the golf carts at a price that they can set. The key difference is that the retailers are not required to sell the golf carts at a particular price.

OTHER UNLAWFUL CONTRACTS

One of the largest industries in this country is gambling. People bet on nearly every activity known to mankind. Despite the popularity of wagering, the activity is unlawful in most jurisdictions. Even friendly bets or employee betting pools are illegal and can not be enforced.

Insurance contracts are a method of shifting risk from the insured parties to the insurance companies. Although there is an element of risk with respect to insurance contracts, these agreements shift risk rather than create it. As a result, they are lawful.

However, one must have some interest in the subject matter of the insurance contract in order to take out the policy. That is, one must suffer an economic loss if the subject matter of the contract is damaged or destroyed. The potential economic loss is called an insurable interest.

The insured must have an insurable interest in the property or life when the policy is taken out. If the policy relates to insurance on another life, it is sufficient that one have insurable interest when the policy is taken out. If the insurance policy relates to property, the insurable interest must also exist when the property is damaged.

> <u>EXAMPLE</u> Mary has a house on Streeker Street. She obtains an insurance policy against fire. On August 1st, she sells the house to Joe. On August 4th, the house catches on fire. Mary may not recover for the damage to the house because she had no insurable interest on the day of the fire.

One may also obtain insurance on one's own life or the life of a person in whom one has an economic interest. For example, one may have a life insurance policy on a spouse, a child, a partner, or a key employee. One must have an insurable interest when one takes out the policy, but the interest need not exist at the time of a person's death.

> <u>EXAMPLE</u> Sarah is the named beneficiary of a life insurance policy on her husband, Bob. Sarah and Bob are divorced on March 1st. The parties agree that the life insurance policy will continue. Bob dies on March 4th. Although Sarah no longer had an insurable interest in Bob's life, she may collect the proceeds of the insurance policy.

The purpose of requiring an insurable interest is to prevent people from obtaining an insurance policy on property or a person in whom they have no economic interest. Such insurance contracts would be illegal because they might encourage people to do damages to a property or a life in which they would suffer no direct loss.

USURY STATUTES

Usury is the charging of interest at a rate higher than the one provided by law. These statutes vary from state to state and may be changed as economic conditions change. As inflation goes up, a low rate may not reflect the cost of capital in a market-driven economy. As a result, borrowers must either obtain money illegally or use other creative measures.

Some people have criticized usury statutes on the grounds that they create artificially low interest rates that force people to go to less than reputable lenders in order to obtain loans. Despite this, such loans would be unlawful.

> EXAMPLE Benny borrows $10,000 from Jill at an interest rate of 24%. The usury rate in the state is 15%. This loan would be unlawful.

In some states the lender will be able to recover the principal and the interest payments, but only up to the amount of the usury rate. In other states, Jill could not recover any of the interest. In still other states, the entire transaction would be void and the lender would not receive any assistance of the court. As a result, the lender may not be able to recover any money.

EXCULPATORY CLAUSES

All persons are responsible for their conduct, and the consequences of their actions. If they fail to use reasonable care and damage to another person or another person's property results, the person causing the damage is responsible. This is the concept known as due care and negligence.

Despite the clear legal liability of persons who fail to use reasonable care, some individuals attempt to place clauses in contracts that relieve them from liability for their own actions. These are called exculpatory clauses.

Generally, these clauses have no legal value because they violate public policy. However, some courts have held that the clauses are valid to the extent that they merely serve to limit one's liability and do not have a substantial impact on the public.

> EXAMPLE Lucy Landlord has every tenant sign a lease that relieves her of liability to any tenant or guest resulting from the landlord's action or lack of action. This clause would be void against public policy.

The landlord's lease would not only prevent tenants from recovering for the landlord's negligence, but it is also an attempt to prevent the public from recovering. This is void against public policy because it would discourage the landlord from exercising the appropriate degree of caution in protecting the public from injury.

> EXAMPLE Splat Parachute School asks all of its new trainees to sign a contract that relieves it from liability if anyone is injured or killed resulting from the negligence of Splat. This clause is more likely to be upheld because people who sign it know that they are engaging in hazardous conduct. In addition, the exculpatory clause does not impact on the general public.

The difference between the two examples is that the first exculpatory clause would excuse a landlord from liability for negligent acts. Such a clause would have an adverse impact on the public safety. This violates the public policy of promoting safety and the clause should be declared invalid.

In the second example, the clause relates to an ultrahazardous activity. It also has very little impact on the general public. If the school could not limit its liability, it might not be able to continue to operate.

BAILMENTS

A bailment is a temporary relinquishment of property from the owner (bailer) to another person (the bailee). These contracts have become increasingly important in a society in which one can rent almost anything. There are firms that rent items to make money (commercial bailers).

These commercial bailers may also attempt to limit their liability by inserting clauses into the rental agreement that limit their liability for defects in the items or for their negligence. These clauses also violate public policy because the items are rented to the general public. As a result, they would reduce the incentive of commercial bailers to take measures that would safeguard the public.

There are certain bailees, such as railroads, that carry people or freight for a fee. While they may not use exculpatory clauses to eliminate their liability, the law does permit the parties to agree on limiting the liability of the carrier.

Hotels and warehouses are also professional bailees. They store people and property for a living. While it is impermissible for them to try to exclude their liability with exculpatory clauses, they may limit their liability by agreement with the other party.

> EXAMPLE Tom's Trucking carries freight from one city to another. It may not totally exclude liability for its negligence. However, it may agree to contracts that limit its liability to a certain amount per shipment.

EXAMPLE The Hotel Hot Street posts a notice in every room that states that guests may store valuables in the hotel safe. If they do not, the hotel's liability for property kept in the guest room is limited to $250. This is permissible under state law.

WORKING AT THE LAW OFFICE

The concept of bailments has become more important because of the explosion of the market for rental items. Some companies are commercial bailers because they rent items for a living. It is important to be able to draft and read these contracts correctly. The rental market is likely to grow in importance. A paralegal could earn a good living by developing specialized knowledge in this area.

OTHER ILLEGAL CONTRACTS

In some jurisdictions, contracts entered into on Sunday are unlawful. Local ordinances may prohibit sales of certain items on Sunday. This is one of the reasons that many shopping malls and downtown business districts are not open on that day. The legal issue raised by such contracts is whether they will be legally enforceable. Courts have interpreted these issues differently depending on the law involved.

If the statute is intended to forbid the sale of products on Sunday, the contract will probably not be enforced if the parties have not carried it out. Conversely, the court is not likely to rescind the contract if the parties have already executed the provisions of the contract.

The courts have generally tended to try to enforce Sunday contracts if possible. The statutes that forbid Sunday sales are primarily designed to prevent excessive commercial activities. As a result, the courts are more likely to enforce Sunday contracts that are essentially private in nature. In addition, the courts will uphold contracts that are reasonably necessary under the circumstances.

Other types of contracts may be unlawful depending on one's profession or state law. For example, it is permissible for an attorney to charge a fee based on the amount of money recovered. This is called a contingent fee and is quite common in the case of negligence suits. However, it would not be permissible for an attorney to charge such fees for representing someone in a criminal action or in other legal matters.

EXAMPLE Alan Attorney charges a fee based on the results of criminal trials in which he defends individuals. He receives 100 percent of the agreed fee if the defendant is found not guilty, 50 percent if there is a mistrial, and nothing if the defendant is found guilty. This would be impermissible and the contract between Alan and his client would be unenforceable. This would be an unlawful contract and could be rescinded by the client.

Contingent fees are seldom permissible for other professions. For example, a physician could not charge different fees depending on whether the patient gets well or dies. An accountant may not charge different fees depending on the opinion she gives regarding the client's financial statements.

> EXAMPLE Alice Accountant, CPA, tells her clients that she will give them a partially qualified opinion for $10,000 and an unqualifiedly positive opinion for $20,000. This is an unlawful contract and could be rescinded by the client.

It may also be unlawful for someone engaged in lobbying governmental officials to agree to fees based on various possible outcomes. It would be unlawful for a lobbyist to charge a contingent fee based on the results of his efforts.

> EXAMPLE Louie Lobbyist agrees to a contract with Sludge Oil to lobby the state legislature. They agree that he will receive $100,000 if the state gas tax is lowered by 1 cent and $200,000 if the tax is lowered by 2 cents. Many courts would treat this contract as unlawful because it might encourage lobbyists to engage in improper conduct. Other courts would uphold the contract if it can be shown that there was no specific wrongdoing by Louie.

EFFECT OF UNLAWFUL CONTRACTS

Although unlawful contracts are generally not enforceable by either party, there are circumstances under which at least one of the parties will be allowed to enforce all or part of the contract. If the statute was designed to protect one of the parties, it would be unfair to deny recovery to the party who was supposed to be protected because the other party violated that statute.

> EXAMPLE The Northovershoe Insurance Company sells an insurance policy without a license to Stewart in the state of Southovershoe. It would be unjust not to allow Stewart to recover. The licensing statute was designed to protect Stewart. It would not be equitable to prevent him from recovering because the contract was illegal.

In some cases, the parties were not equally at fault. In these cases, the party who did not engage in wrongful conduct should be able to recover.

> EXAMPLE Zbo arrived in the United States from another country. He was unfamiliar with the laws of the country when he purchased an undersized fishing net, which was unlawful, from Fred's Fishing Emporium. The net had some defects that made it unsuitable for fishing. When Zbo brought a legal action to recover damages for the defects, Fred argued that the contract was illegal and Zbo should not recover. Fred's position is incorrect. He was, or should have been, familiar with fishing rules and regulations. He was the more guilty party. Zbo should be able to recover because he was not equally at fault.

The contract may also be capable of being divided into several parts. Some of the sections may be unlawful and some may be legal. A court will enforce the sections that are lawful and will not enforce the sections that are not lawful.

However, it may be difficult for the courts to separate the lawful sections from the unlawful. If the courts cannot make the separation, the entire contract will be struck down as unlawful.

> EXAMPLE Jones agrees to buy tables and slot machines from Smith. The contract provides that the tables will be sold for $1,000 and the machines for $500. While the tables could be used for other activities, it is clear that they will be used for the illegal slot machines. If a dispute arises about the contract, the court could enforce the sale of the tables and not enforce the sale of the slot machines. However, the court would be justified in holding that the sales of the tables and slot machines were so linked that the entire contract was unlawful and unenforceable.

UNCONSCIONABILITY

Every contract contains implied covenants of good faith and reasonableness. If the contract is so unfair that it shocks the conscience of the court or the public, it may be declared invalid as being unconscionable. Such a contract is unreasonably oppressive and unfair to one of the parties, who was usually in a much weaker position.

While the doctrine of unconscionability has existed for centuries, it gained new momentum during the middle part of this century when consumers began to build political and legal alliances in order to balance the power of the business community. The person claiming unconscionability must show that the agreement violates common standards of fairness and mutual assent to the contract.

The unconscionability may relate to contracts containing clauses that are not subject to change and tend to strongly benefit one of the parties. These clauses are often called boilerplate and are drafted to favor the party who prepared the contract.

Unconscionability will be found if there is:

1. a belief by the stronger party that there is no reasonable probability that the weaker party will perform;

2. knowledge that the weaker party will be unable to receive substantial benefits from the contract;

3. knowledge that the weaker party will be unable to protect his interests.

Contracts of adhesion are those in which one party is capable of imposing his will upon the other party. Usually, these contracts are written in small print and are often presented to the other party as if there was no choice.

Courts have looked at the bargaining process to determine if each of the parties was able to play a role. If one party was just given the contract and asked to sign it with no real input, the court may find it to be a contract of adhesion and rule it unconscionable and unenforceable.

A contract may also be unconscionable because its provisions are extremely unfair to one party. This may take the form of excessive prices, unfair collection practices, or limitations of remedies. The paralegal should recognize that if the contract is drafted in a way that overreaches, it may be declared unconscionable and void in its entirety.

> <u>EXAMPLE</u> Biggo Department Store drafts contracts that provide that the consumers will make installment payments to pay off loans granted when they made their purchases. The contract further provides that the consumer agrees that Biggo may take and sell all merchandise purchased if an installment is missed. The contract further states that all the loans will come due if any payment is missed. These contracts are so oppressive that they will be set aside as being unconscionable. It permits one party to take unfair advantage of the others. As a result of the overreaching by Biggo, it will not be enforceable at all. This is one danger of trying to accomplish too much in a contract.

A person drafting default provisions of a contract has an obligation to protect the interests of the party for whom he works. However, excessive fees or charges or unusual acceleration provisions may render the contract void. The drafter must find a balance between writing clauses that guard his client's short-term interests and protecting the client's long-term interests.

Contracts may also provide for specific remedies if one party defaults on the contractual duties outlined in the contract. Attempts to limit the remedies of another party or to impose excessively high remedies of one's own are likely to render the contract void as being unconscionable.

WORKING AT THE LAW OFFICE

Kate wants to develop a new line of clothing. She hires several hundred workers to make the clothing. The contracts with the workers provide that they will be paid $3 per hour. These contracts will be set aside because they violate minimum wage laws and are unlawful. While the supervising attorney and the paralegal should protect their client, they should be careful to stay within the law.

PARALEGAL'S "THINGS TO DO"

Student Skill: Students will understand which contractual provisions are legally enforceable.

1. Generally, contracts are legally enforceable if agreed to by the parties. However, there are situations when contracts will be set aside because they violate law or public policy. During the drafting stage, the paralegal working under the supervision of a licensed attorney should check for possible legal problems that might cause difficulties.

2. There are certain professions that require one to have a license in order to practice. For example, one must have a license to practice law, medicine, or accounting.

One may want to ask for the credentials of any professional involved with the contract. While most professionals are genuine, it would be good practice to check the credentials and, if done with tact, this is likely to impress the client.

There are other licensing requirements that may affect the contract. The paralegal should also check on these licenses.

If the contract has already been agreed upon or performed, the paralegal should check to see if the proper licenses are held by the parties. If not, performance may be excused under the law.

3. Certain contractual provisions may violate federal or state antitrust laws. The contract's drafters should check to ensure that the contract does not violate these laws.

> Covenants not to compete must be drafted to reasonably protect the interests of the parties. If they are unreasonable, they will not be valid.

> Contractual provisions that attempt to fix prices or divide up markets by geographical territory are per se unlawful. Agreements that would prevent another person from competing fairly would be unlawful.

> Resale price maintenance agreements are contracts that establish prices below which goods are not supposed to be sold. They are unlawful because they keep prices artificially high. It is permissible to merely suggest resale prices.

> It is unlawful to agree to contracts that may substantially lessen competition. A paralegal who has doubts about any clause should consult an attorney who specializes in antitrust law.

4. Although insurance contracts involve an element of risk shifting, they are lawful as long as the insured has an insurable interest in the life or property being insured. An insurable interest is an economic loss that would be suffered by the insured.

> An insurable interest must exist in a life at the time the policy is taken out.

> An insurable interest must exist in property both when the policy is taken out and at the time the property is destroyed.

5. The paralegal should check any agreement involving borrowing to ensure that it does not violate state usury statutes, which prohibit the lender from charging excessive interest rates.

> This can be a difficult situation for drafters of contracts. In many states, usury statutes set these interest rates artificially low. Economists have stated that when this occurs, borrowers can be driven into the hands of totally unscrupulous lenders.

> If the paralegal is drafting a legitimate loan agreement and the issue of usury arises, she may want to find alternative means of carrying out the loan.

> Some state usury statutes contain various exceptions that should be reviewed by the paralegal.

6. An exculpatory clause is one that attempts to excuse one from liability despite one's own negligence. The law generally does not approve of exculpatory clauses because they tend to discourage the use of reasonable care.

> The drafter of the contract may be able to insert a limited exculpatory clause in the contract. Courts are more likely to approve clauses that merely limit liability rather than attempt to exclude liability. This is particularly true if the clause does not affect the general public and involves high-risk activities.

> The paralegal should also check state and federal statutes to see if they provide for limited exculpatory clauses. This is true for the hotel industry, which is permitted to limit their liability as long as the hotel posts notices that adequately advise their guests.

7. Some jurisdictions prohibit the formation of contracts on Sundays. While these statutes are of doubtful constitutionality, one should seek to avoid any problems by forming the contract on some other day.

> Certain types of contracts are invalid because they violate public policy. Agreements that provide for contingent fees based on the results achieved are often regarded as unlawful. The drafter should be careful not to structure the contract in a manner that would violate public policy.

8. Contracts that violate state or federal law are unlawful. If the contract contains some provisions that are unlawful and some that are lawful, many courts will find the entire contract unlawful. The drafter may want to write separate contracts if there are any doubts about the legality of any portion of the contract.

9. A contract may be held to be unconscionable and unenforceable if it resulted from obviously unequal bargaining positions or unfair overreaching.

> The contract's drafter should seek to protect her client's interest but do so in a way that does not render the agreement invalid.

> Clauses that allow one party to repossess an excessive amount of property to secure a loan tend to be unconscionable.

> Excessive interest rates or other charges also tend to appear unconscionable. The drafter should not take the risk of voiding the entire contract in order to obtain a few additional dollars.

> Clauses that seek to limit the other party's legal remedies are also likely to be held to be void.

10. After the contract has been drafted or performed, the paralegal should check the actions of the parties against the contract's provisions. It is possible that the actions of the parties were unlawful even though the contractual provisions were not.

> The paralegal should look at the specific actions of the parties and the specific clauses. Some of the conduct and clauses may be legal and some may be unlawful. The paralegal must check out all possibilities to protect the client.

QUESTIONS

1. What is a licensing statute?
2. Name some occupations that require a license.
3. What type of violations of licensing statutes will render a contract invalid?
4. Which type of violations of licensing statutes will not render the contract invalid?
5. What is a covenant not to compete?
6. What is a resale price maintenance agreement?
7. What is the effect of a resale price maintenance agreement?
8. Name some contractual agreements that are unlawful per se.
9. What is an insurable interest?
10. When must an insurable interest exist for a person to take out and recover on a property insurance policy?
11. When must an insurable interest exist for a person to take out and recover on a life insurance policy?
12. What is a usury statute?
13. What is a licensing statute?
14. What is an exculpatory clause?
15. Are exculpatory clauses valid?
16. What is a contingent fee agreement?
17. Name some clauses that may cause a contract to be ruled unconscionable.

PROBLEMS

1. Donald has a problem relating to work. He asks Alice Attorney to negotiate several matters for him with his boss. Alice does an excellent job and helps Donald to receive an additional $10,000. Later, it is discovered that Alice never attended law school or passed the bar. Does Donald need to pay Alice's fee?

2. Desmond goes to a local restaurant with his date, Muriel. They eat an expensive meal and drink a bottle of fine wine. When the check arrives, Desmond refuses to pay because the restaurant does not have a municipal license. Is he correct? Why or why not? Explain the difference between this problem and the first problem.

3. Evan and Norman work for separate companies that make similar products. They could be made of higher quality if their two companies were to divide up the country's markets. Evan and Thomas divided the country into North and South. Evan's company took the North and the South was given to the company run by Thomas. What do you think of this agreement?

4. Herb notices that his next-door neighbor is quite elderly. He decides that he would like to take out a life insurance policy on the neighbor. May Herb do so?

5. Hal owns a building on Maple Street. He has a fire insurance policy on the property. He sells the building to Joan on August 1st. A fire burns down the building on August 4th. Hal submits a claim on the policy, which is due to expire on September 30. Can he collect?

6. Bob wants to lend Betty $1,000 at 20 percent interest. He proposes taking the interest payment up front and giving Betty the remaining $800. The state usury rate is 22 percent. Are there any problems with this agreement?

7. Smits sells Lisa a new pool table together with some gambling equipment associated with betting on pool games. Lisa does not pay Smits for the purchases. When Smits seeks to enforce the contract, Lisa claims that the entire sale was unlawful and that she is excused from paying. Who will prevail?

8. Larry sells a variety of items on credit to customers of his department store. He wants to draft a new agreement that he would have his customers sign. Larry has come to you to have you draft the agreement. He tells you to draft a contract "that really sticks it to them." What do you advise him?

8 *Ending the Contract and Remedies*

Students will learn the variety of ways in which the two parties may bring the contract to an end.

Students will learn that the vast majority of contracts are ended when the parties complete their obligations. This means that only a small percentage of contracts will not be completed on the subject of litigation.

Students will learn that certain contracts require different levels of performance depending on the nature of the obligation.

Students will learn that the usual way of compensating a party injured by a breach of contract (failure to perform one's contractual obligations) is to award that party money damages sufficient to place the injured party in the same position she would have been in if the contract had been completed as agreed upon.

Students will learn that another remedy that may be granted by the courts is that of a decree of specific performance. This decree compels the party who breached the contract to perform his duties under the contract.

PERFORMING THE CONTRACT

The vast majority of contracts end with the satisfactory performance of the obligations by both parties. These duties are usually adequately defined by the contract. However, given the frailties of human conduct, it becomes necessary to define the level of performance.

The contract may provide that one party must perform the contractual obligations at a specific time. However, a slight delay in performing the contract may not result in a breach of contract. A party has a reasonable time in which to perform the contract even after the date specified in the contract. A party will not be liable for the other party's lost profits after the period for performance unless there was a time of essence clause in the contract.

> EXAMPLE: Sam has a contract to provide carpentry services to Jones on April 1st. He does not provide the services until April 3rd. Jones argues that he was unable to complete a major construction contract because Sam was late. Jones brings a legal action to recover the lost profits from the construction contract against Sam. Jones argues that Sam was late with his performance and this delay was the direct cause of his loss. Jones will not prevail. Sam's performance was delivered within a reasonable time and he will not be liable for this type of loss, which he could not have expected. The law will not hold one liable for circumstances one could not have reasonably anticipated.

The above example illustrates the importance of drafting the contract carefully. If one wants to hold the other party to the exact date of performance, one should insert a time is of the essence clause in the contract. This places the other party on notice that there is some urgency involved and that she will be held liable if she is late with her performance. A time is of the essence clause allows the injured party to recover lost profits if the other party is late with performance.

A reasonable time for performance depends primarily on the subject matter of the contract and the relationship between the parties. If the subject matter is perishable, a reasonable time for performance is relatively short. If the subject matter is not perishable, a reasonable time would be longer.

One could research the case law to determine if similar facts have been decided by judicial authorities. One could also determine what constitutes a reasonable time from analyzing the past dealings of the parties.

> EXAMPLE: Diane has a contract to provide cleaning services at Frank's house on the first of each month. For the last five months, she has provided the services on the third, fourth, third, fourth, and second of the

month. From their past conduct, the parties have established a pattern in which performance by the fourth appears to be reasonable. Frank is prevented from strictly enforcing that provision of the contract requiring performance on the first of each month because he has permitted a different pattern of conduct. If he had wanted to enforce the date of performance, he should have done so early in the contract.

Another way of determining a reasonable time for performance would be to look at the parties' past dealings before the current contract. For example, the parties may have had previous contracts, and the conduct relating to those contracts could be used to help determine what is reasonable.

Still another way of determining what is reasonable would be to gather information from the marketplace. For example, a reasonable time may be clearly understood and clearly defined in specific markets or trades. One could check with trade organizations or trade magazines to determine if they have an accepted understanding of a reasonable time.

Another way of determining reasonableness is to check prevailing case law. Cases previously decided by judges may present similar facts and the legal rulings should bind the two parties.

OTHER TYPES OF PERFORMANCE

The requirement for reasonable performance as noted above does not apply in many other contract cases. For example, someone who is obligated to pay a particular purchase price may not just pay a reasonable amount. He must pay the full purchase price.

Furthermore, the price must be paid in United States currency, unless the parties agreed to the contrary. If it is paid by check, the payer has not completed her obligation to pay the price until the check is accepted or paid by the financial institution against which it is drawn.

In some contracts, a specific person must approve the performance of the other party. This person may be an architect, an engineer, or some other individual with expertise in a particular field. In these cases, one must act as a reasonable professional would act under the same circumstances.

EXAMPLE: Sullivan has a contract to build a new office building for Fulcomer. The contract provides that Fulcomer's engineer, Nichols, must approve the building's construction before payment is made. Nichols may not act in an arbitrary manner. Nichols must act as a reasonable engineer would perform. That is, Nichols must follow and approve specifications in accord with general engineering standards. If he does not, he has violated the implied covenants of good faith and reasonableness that exist in all contracts.

Other contracts clearly involve matters of personal tastes. Contracts relating to clothing or other items of personal interest such as photographs or portraits clearly fall into this category.

> EXAMPLE: Leon decides to have special riding pants made by Harris for the next major equestrian event. Neither of the parties meets until the pants are completed. When they are done, Leon states that they are too small and he will not accept the pants. The two parties should have looked at the pants as they were being made. As the seller, Harris had the primary duty to ensure that the pants fit properly. Performance relating to clothing is one of personal taste. The buyer may reject the clothing if it does not fit his needs.

Other personal taste contracts would relate to portraits, wedding photographs, and other items as well as clothing. Even in cases involving personal taste, one must act reasonably and in good faith. While a party may reject these items because he does not like them, he cannot reject them simply because he does not want to pay the price.

SUBSTANTIAL PERFORMANCE

Student Skill: The student will understand the requirement for substantially performing the contract and to which contracts it applies.

There are certain types of contracts in which the standard for completion is substantial performance. This is common in contracts relating to the construction of office and residential buildings. In these cases, the builder must make a good faith effort to complete the job and come close to full completion of the contract's specifications.

> EXAMPLE: Carpenter has a contract to build a new professional building for Johnson. The contract has very specific instructions for the specifications relating to the waiting room. Carpenter completes the building, but the waiting room is not built in accordance with the specifications. Johnson argues that there has been no substantial performance. This would be a dif-

ficult question to resolve. While Carpenter has made an effort to complete the contract, he did not finish an important element of the contract.

EXAMPLE: Donald has a contract to build a new house for Dana. He completes the house, but leaves large cracks in the foundation, which leaves the house in an unsettled position. When he brings an action to recover the purchase price, Dana claims that there has been no substantial performance. In this case, Dana will prevail. Large cracks in the foundation undermine the entire structure of the building and this does not constitute substantial performance.

EXAMPLE: Simpson has a contract to build a new fence for George. He completes the fence, but leaves one of the boards slightly out of line. This would be substantial performance. Completion is close to 100 percent and Simpson appears to have acted in good faith.

It is clear that substantial performance must be close to 100 percent and there must have been a good faith effort to conform with the contract's specifications.

OPERATION OF LAW

The courts have also held that contracts may be terminated as a matter of law if the circumstances change such that a reasonable person would believe that the contract would be canceled.

EXAMPLE: Jerry acts as Don's financial adviser. Jerry goes bankrupt after six months. He should recognize that Don would want him to stop being his financial adviser. A reasonable person would expect that the contract would come to an end as a matter of law.

When a person enters bankruptcy, the trustee in bankruptcy has the legal right to cancel all uncompleted (executory) contracts. This means that the trustee may continue the contract, end the contract, or accept part of the contract and reject part of the contract. As a result, the contract could be ended as a result of law. In addition, certain contracts that represent debts will be discharged if the bankrupt person complies with the orders of the court as a matter of law.

When a person dies, certain, but not all, contracts will be terminated.

EXAMPLE: Stoddard has a contract to be Watson's butler. This contract will terminate upon Stoddard's death. It would not be fair to either party to compel Stoddard's heirs to perform the contract. The contract will be terminated as a matter of law.

EXAMPLE: Frank enters a contract to supply Joan with 100 widgets. This contract will not end if Frank dies. His estate will still be required to complete his obligations if the contract so requires. It does not matter to the other party who supplies the widgets. The duties in this case are ministerial in nature and the contract should continue.

A contract may also be ended by the statute of limitations that is applicable in the state. A person must enforce his rights within the time provided by law. If he does not, the contract will be ended as a matter of law. It is important to check the prevailing state statute of limitations.

In addition to the statute of limitations, there is also a doctrine called laches. The principle of laches states that one may not sit on one's contractual rights beyond a certain period of time. A person who does so will lose the right to enforce the contract.

CONDITIONS

Student Skill: Students will learn how to develop clauses that determine whether the parties will be required to perform their contractual obligations.

One or both of the parties to the contract may want to place a clause in the contract (condition) that states that the agreement will terminate upon the occurring of some event.

EXAMPLE: Pat and Bill want to purchase a house. In order to obtain the purchase price, they need to obtain a mortgage from 23rd National Bank. They sign a contract with Mary and Joe to buy their house for $250,000. They place a clause in their contract that states that the completion of the contract is conditional on Pat and Bill's receiving a mortgage. If they receive the mortgage, Pat and Bill must perform the contract and purchase the house. If they do not receive the mortgage, they may rescind the contract to purchase the house.

EXAMPLE: Sally wants to purchase a Donut Deluxe franchise. However, she only wants the shop because it is next to the local police headquarters, from which Sally expects to derive a significant amount of business. She inserts a clause in the contract that states the contract will be rescinded if the police headquarters is closed or relocated within one year. In this way, she protects herself from changing circumstances.

Drafters of contracts should recognize that the careful use of conditional clauses can prove very useful in protecting the parties to the agreement. Conversely, one ought not to use conditional clauses so heavily that they tie up the parties in gridlock.

The condition in the contract may relate to an event before the agreement. This event might either trigger the existence of the parties' duties, or the event might mean that the contract will not be performed.

The condition might relate to a future event. This event might trigger the end of the contract or it might trigger additional duties. Conversely, one could change the contractual duties if the event does not occur.

The condition could also be concurrent with the actual agreement or the time of performance. For example, every contract for the sale of real estate contains an implied covenant that the seller will have good title to the property at the time of closing. If the seller does not have good title, the buyer need not tender the purchase price.

> EXAMPLE: Hanson has a contract to buy Blackacre from Douglas for $100,000 on December 1st. If Douglas cannot demonstrate ownership of the property on December 1st, Hanson need not tender the $100,000.

LEASES

A lease is an agreement between an owner of property and someone else to allow that person to reside in or conduct a business on the property. The owner of the property is called a landlord (lessor) and the other party is a tenant (lessee).

While a lease normally contains a number of terms relating to the property's rental, a lease also contains certain express or implied conditions. Like every contract, there are implied conditions of reasonableness and good faith. The parties must act in ways to make the contract work on behalf of both parties.

Many courts have determined that rental agreements also contain an implied condition that the premises will be habitable. That is, the landlord guarantees that the premises will be fit for the purposes rented.

> EXAMPLE: Don rents an apartment from Alan. When Don moves in, he discovers that the apartment is infested with cockroaches. Don stops paying rent and argues that the landlord has breached his implied warranty of habitability. The premises are not fit for a tenant to live in. Because of the breach, the landlord will not be able to enforce the contract.

> EXAMPLE: Pitty Patty Pet Parlor rents a store from Carl's Commercial Stores. When Pitty Patty moves in, she discovers that the store is infested with fleas. The small insects regularly jump up onto the animals that she sells. Pitty Patty protests to no avail. Finally, she stops paying rent and argues that Carl has breached the warranty of habitability.

Some courts have ruled that a breach of the warranty of habitability has the same effect as an eviction. This has been called a constructive eviction and will relieve the tenant from the obligation of paying rent.

Some courts have also held that tenants may withhold rent and place it into a fund. This fund can be used to make repairs if the landlord does not perform them.

Landlord and tenant law relating to the rental of real property has undergone major changes in recent years. Previously, the law regarded a rental agreement as simply a contract between the parties. More recently, the courts have seen the public interest involved in rental agreements.

People need a place to live. In addition, there is less of an equal relationship between the tenant and landlord. A tenant is an individual, but landlords may be large corporations. Tenants are usually presented by the landlords with printed forms for signature without opportunities for negotiation.

In addition, many tenants have formed groups to lobby for legislation that favored tenants. These state laws have either become an implied part of lease agreements or have affected how the courts have construed them. The balance of power, which was in favor of the landlords, has swung toward the tenants.

The courts are more likely to find reasons that permit tenants to stop paying rent or to leave the premises. Furthermore, many localities have enacted rent control ordinances that limit the percentage of rent increases that may be imposed by landlords.

A landlord has a duty to maintain the structural well-being of the building and the safety of the common areas. The tenant is generally responsible for the safety of the leased property. However, many leases provide that the landlord will make all structural repairs within the premises themselves. In this case, the lease has an implied condition that the tenant will allow the landlord to enter the premises.

WHEN PERFORMANCE IS EXCUSED

Student Skill: Students will learn the legal reasons for which performance of contractual duties will be excused.

There are some cases when a party's performance under the contract will be excused. Although courts want to ensure that there is a high level of certainty associated with contractual promises, certain contracts will be set aside if there is doubt that there was an actual meeting of the minds.

A bilateral mistake is one mutually made by both parties to the contract. In this case, either party may rescind the contract.

> EXAMPLE: Wilson contracts with Johnson for the purchase of a rare antique table that both parties believed to be genuine. Later, it is discovered that the table was merely a good imitation.

This is a bilateral mistake. Both parties believed something that was not true. There was no true meeting of the minds. As a result, there was no meaningful agreement and either party may rescind the contract.

While certainty of contracts is a valuable concept, the contract has little value if it was based on a mistake by the parties. As a result, it would make no commercial sense to require the parties to perform the contract.

A one-party mistake presents a quite different issue. Parties need to be encouraged to perform contractual obligations and to exercise some self-discipline with respect to their contractual duties. Conversely, it would be unjust to require a party to perform the contract under certain circumstances.

> EXAMPLE: Doug asks for bids for the construction of his new luxury home. He receives the following bids:
>
> John, $549,000; Jill, $539,000; Joe, $538,000; Jake, $347,000.
>
> In this case, it looks as if Jake has made a mistake. In addition, Doug should recognize that Jake has probably made a mistake. A reasonable person would ask Jake whether he made a mistake when he submitted the bid. If Doug simply accepts Jake's bid without asking, he is taking advantage of Jake's mistake. The law will not tolerate someone benefiting from another's mistake. Jake will be able to rescind the contract.

The above example illustrates the legal principles relating to one party's unilateral mistake. If the other party knew or should have known of the mistake, the contract may be rescinded. The legal principle is that such circumstances prevented the parties from reaching a true meeting of the minds.

This principle does not mean that a party will be able to rescind a contract simply because she makes a mistake.

> EXAMPLE: Sanders enters into a contract with Brown to supply him with widgets. At the time of the contract, Sanders believed that the materials necessary to make the widgets would cost $1 per unit. Since the date of

the contract, the materials rose to $2 per widget. Sanders argues that he has made a mistake and he should be relieved of his contractual obligations. He will not prevail. This is not the type of mistake that will allow him to cancel the contract.

The above example demonstrates the other side of the legal principles relating to unilateral mistakes. A party is expected to exercise some judgment before he enters a contract. He will not be excused simply because there has been a rise in the cost of materials. If he was, few contracts would have any level of certainty. As a result, few unilateral mistakes are grounds for rescinding the contract.

FRAUD AND INNOCENT MISTAKE

Fraud is a deliberately or recklessly made misrepresentation about a material fact. If a party commits fraud, there has been no true meeting of the minds with respect to the agreement. As a result, the party who is the victim of fraud will be able to rescind the contract.

Innocent misrepresentation is the making of an incorrect statement to another party without the element of wrongfulness associated with fraud. For example, it would be fraud to deliberately lie about the make or year of an automobile. It would be innocent misrepresentation to make a mistake about the year or make of the automobile.

However, in both cases there has not been a meeting of the minds. In both cases, the other party may rescind the contract. If one of the parties committed fraud, the other party may also recover three times the actual damages.

Another interesting area relates to changes in circumstances that make performance very difficult. At common law, performance will be excused only if it has become impossible. This means that routine changes in circumstances will not excuse performance. The change must be unforeseeable and caused by external forces.

EXAMPLE: Simpson has a contract to provide Wilson with 500 widgets. His workers go on strike before the widgets are delivered. Simpson argues that this makes his performance impossible and that he is excused. Simpson is incorrect. Strikes occur on a regular basis. They are not unforeseeable. In addition, strikes are caused by forces internal to Simpson's business. The strike will not excuse his performance.

EXAMPLE: Bronson has a contract to paint Frank's house. There is a two-week period during which it rains every day. Bronson claims that the rain excuses his performance. Bronson is incorrect. Rain is not an unforeseeable circumstance. While the rain may delay Bronson's performance, it does not excuse it.

EXAMPLE: Majors has a contract to provide certain services to Blair on November 15. However, the first hurricane ever to hit the area strikes on November 14. The area's roads are flooded and covered with trees. As a result, Majors is unable to provide these services on the 15th. Majors claims that he was unable to perform the contract. He argues that the hurricane made his performance impossible. In this case, the hurricane was both external and reasonably unforeseeable. Majors' performance will be excused on the grounds of impossibility.

MONEY DAMAGES AND EQUITABLE RELIEF

Student Skill: Students will learn how the legal system awards relief when a party does not perform (breaches) the contract.

If a party breaches (does not perform) the contract, he is liable for money damages. In some cases, the injured party may also obtain equitable relief, which compels the other party to perform the obligations under the contract.

A contract is a civil matter between two parties and the law is seldom concerned with the actions of the parties. However, a party may go to court to recover for injuries if one of the parties did not complete his contractual obligations.

The purpose of money damages is to place the party injured by the other's breach in the same position she would have been if the contract had been completed.

EXAMPLE: Corrine agrees to be Bob's maid for nine months at $1,000 per month. She performs the contract for three months and then stops. Bob finds another maid to do the same work at $1,300 per month. This was a reasonable salary given the marketplace. The appropriate measure of damages would be 6 x $300 ($1,300-$1,000) = $1,800. If Bob receives this amount, it would place him in the same position he would have been in if the contract had been completed.

EXAMPLE: Steve had agreed to sell Blackacre to Rick for $200,000. Rick wants to use the property for commercial purposes. Steve later changes his mind and refuses to convey the property. Rick buys a similar piece of property for $240,000. The appropriate measure of damages is $240,000 − $200,000 = $40,000. If Steve pays Rick this amount in damages, it will place Rick in the same position as if the contract had been completed. In cases involving the sale of real estate, one can also obtain a court order compelling the other party to sell the real estate.

The fundamental measure of damages is illustrated by these two examples. The injured party should receive the amount of money necessary to place him in the position he would have been in if the contract had been completed. These money damages allow the court to affirm the obligations of a party to a contract. On the other hand, the amount of damages is not so high as to penalize any of the parties.

The same principle also applies under Article 2 of the Uniform Commercial Code, which relates to the sale of tangible, movable items (goods). Parties to a contract for the sale of goods may deal with the other party's noncompliance by buying or selling the goods from another party.

In these cases, the measure of damages is relatively easy to compute. One simply uses the contract price as the base and calculates the damages around the difference between it and the new price.

> EXAMPLE: Don has a contract to buy 300 desks from Dan. However, Dan does not deliver the desks. Don then buys the desks from Doris. The contract price was $30,000. The purchase price from Doris is $40,000. The difference between the two is $10,000. This is the appropriate amount of money to award to Don because it would place him in the same position as if the contract had been completed.
>
> EXAMPLE: Assume the same facts as the above example, except this time Don calls Dan to tell him not to deliver the desks. Dan sells the desks to Doris for $25,000. The appropriate level of damages is $30,000 - $25,000 = $5,000. If Dan receives $5,000, it would place him in the same position he would have been in if Don had completed the contract. This is the appropriate measure of damages.

A party may also receive other types of money damages. Punitive damages are those that are designed to punish the person against whom they are assessed. While punitive damages are more common in tort (injury) cases, they are sometimes applied in contracts cases.

Punitive damages may be applied in the case of fraud. This represents deliberate misconduct by one party. As a result, punitive damages will be assessed in order to punish that party and deter future misconduct by the party who committed the fraud.

In some antitrust cases, punitive damages will also be applied. Engaging in actions that violate antitrust laws harms the process of free competition and constitutes wrongful conduct. Again, the imposition of punitive damages is designed to deter such conduct in the future.

Liquidated damages are amounts of money that the parties have determined will constitute an appropriate amount of damages in the event of a breach. These damages will be upheld as long as they are reasonable. For example, leases often contain liquidated damages clauses relating to late payment of rent. These payments will be upheld as valid as long as they bear a reasonable relationship to the amount of rent.

EQUITABLE REMEDIES

Student Skill: Students will learn the appropriate legal remedy in cases involving land and unique items.

A party injured by a breach of contract may also seek the equitable remedy of specific performance in certain cases. This remedy is a court order that compels a party to perform his obligations under a contract.

A degree of specific performance will be granted in contracts involving the sale and purchase of real estate.

> EXAMPLE: Dolly contracts to buy a specific house in Anytown, U.S.A. from Dave for $69,000. Dave later refuses to convey the real estate to Dolly. She may go to court and obtain a court order of specific performance that would compel Dave to sell the house to her. The decree will be granted because money damages will not place her in the same position as if the contract had been performed. Each parcel of real estate is considered unique and telling Dolly to buy another piece will not place her where she wants to be.

A decree of specific performance will also be granted in contracts involving unique items.

> EXAMPLE: Smith has a written, express contract to buy Elvis Presley's guitar from Priscilla. When Priscilla refuses to convey the guitar, Smith can go to court and obtain an order of specific performance to compel Priscilla to sell the guitar to him. The reason for the relief is that no remedy other than such a decree will place him in the same position. The guitar is a unique item and cannot be easily purchased in the marketplace.

The items under the contract must be actually unique. They may not just be unusual or different. If they can be commonly bought in the marketplace, they will not be regarded as unique. For example, a wide-screen television set may be different, but it is not unique.

Orders for specific performance will not be granted in contracts for personal services.

> EXAMPLE: Smith plays baseball for the New Mexico Cactuses. One season he decides not to play and to negotiate a contract with another team. The Cactuses go to court and ask for an order for specific performance that would compel him to play for them. The Cactuses will not receive the order of specific performance to compel him to play. They may ask for a court order (injunction) that would prevent Smith from playing for another team. This order would probably be granted.

There are good reasons for not granting an order of specific performance in personal service contracts. Such an order would make a virtual slave of one of the parties. In addition, such orders would be extremely difficult to enforce. The court would be compelled to supervise all aspects of Smith's performance. This would be an enormous burden on the court and on the parties involved. The parties would likely find themselves coming back to court again and again as disputes occurred about Smith's play.

RESTITUTION AS REMEDY

If the party is not able to recover money damages or obtain equitable relief, it still may be possible to bring an action for restitution. The remedy is designed to allow the plaintiff to recover for any benefit conferred upon the defendant. The premise is that it would be unjust to allow the defendant to retain the benefits conferred to him by the plaintiff.

> EXAMPLE: Patricia, an attorney, drafts a will and a trust agreement for Frank. However, Frank dies before he can execute either the will or the trust. It would be appropriate for Patricia to bring an action to recover for the value of drafting the will and the trust. She could recover the fair value from Frank's estate.

REAL ESTATE

The general common law rule is that one may not recover any partial payment one has made with respect to the purchase of real estate if one does not perform the contract.

EXAMPLE: Victoria has a contract to purchase Brownacre from Jones. She makes a ten percent down payment before the closing date. Victoria later refuses to buy the land. Under the traditional common law theory, Jones could keep all of the down payment.

This legal principle has been criticized by many legal scholars as being excessively harsh. If the down payment was a large percentage of the purchase price, one could argue that the retention of the down payment constitutes an excessive penalty. The person keeping the down payment may be receiving a benefit in excess of the loss resulting from the failure of the other party to complete the contract.

The courts have also held that the party seeking the restitution of the payment has the burden of showing that the retention of the payment would exceed the loss suffered by the seller.

EXAMPLE: Smith makes a down payment of $10,000 to buy Greenacre from Watson for $200,000. Smith refuses to perform the contract and asks for the payment to be returned. Smith will have the burden of showing that Watson should not retain the down payment because it exceeds any loss caused by his failure to perform the contract.

The lesson for the paralegal is to check the state statutes and case law as well as the contract carefully to determine the rights of the client. It may be useful to place a specific clause in the contract to deal with this matter. The seller will want to keep the deposit and the purchaser will want to have it returned. It may be useful to find a middle ground that directly relates the portion retained to the actual losses suffered by the seller.

SALE OF GOODS (UCC)

The traditional common law rule has been changed with respect to the sale of goods under the Uniform Commercial Code. Section 2-718 requires the seller to return to the buyer any deposit or down payment in excess of the actual damages suffered by the seller.

WORKING AT THE LAW OFFICE

It is important for the paralegal to understand the remedies available to a party who has been injured by a breach of contract. While law books discuss points of law, the practical world of the law office demands payment or other remedy for a breach of contract. Clients need to receive a remedy and law offices need to be paid. A paralegal who can bring about these events will be an important part of the law office team.

ELECTION OF REMEDIES

In some cases, one may be compelled to choose among the various remedies. A party may look at a number of factors to help her choose the most appropriate one. This can be an important decision because she may not be able to ask the court to change at a later time.

Money damages should place the injured party in the same position they would have been in if the contract had been performed satisfactorily. The selection of money damages permits the plaintiff to obtain cash, which permits a cleaner parting from the contractual relationship. The collection of money damages is relatively easy to enforce.

The equitable remedy of specific performance compels the other party to perform the duties in the contract. This would be an appropriate remedy to request if the contractual duties are for the sale of real estate or for personal property of a unique nature. It will not be granted in contracts related to the performance of personal services.

An injunction may be issued by a court to stop a party from performing certain activities. It would be appropriate to ask a court to impose an injunction to prevent a party from engaging in personal services for someone else.

PARALEGAL'S "THINGS TO DO"

Student Skill: Students will learn drafting skills relating to the performance and termination of contracts.

1. The paralegal should recognize that the law allows the parties to draft their own agreement. This also permits them to define their own levels of performance, measure the severity of the breach, and determine the amount of damages.

> The paralegal should define the level of each party's performance with a high level of specificity.

> The paralegal may also want to specifically draft remedies relating to the breach and the degree of breach. The courts will permit parties to

develop their own remedies as long as they do not allow one party to take unfair advantage of the other.

2. The paralegal should consider inserting a time is of the essence clause if it is important that one or both of the parties' performance be made as of a specific date. If this clause is not included in the contract, a party will not be able to recover damages for lost profits or other losses that would not have been foreseeable.

> Conversely, such a clause clearly places the other party on notice that the date of delivery is extremely important and that damages will be assessed if delivery is late.

3. While payment of the purchase price should normally be made in U.S. currency (cash), it may be useful to indicate the appropriate method and manner of payment.

4. Some contracts require the services of an expert to review the performance of one of the parties. For example, the parties may bring in a specialist who will review the goods, level of service, or some other aspect of the level of performance.

> If the contract calls for approval of performance based on an expert or personal taste, the parties may want to outline how this will be accomplished. It is good practice to make arrangements for partial payments in these cases. For example, one could divide the payments so that they are made as certain levels of performance are completed. If the contract calls for approval, the payments would be made at each stage. This prevents an all or nothing approach at the end of the contract, which is also likely to lead to disputes.

> If possible, one should try to outline how these judgments based on expertise or personal taste ought to be made. This is likely to reduce the possibility of disputes about the criteria to be used in making these judgments. One could also make reference to specific standards that are often found in the various professions. Often, the professions have very precise standards as to how performance should be carried out.

5. The contract's drafter may also wish to include provisions as to whether the contract will terminate based on certain events.

> Will the contract end if one or both of the parties go bankrupt?

> Will the contract end if one or both of the parties die?

6. The drafter may also want to put a provision in the contract that states the time period within which one must bring an action for breach of contract.

> Compelling parties to bring an action sooner rather than later is more likely to keep the relationship going.

7. A condition must be fully satisfied. If not, there is no contract. Therefore, the drafter should be very precise in outlining a condition. For example, one should specify if obtaining a mortgage by the buyer is a condition to the performance of a contract for the purchase of real estate.

> Particular attention should be given to an event that may have an impact on a client's customer base. If the event's occurrence would harm the client's ability to earn a living, it should be referenced in the contract. The event could be a condition that changes the responsibility of the parties. This is a matter for negotiation between the parties. It is the paralegal's responsibility to find a position that best protects the client's interests.
>
> The paralegal should anticipate events that might have an impact on a client's business. She should strive to include provisions in the contract to deal with that event.

8. There are situations under the law in which a contract will be excused as a matter of law. However, the parties may provide for these situations with their own solutions.

> Situations involving mistakes are quite common in matters relating to contracts. The parties could provide for their own remedies if they discover a mistake has been made. The parties could agree to rescind the contract, provide for changes in consideration, or take some other action.

9. The parties may also provide for their own remedies. If they are reasonable remedies and are not oppressive, the courts will uphold them.

> The parties may not bind the courts but they could provide for liquidated damages or other remedies that are fair and reasonable to the parties.

QUESTIONS

1. What is a time of the essence clause?

2. What is the purpose of such a clause?

3. What are the consequences if such a clause is not included in the contract?

4. What is performance within a reasonable time?

5. How would one determine a reasonable period of time?

6. Name some situations in which a contract will be terminated as a matter of law.

7. What is a condition?

8. How does the failure of a condition affect the parties' duty to perform the contract?

9. List some conditions you might want to include in a contract for the sale of real estate.

10. List some conditions you might want to include in a contract to buy a business.

11. Name some conditions that a landlord might want to include in a lease.

12. Name some conditions that a tenant might want to include in a lease.

13. What is a bilateral mistake?

14. What are the consequences of a bilateral mistake?

15. What is a unilateral mistake?

16. What are the consequences of a unilateral mistake if the other party knew. What are they if the other party did not know?

17. What is fraud?

18. What is the difference between fraud and innocent misrepresentation?

19. Name some unforeseeable circumstances that would excuse a party's performance under a contract.

20. Define the appropriate amount of money damages that should be awarded for a breach of contract.

21. What is a decree of specific performance? When will it be granted?

PROBLEMS

1. Rob and Joe are working on an agreement for the purchase and sale of real estate. Rob would like Joe to make a substantial down payment. What should he do?

2. Frank and Ron are working on an agreement under which Ron would build an office building on Frank's land. They would like to avoid any disputes about the construction. What should they do?

3. Mary and Sally are working on an agreement. Sally needs Mary to perform her duties on the exact date specified in the contract. What should she do?

4. Jill and Jan are working on an agreement. They would like to provide that each has a reasonable time to complete their duties under the contract. How should the contract be drafted? Where else might they go to look for guidance?

5. Sandra is working on an agreement to make a number of dresses for Molly. The two of them would like to maintain an amicable relationship during the period of their contract. If you were Sandra, what would you do? If you were Molly, what would you do?

6. Theresa has a contract to make 100 gift baskets for Gertie's Gift Store. She makes the baskets but leaves out the gingerbread men that were in the sample she had shown to Gertie. Gertie refuses to pay Theresa. What is her legal remedy?

7. Joan has a contract to act as a fire prevention consultant for Cathy's Curtain Company. Joan's office catches fire and burns down. Cathy tells Joan that she is relieving her of her contractual duties as a fire prevention consultant. Joan brings a legal action to recover damages and to be reinstated. Who will prevail?

8. Fred has a contract to supply potatoes to Al. A potato famine hits Fred's farm and wipes out most, but not all, of his crop. Does Fred have to perform his contractual obligations?

9. John and Jane had a written contract to buy a home in Springfield. The seller decides not to perform the contract and offers to return their deposit. However, John and Jane want this house. What is their legal remedy?

9 *Sale of Goods (UCC)*

Students will learn that a merchant is someone who regularly deals in goods.

Students will learn that the Uniform Commercial Code (UCC), Article 2, applies to the sale of goods as opposed to land or services, which are still covered by common law. Principles under the UCC may be different from those under common law.

Students will learn that goods are tangible, movable items that are regularly sold in the marketplace.

Students will learn that the Uniform Commercial Code (UCC) has gap-filling provisions that complete the terms of a contract if the parties do not, and is significantly different from the common law.

SALE OF TANGIBLE, MOVABLE ITEMS

Goods are movable, tangible items that are commonly sold in the marketplace. Because of the nature of goods, the drafters of the Uniform Commercial Code (UCC) believed that many of the older common law provisions were inadequate to address the needs of people who regularly trade in goods.

For example, the older common law required an extremely high degree of definiteness with respect to every element of the contract. While this may be useful with respect to agreements relating to land and services, it is far less important with respect to contracts for the sale of goods.

The major reason for this is that many items relating to the sale of goods can be found in the marketplace. As a result, they do not have to be included in the contract itself. In addition, the UCC provides a series of gap-filling provisions that provide many of the terms that normally need to be included in a contract under the common law.

The result is that contracts under the UCC are more flexible than under the common law. In addition, it is more likely that a contract will be upheld under the UCC than under the common law. It becomes extremely important, therefore, to determine which law should apply.

DETERMINING THE LAW

As noted, it is important to determine whether the common law, a statute, or the Uniform Commercial Code is applicable under the circumstances. In some cases, it is difficult to determine which applies because the contract is a mix between goods and either real estate or services. Article 2 of the UCC will apply if the major element of the contract relates to the sale of goods. Otherwise, common law will apply.

> EXAMPLE Mary buys a new computer from Computer City for $1,500. Part of the contract is for annual maintenance and checkup of the computer. The sales contract also provides for other services.

Although there are a significant number of service features associated with this contract, the main portion is associated more with the sale of goods than with the provision of services. As a result, the Uniform Commercial Code applies to the entire contract.

> EXAMPLE John agrees to buy Blackacre from Joe. As part of their written contract, John also agrees to buy some furniture that is located in the house. Although this contract contains some provision for the sale of

goods, the major thrust of the contract relates to the sale of land. Contracts for the sale of real estate are governed by common law. This contract would be governed by common law.

The common law is quite different from Article 2 of the UCC. As importantly, there is less likely to be a legally enforceable contract under common law than under the UCC. Common law requires a definite agreement on all terms. The UCC provides terms for the parties if they are left out of the agreement.

> EXAMPLE In the above example, the parties decide to separate the transaction into parts. They put together a written contract for the sale of the land and another written contract for the sale of the furniture. In both contracts, the parties leave out the price. The agreement for the sale of the land will not be a legally enforceable contract. There is no practical way for the court to determine the price of the land. Conversely, there is a legally enforceable contract for the sale of the furniture. The court can look out into the marketplace to determine a reasonable price for the sale of the pieces of furniture.

Price is one of the terms that can be deduced from a variety of sources. One can look into the marketplace to determine the reasonable price for goods of that type. In addition, one can look at previous transactions of the parties or at similar transactions in the marketplace. Under the UCC, it is a relatively easy term to determine. Under common law, one has no contract if the price has been left out of the agreement.

OTHER DIFFERENCES FROM COMMON LAW

Another major difference between common law and the Uniform Commercial Code relates to offer and acceptance. Under common law, there must be a definite offer and an acceptance. The offeror can control the offer, and the offeree must accept it exactly as made.

Under the UCC, the offeree may offer changes without terminating the offer. At common law, an attempt to change the offer is called a counteroffer and is equivalent to a rejection, which ends the offer.

Under the UCC, an offeree may send the offeror new terms to consider. If the offeree sends new terms to an offeror who is a merchant, the offeror must object to the new terms or they will become part of the contract unless they would materially alter the terms of the offer.

In addition, if the offer calls for the shipment of goods, the offeree may accept the offer in a number of ways. The offeree could reply that he will ship the goods requested in the offer. The offeree may also accept the offer by sending either conforming or nonconforming goods.

The sending of conforming goods means that the contract has been satisfactorily executed. If the offeree sends nonconforming goods, it means that there is an acceptance but a breach of contract.

The concepts discussed above are generally not known at common law. One must accept an offer exactly as made at common law. If one does not, there is no contract. As noted above, this is quite different from the methods of acceptance under the Uniform Commercial Code.

At common law, one could revoke an offer at any time prior to acceptance by the offeree. This was true even if the offeror had promised to keep the offer open (an option). This law was based on the doctrine of consideration that stated that one must give something of value to another in order to enforce a promise.

The Uniform Commercial Code changes this law as it relates to offers made by a merchant. If a merchant places an offer into writing, it is valid for a period of up to three months even if there was no consideration given to the merchant from the other party. This is known as the firm offer rule and is a substantial departure from the common law option rule, which states that an offeror may revoke an offer at any time prior to acceptance unless the offeree gave the offeror some consideration.

GAP-FILLING PROVISIONS

The common law requires that the two parties agree on every major term in the contract. If they do not, the discussions were meaningless because there is no enforceable contract. The UCC handles these problems differently.

Article 2 of the Uniform Commercial Code provides a series of gap-filling measures that serve to complete the contract. They are discussed in more detail below.

Section 2-305 of the code provides that the price need not have been determined by the parties at the time of agreement. The parties can determine the price at a later time or use the market standard or some other standard. If the parties do not agree, the price will be a reasonable price at the time of delivery.

Section 2-309 states that the time for delivery, if not agreed upon by the parties, will be a reasonable time. A reasonable time will be determined by what constitutes an appropriate period of time given commercial standards and the dealings of the parties.

The court may look at a number of factors in determining what is a reasonable time. These are listed below:

- The previous dealings of the parties provide the best evidence of what constitutes a reasonable time for performance. If the parties have continuously accepted six days as an appropriate time, that time is likely to be regarded as reasonable.

- The court can also look at the dealings of the parties with respect to other contracts in order to establish a reasonable time. For example, a prior contract may have established eight days as a reasonable time. This would constitute valuable evidence with respect to establishing a reasonable time for delivery.

- One could also look out into the marketplace to determine what constitutes a customary commercial practice. For example, certain trades have established common usage with respect to time periods for delivery of goods. While not necessarily definitive, these practices can help the courts determine a reasonable time.

- Payment for the goods is generally due at the time of the delivery of the goods. In a Cash on Delivery (C.O.D.) shipment, the cash payment is due at the time of the delivery of the goods. However, a person has a reasonable time to inspect the goods before accepting them.

Working at the Law Office

Legal offices that draft contracts often spend a considerable amount of time defining the terms because of the common law requirement for a precise meeting of the minds. Contracts for the sale of goods do not require the same level of definiteness. While it is still extremely useful to draft contractual provisions with precision, the Uniform Commercial Code provides gap-filling provisions. It is also important for the paralegal to be able to distinguish between contracts whose predominant purpose is for the sale of goods and those that fall under common law.

REQUIREMENTS AND OUTPUTS CONTRACTS

The parties may leave the quantity open if they agree that one party will buy all of his requirements or all of the other party's outputs from the other. The requirements of good faith and reasonableness apply to these contracts. The first of these contracts is called a requirements contract and the second is an outputs contract.

A requirements contract provides that a person will buy all of a particular product she requires from the seller. An outputs contracts states that the buyer will purchase everything made by the seller. In other words, he will buy all of the seller's outputs.

These contracts are very common in certain areas where it is useful to obtain all of someone's products. For example, one might want to obtain the entire output of a particular designer or of a specific design. Conversely, a requirements contract might permit the buyer to obtain all of his requirements of a specific item at a relatively inexpensive price.

If a party tries to take advantage of the other by ordering or supplying more than a reasonable amount, the covenants of good faith and reasonableness will prevent one party's misconduct. The requirement for consideration is also satisfied by the covenants of reasonableness and good faith.

DELIVERY OF GOODS

The parties may agree on the place for delivery of the goods. If they do not, Section 2-308 of the UCC provides that the seller's place of business, or if none, the seller's residence is the appropriate place for delivery. The parties may also provide that the buyer pick up the goods at some other location.

It is quite common for the parties to provide that the buyer is to pick up the goods at a location known to both parties. There may be someone such as a warehouser who is holding the goods. In this case, the seller is obligated to deliver a negotiable document of title to the buyer or ensure that the bailee knows that the buyer is entitled to the goods.

If the goods are in a warehouse, the seller may negotiate a warehouse receipt to the buyer. This transfers ownership of the goods to the buyer. The buyer can then take delivery of the goods by giving the receipt, as endorsed, to the warehouser.

The seller must present conforming goods in order to have a completed delivery. In addition, the seller must give the buyer any reasonable notification necessary to permit the buyer to take delivery. Each of the parties must act reasonably, which means that the seller must deliver the goods at a reasonable time and that the buyer must furnish suitable facilities to receive the delivery.

FIRM OFFER

At common law, an offer can be revoked at any time prior to acceptance. This is true even if the offeror promised to keep the offer open for a period of time unless the offeree gave the offeror something of consideration.

The Uniform Commercial Code provides that a merchant will be bound for a period of up to three months if the merchant puts the offer into writing. This is sometimes called the firm offer rule.

> EXAMPLE Big Bob's car lot regularly sells automobiles. Often, the potential buyers are undecided about whether to make a purchase. The salespeople often put price quotations into writing. These state that the buyer will have a certain period of time in which to make the purchase at the price quoted. This is a firm offer and cannot be revoked prior to the time stated in the offer.

The paralegal should be aware that the firm offer will be enforced even if the offeree provided nothing of consideration to the offeror. This is different from the common law. As a result, the outcomes will be different for an offer relating to goods than for one relating to real estate or services.

DELIVERY TERMS

Free on Board (F.O.B.) is a term that is followed by a place. It usually means the location to which the seller is obligated to ship the goods. If the seller is obligated to ship the goods to the buyer, it is called a destination contract. If the seller is only obligated to hand the goods over to a carrier for delivery to the buyer, it is called a shipment contract.

> EXAMPLE Jones agrees to purchase some blodgies from Grant. The two parties agree that Grant has the obligation to ship the goods to Jones in New York. This would be a destination contract and the shipping terms would read F.O.B., New York.
>
> EXAMPLE The same parties as in the previous example agree to another shipment of blodgies. This time they agree that Jones will bear the cost of shipping the blodgies from Grant's place of business in Cleveland. This time the shipping term would read F.O.B., Cleveland. This is a shipment contract.

The term F.A.S. Vessel (free alongside) at a named port means that the seller must deliver, at his own expense and risk, the goods alongside the vessel at the port designated by the buyer. C.I.F. means that the price includes the goods as well as the freight and the insurance to ship them to the named destination. The seller must obtain the insurance policy for the benefit of the buyer. The seller must tender the proper documents to include a negotiable bill of lading and an invoice for the goods. The buyer must make payment upon tender of these documents.

REQUIREMENTS FOR WRITINGS

Under the statutes of frauds that were passed by the English Parliament and United States state legislatures, various oral contracts such as those relating to the sale of land had to be evidenced by a writing in order to be enforced. Under the UCC, contracts for the sale of goods for less than $500 do not need to be in writing.

However, under Section 2-201, contracts for the sale of goods of $500 or more must be in writing and signed by the defendant. The section discusses this requirement in more detail, and also states some exceptions to the requirement for the writing.

The statute provides that a written confirmation of oral agreements between merchants may constitute a writing necessary to satisfy this section. If the merchant receiving it has reason to know its contents, and does not object to it within ten days after receipt, the parties will have a binding contract.

There are several exceptions to the UCC requirement for writing. The first is when the goods have been especially made for the buyer and would not be suitable for sale to others in the ordinary course of business.

The second is when the defendant admits in his pleadings or in court that there was a contract. In this case, there is a contract to the extent that one admits to a certain quantity.

The third exception also relates to partial performance. If the goods have been accepted or payment has been made for them, the contract will be enforceable.

The UCC requirement for a writing bears similarities to the statute of frauds relating to common law contracts. Since the provision is one that relates to evidence as to whether an agreement existed, other evidence such as the partial performance of the contract or making special goods for the buyer will substitute for the writing. This fulfills the essential purpose of the statute of frauds because it provides evidence that a contract existed.

MODIFYING THE CONTRACT

The common law required further consideration by the parties in order to modify the contract. The prior contract constituted a preexisting obligation so that it could not constitute consideration for an exchange of new promises. The UCC better reflects the practices of merchants and does not require additional consideration.

Under the UCC, modification to the same contract may be made orally unless the parties have agreed to the contrary. In those cases, the modification must be in writing. In addition, the UCC requires that if the modification raises the contract amount to $500 or more, the modification must be in writing. This is consistent with the UCC statute of frauds provision. However, the modification need not be in writing if the amount of the modified contract is below $500.

> EXAMPLE Clark and Melanie have a contract for the sale and purchase of 500 nail files. They later reduce the price from $500 to $450. The later modification need not be in writing.

RENTALS AND LEASES OF GOODS

The leasing and rental of various goods has become quite popular in recent years. This has resulted in some changes in the law as the courts have sought to define the various responsibilities of the parties to rental and leasing arrangements.

An agreement to rent goods is a type of bailment. The law relating to rental agreements of goods has been somewhat of a mixture of the law of bailments and the law of the sale of goods. In the case of rental agreements, the lender is the person who relinquishes the property, the bailor, and the person borrowing the property is the bailee.

The bailee is liable to return the property in the same condition as he received it. If the property is damaged before it is returned to the bailor's possession, it will be presumed that the damage was caused by the bailee's negligence.

The organization that rents the property also has certain liabilities. This is particularly true if it is a commercial bailor. A commercial bailor must disclose any defects in the property to the bailee. In addition, some state courts have held commercial bailors to the same standards as a merchant. That is, a commercial bailer will be held liable for injuries that result from any defect in the rented product. This places the burden on the bailor to check the rented products to ensure that they are safe.

> EXAMPLE Rent a Tool rents a hammer to Jack. While he is using it, the head flies off and hits him in the chest. If Jack was using the hammer properly, he may recover damages for his injuries from Rent a Tool.

The commercial bailor will still have the same defense of product misuse that is available to a merchant. The courts have held that the defendant will be held liable if it could have reasonably anticipated that the plaintiff would use the product in that manner.

Similarly, the commercial bailor will be liable to people injured by the product if it could have reasonably anticipated that the other person might use the product or be injured by its use.

> EXAMPLE Jeff rents a power saw from Saw City. While he is using it, the blade jumps out of the guard and injures Bert, who is standing nearby. Saw City will be held liable. It could have reasonably anticipated that a person standing next to a defective saw might be injured.

While leases of goods have been rather common, the law relating to leases was unclear. UCC Article 2A has been adopted by more than a majority of the states. Article 2A regulates the performance of the parties to a lease. UCC Article 2A Section 103 defines a lease as the transfer of the right of possession of the goods for a period of time in return for consideration.

Many of the provisions of Article 2A are the same as Article 2. However, Article 2A reduces the ability and extends the time that one has to bring a legal action for remedies. The remedies under Article 2A are similar to those found under Article 2.

PARALEGAL'S "THINGS TO DO"

Student Skill: The student will learn how to draft contractual provisions relating to the Uniform Commercial Code.

1. The paralegal should understand that a sale of goods (tangible, movable items) is governed by the Uniform Commercial Code, which is different from the traditional common law.

> The sale of goods is heavily influenced by the marketplace. As a result, the Uniform Commercial Code attempts to give the parties a climate where the terms of agreement may be established by the marketplace.
>
> The requirements for the offer and acceptance under the UCC are quite different from those under common law.
>
> The common law required an exact meeting of the minds between the two parties. This resulted in situations in which very minor deviations

between offer and acceptance resulted in the courts finding no contract.

While the drafter should still search for precise agreements, she should recognize that a contract for the sale of goods may exist although there are differences between the parties.

2. The paralegal should first determine which law applies. The common law applies if the contract is primarily for real estate or services, and the UCC applies if the contract is for the sale of goods.

3. The paralegal should be familiar with the major provisions of Article 2 of the Uniform Commercial Code.

The price of the goods will be the price found in the marketplace if the parties have not agreed on the price.

The UCC provides that the parties must act in accordance with the standards of reasonableness and good faith, but the drafter may wish to include this in the contract.

4. The contract's shipping terms are critical to determine the risk of loss when the goods are being transported from the seller to the buyer.

If one represents the seller, one should try to draft a shipment contract, which places the burden on the buyer to have the goods transported. This also means that the buyer bears the risk of loss.

Conversely, if one represents the buyer, one should draft a destination contract, which places the cost of transporting the goods and the risk of loss on the seller.

5. The paralegal should check the intention of the parties with respect to whether the goods will be purchased or leased. The rental or lease of the goods will result in a different type of contract than one for the purchase of goods.

A contract for the rental of goods creates a bailment. If the person or organization that rents the goods does so on a regular basis, it is a commercial bailor.

A bailee has the obligation to safeguard the rented property and to return it in the same condition as it was received.

A commercial bailor has the obligation to warn the bailee of latent defects in the goods. It will be held liable if any injury results from not doing so.

Many courts have held that commercial bailers have given a warranty of merchantability that the goods will be fit for normal use. If an injury results from a defect in the goods, the commercial bailor will be liable for the injury.

Commercial bailors may attempt to eliminate their liability through exculpatory clauses. The courts generally do not approve of such clauses. They are more likely to approve clauses that put limits on the bailor's liability rather than exclude it entirely.

The contract's drafter may also want to outline liquidated damages of specific amounts of money if the bailee is late returning the goods. For example, a commercial bailor may want to assess some percentage of the rental fee as liquidated damages for every day that the bailee is late.

Given the potential liability of the bailor, the drafter may specifically want to explain the proper use of the product as well as uses that are not proper. For example, one might wish to note that hammers are for driving nails, but not for driving screws.

QUESTIONS

1. What are goods?
2. The Uniform Commercial Code, Article 2 applies to the sale of what?
3. What is a merchant?
4. What are some of the gap-filling provisions of Article 2 of the Uniform Commercial Code?
5. Name some of the differences between the UCC and common law.
6. What is a firm offer?
7. What is a requirements contract?
8. What is an outputs contract?
9. What is the consideration found in these type of contracts?
10. What is a shipment contract?
11. What is a destination contract?
12. Which contracts for the sale of goods must be placed into writing?
13. Must a contract modification under the UCC be in writing?

PROBLEMS

1. Smith buys a new deluxe pool table for $5,000 from Billiards City. Their contract also provides that Smith will receive three pool lessons from a Billiards City instructor. Is this contract governed by the UCC or common law?

2. Grant and Jackson agree that Grant will sell 1,000 chairs to Jackson with a delivery date of August 31. The two of them neglect to include the price in their agreement. Grant later claims that the failure to include the price means that the two parties have no legally enforceable contract. Is he correct?

3. Campbell buys a new soup stirring machine from Soup City for $900. Soup City delivers the machine to Campbell. After using the machine for five days, he returns it and claims they had no contract because there was no writing. Is he correct?

4. Jim and Lynda have a contract under which Jim is to deliver 1,000 ashtrays to Lynda. Their contract neglects to include the time for delivery of the ashtray. What is the appropriate time? Where could they look to determine this?

5. Jones has an oral contract to make a very large countertop for Dotson. Jones makes the countertop but Dotson claims that their agreement is not legally enforceable because it was not in writing. Is Dotson correct?

6. Forest makes shrimp nets every six months and sells them to friends. Is he a merchant?

7. Johnson and Burton have a contract under which Johnson will sell 500 combs to Burton for $600. They later orally modify the contract to 400 combs for $480. Johnson later claims that the modification was not valid because it was not in writing. Is Johnson correct?

10 *Performance, Termination, and Breach (UCC)*

Students will learn the various types of performance associated with contracts for the sale of goods under the UCC.

Students will learn that each party must perform her obligations under the contract in order to receive the performance of the other party to the contract. If a party does not perform his obligations under the contract, he has breached the contract and the other party has a legal remedy.

Students will learn that there are ways of terminating the contract other than by full performance or complete breach. These may include terminating contractual duties when neither party has performed, terminating a duty when one party has performed, terminating a noncontractual duty, accord and satisfaction, and novation.

Students will learn the law relating to special sale situations such as sales on approval, sales or return and auctions.

Students will learn that a bulk transfer is the sale of all or a substantial portion of the seller's inventory. There are special requirements that require the parties to a bulk transfer to give notice to the seller's creditors of the sale in order to fully terminate the parties' responsibilities under the sale.

SELLER'S PERFORMANCE OF SALES CONTRACT

Both parties to a sales contract have certain obligations and duties. Each of them must perform their duties in order to receive the performance of the other party. When both parties have performed their obligations under the contract, the contract has been completed and the parties are discharged.

The basic duty of the seller is to tender and deliver goods that conform to the contract. Section 2-503 of the UCC requires that the seller place conforming goods at the buyer's disposition and give the buyer any documents required to take the goods.

The seller must tender the goods at a reasonable time and must furnish facilities to allow the buyer to take possession. The seller may also deliver the goods by means of transporting them by common carrier or by permitting the buyer to obtain them from a professional bailee such as a warehouser.

A common carrier is a person or an organization that transports goods for the public. If the contract provides for delivery by common carrier, the seller must conform with the shipping requirements under the contract. The contract may provide that the seller has the obligation to ship the goods to the buyer or the seller's duties may be to deliver the goods to a carrier.

A shipment contract requires the seller to only deliver the goods to the common carrier. The buyer must bear the costs of shipping and the risk of loss after the seller has accomplished this act. A destination contract requires the seller to bear the costs of shipping and the risk of loss until the goods reach the buyer. If the goods are delivered in conformity with the terms of the contract, the seller has completed his obligations and is discharged.

Delivery to a buyer may also be made to a bailee. A bailee is a person who holds goods for another. The seller may then accomplish delivery by giving the buyer the appropriate documents that will allow the buyer to take possession of the goods.

Section 2-503(4)(a) and (b) provides that when the goods are in the possession of a bailee, the seller should tender a negotiable document of title to complete his obligations under the contract. If the seller tenders a non-negotiable title, the buyer may object. The difference between the two is that a buyer may simply give the bailee a negotiable document of title and the bailee will turn over the goods. The bailee does not have to deliver the goods against a non-negotiable document without adequate proof of one's identity and other information properly requested by the bailee.

DELIVERY

If the contract does not specify the place of delivery, the UCC provides that the proper place of delivery is the seller's place of business. If the seller has no place of business, the proper place for tender by the seller is the seller's place of residence.

This places the burden on the buyer to come pick up the goods after reasonable notification by the seller. This is reasonable as it is similar to the process when one obtains goods at a store. If the seller is a merchant, he retains the risk of loss until the goods are actually taken by the buyer. If the seller is a nonmerchant, the buyer has the risk of loss when the seller makes them available to the buyer.

The seller must perform his duties in accordance with the standards of reasonableness and good faith. If there is some difficulty with performance, the seller should make alternative arrangements in accordance with these standards and attempt to meet his obligations as best as he can.

THE BUYER'S DUTIES

If the seller delivers conforming goods, the buyer's obligation is to accept and pay for the goods. There are several ways in which the buyer may accept the goods. Acceptance means that the buyer has agreed to be liable to pay the price for the goods. Acceptance may occur in one of the following ways:

1. The buyer explicitly informs the seller either orally or in writing that the goods conform to the contract and that she will accept them.
2. The buyer holds the goods beyond a reasonable time in which to reject them.
3. The buyer acts in a manner inconsistent with the seller's ownership. Such acts might include altering the goods or reselling them.

If the buyer accepts the goods in any of these ways, he becomes liable to pay the seller the price in the contract.

Before the buyer accepts the goods, she has a reasonable opportunity in which to inspect the goods to determine if they conform to the contract.

BUYER'S RIGHT TO INSPECT

Section 2-513 of the UCC provides that the buyer has a reasonable time in which to inspect the goods subject to the contract. Expenses of the inspection are to be borne by the buyer. However, if the goods do not conform to the contract, the seller will bear the costs of inspection.

The buyer of goods sent by C.O.D. (cash on delivery) must pay cash on the goods' delivery. However, the buyer has the right to inspect the goods after taking them. The mere fact that the buyer took the goods does not constitute acceptance. If the goods are not conforming, the buyer may reject them and require the seller to take them back.

The buyer must normally inspect the goods upon delivery. However, if the buyer later finds a material defect, the buyer may notify the seller. This gives the seller the opportunity to cure. If the seller does not cure the defect, the buyer may revoke the acceptance.

> EXAMPLE   Joe has a contract to deliver a new automobile to Joan. When the automobile is delivered, Joan conducts a reasonable inspection of the car. Later, she finds a crack in the transmission that makes driving the car dangerous. Joan calls Joe and notifies him of the defect in the transmission. Joe has a reasonable time in which to cure the defect. If he does not, the buyer may revoke her acceptance.

Generally, sellers have a right to cure nonconformities up to the date for delivery of the goods. The buyer may, of course, permit the seller additional time in which to cure. If the seller sent goods that he reasonably believed were conforming based on past dealings or other factors, the seller has a reasonable time in which to cure the defect beyond the delivery date.

PAYMENT BY BUYER

If the goods are conforming and the buyer accepts them, the buyer is obligated to pay the price agreed upon. The buyer may pay cash or pay by a draft (check). If the bank on which the check is drawn dishonors it, the buyer has not completed his obligations under the contract and is not discharged.

If there are reasonable questions raised about the buyer's credit, the seller may demand that payment be made in cash. The code gives the buyer a reasonable amount of time to raise cash in this instance.

A letter of credit is an instrument issued by a financial institution. A seller who is unsure of being paid may ask the buyer to obtain a letter of credit, which substitutes the bank's credit for the buyer's credit. The buyer may instruct the bank to pay the seller when the buyer makes the decision that the proper documents or conforming goods have been delivered.

The letter of credit may be irrevocable. This means that the bank may not revoke it. The letter of credit may also be revocable: The financial institution may revoke upon giving notice to its customer.

Contracts for the sale of goods under the Uniform Commercial Code are increasingly important. It is useful for the paralegal to understand the legal provisions that govern contracts for the sale of goods. The provisions of the Uniform Commercial Code have been copied by many of the legal systems in other countries. An understanding of the UCC will also help the paralegal deal with sales transactions in other countries.

SPECIAL TYPES OF SALES SITUATIONS

A sale on approval is one in which the seller transfers the goods to the buyer for a trial period. During this trial period, the seller retains the risk of loss. The buyer may return the goods at any time.

If the buyer decides to keep the goods, she may accept them in any of the ways discussed previously. After acceptance, the buyer bears the risk of loss and the obligation to pay for them.

> EXAMPLE Stanley sends Myra some books about Africa as a sale on approval. Myra holds them for five days. During this period, Stanley remains liable for the books in the event they are damaged or destroyed. After Myra accepts the books, she must now pay for them. She also is liable if they are damaged in some way.

A sale or return is different because the buyer is taking the goods with the purpose of reselling them. In this case, the buyer is liable for damages to the goods. The buyer must pay for any goods sold, but may return goods that are not resold to another party.

> EXAMPLE Biff sends Barb some dishes on a sale or return basis. Barb bears the risk of damage or loss while the goods are in her possession. She must pay for the goods she is able to resell to others. She must return the remaining goods to Biff.

AUCTIONS

An auction is a sale of goods made at a public sale at which numerous members of the public make bids on items offered for sale. Section 2-328 of the UCC governs auction sales.

At an auction held without reserve, the seller must accept the highest bid. At an auction held with reserve, the seller need not accept the highest bid. Auctions are important because they may be used to sell goods that have been the subject of an action allowing one to seize the goods of another and then to resell them in order to pay off the owner's debts.

BULK TRANSFERS

Student Skill: Students will understand the special requirements associated with the sale of a major portion of a seller's inventory.

A transfer of a major portion of a seller's materials, supplies, merchandise, or other inventory is known as a bulk transfer. There are special notice requirements relating to bulk transfers, which are outlined in Article 6 of the Uniform Commercial Code. The buyer will be able to retain possession of the goods or inventory only if these requirements are met. They are listed below:

1. *Prepare list of creditors.* The seller must prepare a list of existing creditors with their addresses and the amounts due and owing to the seller. The seller must give the list of creditors to the buyer and file a copy with the appropriate state office.

2. *Prepare list of items to be sold.* The seller should prepare a list of the property to be transferred from the seller to the buyer.

3. *Buyer notifies creditors.* All creditors are entitled to 30 to 45 days' notice. This notice should be sent by certified mail. This provides notice to the creditor and gives her the opportunity to demand payment for the goods. A creditor who does not receive notice may exercise any other remedies available to her.

4. *The buyer pays the net contract price.* Article 6 provides that the buyer will distribute the net contract price to either the seller or the creditors. Failure to comply with the provisions of Article 6 results in liability for the buyer to the seller's creditors.

WAYS OF ENDING THE CONTRACT OTHER THAN BY PERFORMANCE

The contract may be ended in a number of ways other than by performance or by breach. The parties may decide that the performance of their contractual duties is no longer in their interest and that the best course of action is to terminate the contract. They may decide to rescind the contract, but a rescission is another type of contract and the parties must follow all the rules relating to the formation of the contract. There must be an offer to rescind the contract and acceptance of the offer. In addition, there must be some exchange of consideration by the parties in order for the contract to be rescinded.

> EXAMPLE Bob has a contract to sell 100 desks to Bert. The two of them regularly discuss their mutual business affairs. When they do, Bert realizes that Bob could probably obtain a higher price selling the desks to someone else and that he no longer needs the desks. Bert explains these changes in the situation to Bob. He offers to rescind the contract. Bob agrees to accept Bert's offer to rescind the contract.

Now there is an offer and acceptance. The consideration exchanged by the parties is to rescind the contract. Essentially, there is a new contract to rescind the prior contract.

The parties may also agree to modify the contract if they wish. While the parties do not need to have additional consideration for the modification of a contract under the UCC, they do need to have an offer and acceptance. This is different from the common law, under which consideration must be exchanged by the parties.

> EXAMPLE Jim and Bob have a contract for the purchase and sale of Blackacre. The original contract only provides for the sale of the land and the house. Jim decides he would also like to obtain the furniture in the house. Bob agrees to sell Jim the furniture. They also agree that Jim will pay an additional $7,500 for the furniture. There has been an offer and acceptance and an exchange of values as consideration.

> EXAMPLE Stan has a requirements contract with Susan to purchase a certain type of pipe for $25 per pipe. Susan decides to raise the price to $26 per pipe and Stan consents. This is a UCC contract and it does not require additional consideration to alter the price.

OTHER TERMINATION ISSUES

A party who has performed a contract may terminate the other party's obligation. In this case, one party is making a gift to the other because there has been no exchange of consideration.

> EXAMPLE Bobby sells band candy door-to-door. Sam agrees to give him $50 for ten cartons of peanut brittle. Bobby has only eight cartons. Sam gives him the $50 and tells him to forget about the remaining two cartons.

One may also terminate other obligations by creating a new contract.

> EXAMPLE Don has some rather vague discussions about buying some wastebaskets from Donna. Despite the failure of the parties to reach a meeting of the minds, Donna sends Don 100 baskets. Donna later claims that Don owes her $600 for the baskets. The two of them argue about the amount owed. Don finally gives her $400 and the two of them agree that the amount will settle any obligation owed by Don to Donna.
> EXAMPLE Bill eats dinner at a local restaurant. He bites down on a foreign object and breaks one of his teeth. He brings a lawsuit based on a breach of the implied warranty of merchantability. Bill and the local restaurant have considerable discussions about damages owed by the restaurant to help pay for Bill's broken tooth. The restaurant pays Bill $10,000 and he signs a contract (a release) in which he releases the restaurant from any further liability relating to the incident and his injuries.

ACCORD AND SATISFACTION

An accord and satisfaction is an agreement between the parties to substitute another type of performance for the original performance in the contract. An accord and satisfaction is another contract that also must conform with all the requirements for a valid contract. There must be an offer and an acceptance and there must be an exchange of consideration. The agreement for substitute performance is usually the consideration that is exchanged.

> EXAMPLE Jan and Jean have a contract under which Jan was to sell her 1976 Chevy to Jean. Jan decides that she would prefer to sell her 1977 Ford to Jean. She calls Jean to discuss the transaction. Jean agrees if Jan reduces the price by $500. The two of them agree to substitute the Ford for the Chevy at the price of $9,500 rather than $10,000. In this case, there has been an offer and acceptance. The consideration is the reduction in the price in exchange for the change in the automobiles.

One of the more interesting situations occurs when there is some dispute about the amount of money owed from one person to another. A settlement of this amount may also be regarded as an accord and satisfaction. Whether an agreement on the amount of debt will be treated as a final accord and satisfaction depends on the circumstances.

> EXAMPLE Jones has a contract to sell 100 chairs to Smith for $3,000. He delivers the chairs on August 1, 199X. Unfortunately, the chairs have some defects, and there is some dispute about the actual amount due. Smith sends Jones a check for $2,500. He writes "Payment in full for delivery of 100 chairs on August 1, 199X from R. Jones." If Jones accepts and deposits the check, he has agreed that the amount is an accord and satisfaction, and it settles the debt.

The above example is based on a disputed debt. If there is a debt that is actually in dispute, there is adequate consideration involved in the settlement of the debt. Therefore, the acceptance of the check settles the matter.

This is not true if there is no genuine dispute about the debt. In these cases, attempts to eliminate the debt by sending a check marked "Paid in full" will fail because of lack of consideration. A party must give up something in order to get something under contract law.

> EXAMPLE Bernie has a mortgage with 39th National Bank. He still owes $100,000 to the bank on his loan agreement. If he sends a check to the bank marked "Paid in full related to my mortgage with 39th National Bank" for less than $100,000 it will have no effect. He has given the bank nothing beyond what was owed.

In the above example, there was no genuine dispute about the amount that Bernie owed to the bank. As a result, he has provided no consideration to the bank and may not be released from his debt.

This is the general rule with respect to debts not in dispute (unliquidated debts). One must give some consideration in order to be released from an unliquidated debt. The same general rule is true with respect to the reduction of an unliquidated debt. The debtor must give some consideration in order to obtain a reduction of the debt. However, almost any consideration will be sufficient to permit the reduction.

> EXAMPLE Danny owes Donny $50,000, which is payable on August 1, 199X. Danny would like to have the debt reduced. He suggests that the debt be reduced by $1,000 to $49,000. Donny states that he would be willing to reduce the debt if Danny would be willing to pay the debt six months earlier. Danny states that he would be willing to pay off the debt four months earlier. The two parties discuss the matter and agree that Danny will pay $49,000 five months earlier. Both parties have given sufficient consideration for the reduction of the debt.

The above example demonstrates that almost any consideration will be sufficient to support the reduction of the unliquidated debt.

> EXAMPLE   Frank owes Freida $15,000. He tells her that he would rather give her goods valued at $20,000 than pay her the debt. Freida agrees to accept the goods rather than the debt. The exchange of goods for the debt is sufficient consideration for the reduction of the debt. Each party has provided something of value to the other.

In the above example, the parties have found consideration in the exchange of a somewhat speculative value of the goods in exchange for the certainty of the debt. One party received goods worth more than the debt, and the other party has disposed of the goods in exchange for a specific amount of money.

PARALEGAL'S "THINGS TO DO"

1.   After the buyer has accepted the goods, she has an obligation to pay for them. Normally, the buyer must pay for them in U.S. currency.

> Getting paid can be a problem for many sellers. This may be particularly true for international transactions.

> One way of increasing the likelihood of getting paid is to require the buyer to pay some portion of the price during manufacture of the goods and before delivery.

> Another way of increasing the likelihood of getting paid is to require the buyer to obtain a letter of credit from a reputable financial institution. In this way, the financial institution's credit is substituted for the buyer's, which means the seller will get paid. This is a common practice in international transactions.

> The paralegal might also want to look for creative ways to permit the seller to be paid.

2.   If the paralegal represents the buyer, she should ensure that the goods delivered by the seller will conform with the contract.

> The buyer may want to require spot inspections or partial payments as the goods are being made.

> The buyer may also want to check the specifications of the contract very carefully and inspect the goods quite closely. Beyond a certain time, the buyer will have accepted the goods.

3. A person who is engaging in either the purchase or sale of a bulk transfer must exercise special caution in carrying out the transaction.

> The buyer and seller must prepare a list of the seller's creditors. While this is primarily the responsibility of the seller, the buyer must check the information carefully to avoid liability.

> The buyer should then prepare a list of the property to be transferred from the seller to the buyer. It is important to include all of the property in the list to avoid future liability.

> The buyer should then send a registered mail notice to creditors that informs them of the sale. A creditor who did not receive a notice may pursue the normal remedies available to him. The seller should ensure this is accomplished.

4. The buyer may pay the creditors or the seller may take the purchase price and pay the creditors.

5. The paralegal should also be aware that there are methods of changing the responsibilities of the parties to the contract.

> An accord and satisfaction is an agreement by the parties to change the obligations of at least one of the parties. While it is permissible to make changes in the original agreement, it may be better to redo the entire agreement.

> A novation is the substitution of one party for another in the original contract. It may be useful to draw up another agreement with the new parties.

> A release is an agreement that states that in exchange for value, one will not pursue a claim.

QUESTIONS

1. Name some seller's duties under a contract for the sale of goods.
2. What are some of the buyer's duties under a contract for the sale of goods?
3. What is acceptance?
4. What are some methods that a buyer could use to accept goods?
5. What is the buyer's right to inspect the goods?

6. What is a letter of credit?

7. What are the benefits of a letter of credit?

8. What is a common carrier?

9. What is a sale on approval?

10. What is a sale or return?

11. What is a bulk transfer?

12. What are the duties of a seller in a bulk transfer?

13. What are the duties of a buyer in a bulk transfer?

14. What is an accord and satisfaction?

15. What is a novation?

16. What is a liquidated debt?

17. What is an unliquidated debt?

18. What are the differences with respect to the requirements for consideration in settling an unliquidated debt in contrast to a liquidated debt?

PROBLEMS

1. Watson has a contract to supply goods to Hanson. The goods would be accepted by most people, but Hanson rejects them because there is a slight nonconformity in the goods that deviates from the specifications in the contract. Watson brings an action to recover the price for the goods. Will he recover?

2. James has a contract with Robert for the delivery of goods. The contract neglects to state the place for delivery. What is the appropriate place for the delivery of the goods?

3. Johnson delivers the goods to Buttle, who does not like the way they look. Buttle makes a number of alterations to the goods. After holding them for two weeks, Buttle sends them back to Johnson on the grounds that they do not conform with the contract. Johnson brings a legal action to recover the price of the goods. Who will prevail?

4. Gertie wants to do business in another country. She worries that she will not be able to be paid. How should she do this?

5. Gardner wants to buy a large amount of the inventory of Donaldson. He wants to protect himself against Donaldson's creditors. How should he do this?

6. Mary owes Dolly $3,000. The debt is payable on July 1, 2005. Mary would like to repay the loan for a lesser amount, but she does not know how she will find the consideration to do so. Does she need additional consideration to do so?

11 *Uniform Commercial Code (Title, Risk of Loss, Warranties)*

Students will learn that title represents ownership of goods. While the concept of title is less important than previously, it may be significant in the determination of certain issues.

Students will learn that the passage of the risk of loss is important in determining who has the responsibility for damage to the goods.

Students will learn when the risk of loss shifts from the seller to the buyer.

Students will learn that a warranty is a type of guarantee regarding the goods from the seller to the buyer. Warranties can be either express or implied.

Students will learn that under the UCC, every merchant warrants to every buyer that the goods are fit for the purpose for which they were bought. This is called the warranty of merchantability, and states that the seller will be liable if a defect in the product causes injury to a person whom the seller could have reasonably expected would be affected by the product's use.

Students will learn that the UCC also provides for a number of other warranties including a warranty that the goods will be fit for specific purposes designated by the buyer. This is a warranty that the goods will be fit for a particular purpose.

TRANSFERRING TITLE AND RISK

Title is evidence of ownership of goods. While the concept of title is less important under the UCC than previously, it still may be significant with respect to certain issues. More important is the question of when the risk of loss has shifted from the seller to the buyer. Generally, the risk of loss shifts from the seller to the buyer when the seller completes his shipping obligations under the contract.

A destination contract is one in which the seller has agreed to ship the goods from the seller to the buyer. In this case, the obligations of the seller do not end until the goods reach the buyer. As a result, the seller bears the risk of loss until the goods reach the buyer. If they are damaged or destroyed in his possession or in transit, the seller will bear the loss.

A shipment contract is one in which the buyer has the shipping obligation. In this case, the buyer bears the risk of damage or destruction of the goods while they are in transit to the buyer. The shipping terms of a destination contract are F.O.B. (free on board), buyer's location. The shipping term for a shipment contract is F.O.B., seller's location.

There are some special provisions that relate to the transfer of risk when there is a breach of contract. The general rule is that the risk of loss remains with the party who breached the contract.

> EXAMPLE Richard has a contract to deliver 1,000 desks to Harold. The desks are not in conformity with the contract. If they are damaged or destroyed either in transit or in the possession of the buyer, the seller will still bear the risk of loss.

> EXAMPLE Same facts as the above example, except that the goods are in conformity with the contract. Harold refuses to pay for them because he is having a cash flow problem. This is a breach of contract. Harold will remain liable if the goods are destroyed or damaged. The risk of loss remains with the party who breached the contract.

PROBLEMS WITH TITLE

Student Skill: Students will understand the concepts of title to goods and the special protection given to a bona fide purchaser for value.

The seller must have good title to the goods to transfer rightful ownership to another. Sometimes, there could be a situation in which an owner sells the goods to a party who wrongfully acquires them. The buyer may sell the goods to another party. In these cases, the question of true ownership will arise.

> EXAMPLE Donald sells goods to Joe, who pays with a bad check. Joe then sells the goods to Sally, who pays reasonable value for them and has no knowledge of the transaction between Donald and Joe.

Before the UCC, Sally may have had some problems in retaining the goods. Joe had never obtained good title to the goods because he had paid for them with a bad check. As a result, he would have had some difficulty in passing good title to another person.

The UCC, however, places great emphasis on facilitating the stream of commerce. If buyers of goods were required to check on people's title, the stream of commerce would be slowed considerably. The UCC solves this problem by providing that someone who purchases goods for reasonable value and with no knowledge that there were problems with the title will prevail over the original owner. This person is a bona fide purchaser for value.

In the above example, Sally is a bona fide purchaser for value. She will prevail over Donald. He is the person who took the risk by placing the goods into the stream of commerce. He should bear the risk of loss if something should go wrong with the various transactions.

This does not mean that the original owner will never prevail. The person who sells the goods must have at least voidable title to transfer some title to the bona fide purchaser. If the goods were stolen from the original owner, future purchasers can only acquire void title. Because the original owner did not place the goods into the stream of commerce, he should prevail against future purchasers.

> EXAMPLE Jim has two wide-screen television sets in his house. A thief breaks into the house and takes the sets. He then sells the television sets to Sally, who is a bona fide purchaser for value. In this case, the original owner, Jim, will prevail over Sally. The thief can only pass void title to Sally. This is not sufficient to defeat the original owner.

ENTRUSTMENT DOCTRINE

The same principle of facilitating commerce applies when a person entrusts an item to a merchant for repair or servicing.

> EXAMPLE Betty brings her typewriter to Typing City for repair of the keys. The owner of Typing City sells the typewriter to Ralph without Betty's permission and then skips town. Betty brings suit against Ralph to recover her typewriter. Betty will lose her suit against Ralph. She entrusted her typewriter to Typing City and put it into the stream of commerce. Ralph was a good faith purchaser with no knowledge that Typing City was engaging in improper conduct.

This result seems unfair to many people. However, it would be impractical to require people to research title to goods before they can purchase them. Such a process would have a very detrimental impact on the flow of commerce. Throughout all of the UCC the emphasis is on allowing a good faith purchaser to prevail over other individuals. This permits people to participate in the economic system with a high degree of confidence.

ACCEPTANCE BY THE BUYER

Student Skill: Students will understand how the buyer accepts goods under the UCC.

A buyer's acceptance of the goods is an important part of the sales process. When the buyer accepts the goods, he becomes liable to pay the price agreed to in the contract. There are a number of ways in which the buyer may accept the goods.

The buyer may accept the goods by explicitly informing the seller that she accepts the goods.

> EXAMPLE Stuart has a contract to sell widgets to Sally. When Sally receives the goods, she inspects them and sends a letter to Stuart that states that the goods are in conformity with the contract. This constitutes acceptance and Sally is now obligated to pay Stuart the price designated in the contract.

The buyer may also accept the goods by waiting beyond a reasonable time to reject them.

> EXAMPLE   Gerry has a contract to supply Jerry with blodgies. She sends
> blodgies to Jerry. He does not send any information about the blodgies to
> Gerry for more than one month. Jerry has waited too long to reject the
> blodgies and is deemed to have accepted them.

The purpose of this provision is to allow the seller sufficient time to cure
any defects before the goods deteriorate.

A third way a buyer may accept the goods is to resell them or alter them
in some way.

> EXAMPLE   Sam has a contract to deliver widgets to Joan. He sends the
> widget. to Joan, who adds a new coat of paint and resells them to Frank.
> Joan has effectively accepted the goods and now must send payment to
> Sam.

The reason for this provision is that a person who alters or sells goods is
acting as if he was the owner. This is the equivalent to acceptance by the buyer.

A buyer is allowed a reasonable time to inspect the goods after receiving
them. This is true even for C.O.D. (cash on delivery) shipments.

Although the person receiving the goods must pay for the goods when received, the buyer still has a reasonable time in which to inspect them. If the
buyer discovers a defect in the goods, she may still reject them.

Under the UCC, the seller has a chance to cure the goods even after he has
delivered them. If the seller reasonably believed that the goods conformed to
the contract, the seller may cure the defect before the date specified in the contract for delivery.

> EXAMPLE   Hanson has a contract to deliver ashtrays to Johnson. Of the
> 1,000 delivered, 950 are in good condition, but 50 were chipped, unknown
> to Hanson. The buyer notifies Hanson about the problem before the con-
> tract's delivery date. Hanson may cure the problem by delivering 50 new
> ashtrays before the delivery date. If he does, the buyer has not been
> harmed.

If the seller has reason to believe that the goods were conforming, he will
have a reasonable time after the delivery date to cure any defects.

> EXAMPLE   Bobby has a contract to provide 100 refrigerators to John. He
> delivers the refrigerators to John on the contract's delivery date. Ten of
> the refrigerators have some defects of which Bobby was unaware. John
> rejects the delivery of the refrigerators.

Because Bobby believed that the refrigerators conformed to the contract, he has a reasonable time in which to cure these defects. The purpose of this provision is to allow the parties to maintain the contractual relationship even if there is some defect in the delivery. This allows the parties to find a way to correct defects and to maintain the relationship.

WARRANTIES

Student Skill: Students will understand how warranties are formed and their importance to UCC contracts.

A warranty is a guarantee that the seller gives to the buyer about the goods. The warranty may be express or implied. An express warranty is a specific guarantee that the seller gives to the buyer about the goods. This guarantee may be related to the goods generally or to a specific feature. The warranty may be in the form of a written description, a sample, or a model.

> EXAMPLE Sam buys a refrigerator from Joe, who tells him that the refrigerator has five shelves and three extra shelves on the door. Joe further states that these shelves will be sufficient for a large family. When Sam obtains the refrigerator, he discovers that there are only three shelves and one on the door. Furthermore, the refrigerator does not meet the needs of a large family. This would be a breach of the warranty given from Joe to Sam by description.

The warranty could also be made by model or by sample.

> EXAMPLE Joe shows Sam a model of the refrigerator he will obtain as a result of the purchase. The model contains five shelves and three additional shelves on the door. Sam buys the refrigerator on the basis of the model shown to him. When the refrigerator arrives, it bears little relationship to the model shown to Sam. This is a breach of the warranty that was created by the model shown to Sam.

The warranty could also be based on a sample that the seller shows to the buyer. In this case, the seller warrants to the buyer that the entire shipment will be similar to the sample.

> EXAMPLE Sam is selling tomatoes to Joe. Sam shows Joe a tomato that he says will represent the entire shipment. The tomatoes are nothing like the sample shown to Joe. Sam has breached his contract to Joe. This is

a breach of warranty with respect to the sample shown by Sam to Joe. This is both a breach of warranty and a breach of contract.

The parties may also agree to warranties with respect to specific items relating to the goods. A warranty of fitness for a particular purpose is a guarantee that the goods will work in accordance with specifications agreed to by the seller.

> Example Tom agrees to sell an oven suitable for commercial use to Tara. When the oven arrives, it is useful for regular, but not for commercial, purposes.

This is a breach of the warranty of fitness for a particular purpose. Tom has breached the contract with Tara and she may recover money damages as a result.

The Uniform Commercial Code provides for certain implied warranties. Every seller of goods guarantees that she has ownership of the goods and can pass along good title (ownership) to other parties. The seller and the buyer both agree to act in good faith and in accord with how a reasonable person would act under the circumstances. This means that the parties can work out details that may arise later, or they may refer to the provisions in the code to determine how they might proceed.

IMPLIED WARRANTY OF MERCHANTABILITY

Student Skill: Students will understand the meaning and importance of the warranty of merchantability under the UCC.

One of the most important legal developments in recent years is the implied warranty of merchantability, which imposes liability on merchants who sell products if a defect in the product results in injury to a person whom the merchant could have reasonably expected would be affected by the product.

The purchaser may recover contractual damages and pursue the usual remedies relating to breach of contract if the product contains a defect. The amount of damages would be the difference in value between the product without the defect and the product with the defect. In addition, the buyer could rescind the contract.

However, the most interesting aspect of the warranty of merchantability relates to tort liability. The merchant will be held liable if a defect in the product causes either damage to a person's property or injury to a person. Not only is the merchant liable to the person who purchased the product, but he is also liable to other parties who the merchant could have foreseen would be affected by the product's use.

Many jurisdictions have held that the merchant is strictly liable for any defect that causes injury to another. Under common law, a person had to show some negligence by the merchant in order to recover for the injury. This is no longer necessary in many jurisdictions.

> EXAMPLE Sam buys a hatchet at Hatchet City. When he is chopping some wood, the head of the hatchet flies off and injures him and Ralph, who was standing in the area. Both Sam and Ralph can prevail under the implied warranty of merchantability. The hatchet was not fit for the purpose for which it was purchased and a defect resulted in an injury to the purchaser. Sam does not need to show any negligence. A showing of proper use, the defect, that the defect was the cause of the injury, and the damages suffered as a result of the injury will be sufficient to permit Sam to recover. Ralph may also recover based on the same showing. Although he did not purchase the hatchet, the seller could have reasonably expected that a person nearby would be injured if the head flew off.
>
> EXAMPLE Joan buys a chair at Chair City. She brings it home and sits down to type her presentation for work. When she does, the chair breaks and she is injured. Sarah, who is Joan's daughter, was also injured when Joan fell on top of her. Joan may recover for her injuries. There was a defect in the chair that resulted in her injuries. She was using it for the purpose for which she purchased it. Sarah may also recover because a chair manufacturer could reasonably expect that a person would be standing near someone sitting in a chair.

The merchant has few defenses if the injured party can prove that a defect in the product caused the injury. One defense is that the plaintiff used the product improperly. While there are cases of clearly proper use and others of clearly improper use, the tough cases are usually found in between.

> EXAMPLE Bob buys a new portable hair dryer from Hair City. After washing and drying his own hair, he uses the dryer on his cat. The cat is injured. Can Bob recover for the injuries to the cat?
>
> EXAMPLE Joe buys a new hammer from Hammer Heaven. Joe uses the hammer to drive in a large screw that he was unable to screw into a large board. The head of the hammer flies off and hits him in the head. Can Joe recover for his injuries?

These two cases illustrate the difficulty in resolving the issue of proper use. In the above two examples, the issue of proper use is not clear. The courts have resolved this by employing a reasonable expectation test. That is, could the manufacturer have reasonably expected that a buyer would use the product in this way?

This test is one that is usually left for a jury to decide. While it is still not an easy issue, the reasonable expectation test does at least provide some guidance for sellers of goods. They would be well served to advise their customers of uses that should not be attempted with a product. Lawyers and paralegals could help their merchant clients by including provisions in sales contracts that outline appropriate uses.

The plaintiff must also show that the defect was the proximate cause of the injury. The defect was the proximate cause if it was a direct enough cause. If the defect was not a sufficiently direct cause, the seller will not be liable.

> EXAMPLE Bobby buys a toaster from Toast City. When he puts two slices of bread in the toaster they spring out too far, bounce off the kitchen cabinets and then onto a bottle of milk, balanced precariously on the counter's edge, which falls to the floor. The glass from the bottle cuts Bobby's feet. He brings suit against Toast City for his injuries and argues that the defect was the proximate cause of his injuries. In this case, it appears that the defect was not the proximate cause of the injuries because the intervening precariously balanced bottle appears to have been a more direct cause of the injury.

The warranty of merchantability also applies to cases involving the sale of food in restaurants or other locations. If an object in the food results in an injury, the food server may be held liable for the injury.

If the object in the food that caused the injury was foreign to the food, the server will be held liable for the injury.

> EXAMPLE Smitty orders a hamburger at Mom's Diner. He bites down on the burger and chips three teeth. When he opens the burger, he finds a large bolt with bite marks on it. Smitty brings a suit against Mom's Diner for his injuries. He will be able to recover damages from Mom's Diner because it is a breach of the warranty of merchantability to permit a foreign object to be in the food.

If the object in the food that caused the injury was natural, the plaintiff may recover if the object was not one that the plaintiff could have reasonably expected would be in the food.

> EXAMPLE Harvey orders a turkey for Thanksgiving from Turkey Town. When he is eating the turkey, he bites down on a bone and injures his

teeth. Harvey could have reasonably expected to find a bone in a turkey. He will not be able to recover for his injuries.

EXAMPLE Hank orders a bowl of turkey soup at Turkey Town. He takes a couple of sips and then catches a turkey bone in his throat. Hank brings a suit to recover for his injuries. One would not have reasonably expected to find a bone in turkey soup. Hank will be able to recover for his injuries.

Paralegals should be aware that it is possible to disclaim the warranty of merchantability. In order to do so, one must place the disclaimer either in bold print or in a different color ink. The words usually used are "AS IS" or "This contract contains NO WARRANTIES." One should recognize that a disclaimer of the warranty of merchantability will substantially reduce the value of the goods.

ADDITIONAL WARRANTIES

The UCC also recognizes a warranty of fitness for a particular purpose. In this case, the buyer asks the seller to make goods for a specific purpose and the seller agrees. The buyer is relying on the seller's particular skills in making the goods.

EXAMPLE Schmidt is the owner of a very large, fine German restaurant. He asks Otto to make a stove that would be suitable for cooking large amounts of food for his customers. Otto, who is the chief executive officer of Otto's Ovens, agrees to make the stove. Schmidt and Otto spend a considerable amount of time discussing the specifications for the stove. When a stove is delivered from Otto to Schmidt, he determines that while it is suitable for many restaurants, it does not meet the specifications agreed upon for a very large German restaurant. This is a breach of Otto's warranty of fitness for a particular purpose.

This does not mean that the seller has given the buyer a warranty if the buyer provided the specifications for particular goods that do not work as intended. In this case, the buyer has assumed the risk with respect to the goods.

EXAMPLE Spangio races a certain type of automobile on country roads. He designs a new type of automobile. He furnishes this design to John Gord, who manufactures automobiles. The contract between Spangio and Gord specifically states that Gord must make the automobile in accordance with Spangio's design. Gord does make the car in accordance with the design.

However, the automobile does not work as Spangio intended. He does not have a claim against Gord.

Both parties give other warranties to each other that they have not violated another's right to ownership. In addition, both parties warrant that they will not violate each others' or third parties' rights to copyrights, patents, or other property.

DISCLAIMER OF WARRANTIES

Student Skill: Students will understand how to disclaim warranties.

The seller may not disclaim any express warranties given to the buyer. It would make no sense to permit a seller to give the buyer an express warranty based on a description, a model, or a sample and then allow him to disclaim it.

However, as noted earlier, a seller may disclaim warranties implied as a matter of law. The seller may do so by noting the disclaimer either in **bold print** or in some other conspicuous manner that would draw the reader's attention to it.

The law generally does not like provisions that attempt to disclaim implied warranties. Therefore, the paralegal should be careful not to overreach. However, the paralegal should also be careful to draft the disclaimers in a way that satisfies the law's requirements for conspicuous language and appropriate methods for bringing the disclaimers to the buyer's attention.

Disclaimers are usually made with older or damaged goods. It would be unusual to associate disclaimers with new goods. Disclaimers of warranties of title or merchantability would be strong indications that the seller does not place great value on the goods being sold.

MAGNUSON-MOSS ACT

This law, passed by Congress, gives additional protection to consumers. The act requires that the seller provide the buyer with certain presale warranty information. It also sets forth procedures to help buyers to obtain the benefits of the warranty protection. In addition, it outlines the differences between a full and a limited warranty.

When goods are sold for more than $10:

1. The warranty has to be available prior to the purchase.
2. The warranty must be in easily understood English.
3. The warranty must state whether it is full or limited.

The Magnuson-Moss Act provides four basic requirements for a full warranty. These are:

1. Defects will be corrected within a reasonable time.
2. Exclusions or limitations of consequential damages must be conspicuously stated.
3. An implied warranty cannot be limited in time.
4. The product's defects must be corrected. If not, a replacement or refund must be provided.

The full warranty must also state a specific time of duration. If the warranty does not meet these criteria, it will be regarded as a limited warranty. The agreement must set forth whether the warranty is full or limited.

PARALEGAL'S "THINGS TO DO"

1. The paralegal should check to determine which warranties the seller may want to give or has given to the buyer.

> If the paralegal represents the buyer, she should determine the extent to which the seller gave any express warranties to the buyer. These should be placed into writing to avoid later misunderstandings.

> The warranties may have been granted as a result of a description, the demonstration of a model, or a sample.

> The seller must carry out the warranties given in the contract. If he does not, he will be in breach of contract.

2. The implied warranty of merchantability is given by every merchant to each buyer. The seller may disclaim this warranty by doing so in clear and conspicuous language.

> The paralegal should be aware that the implied warranty of merchantability means that the seller guarantees that the goods will work as intended.

A disclaimer of the warranty of merchantability by the seller seriously undermines the value of the goods. The paralegal should be aware of the perception of a lack of value when the warranty is disclaimed.

The seller should realize that the seller's disclaimer of the warranty of merchantability protects him from certain liabilities, but will also likely result in the reduction of the sales price.

If the buyer purchases goods without a warranty of merchantability, she is giving up the ability to recover damages if the goods do not work as intended. She also gives up her right to recover if a defect in the goods results in an injury to the buyer or someone else.

3. The warranty of fitness for a particular purpose extends beyond the concept that the goods will work as intended. This warranty guarantees that the goods will be fit for a specific use.

If the goods do not work as intended, the seller has breached the contract and the buyer may recover damages.

A warranty of fitness for a particular purpose would be especially useful if the goods are to be employed commercially. It would help protect the buyer if she wishes to utilize the goods for a commercial purpose.

4. The provisions of the UCC make the checking of the seller's title less important than previously. However, in very large purchases, it still may be useful to check the right of the seller to convey the goods to the buyer.

Every seller gives the buyer a warranty of title under the UCC. If it is later discovered that there is some problem with the title, the seller will have breached the contract.

If a dispute arises over the title, the paralegal should recognize that a bona fide purchaser for value will generally prevail over others as to the goods ownership.

5. The buyer will become obligated to pay the purchase price after acceptance. The paralegal should advise the buyer that if she waits too long before rejecting the goods, alters them, or resells them, she will be held to have accepted them and will be liable to pay the price.

The buyer may reject the goods for any nonconformity. It is important for the buyer to make a reasonable inspection. Failure to do so will mean that the buyer has lost the right to object to the nonconformity.

The buyer may also revoke her acceptance if she later discovers a material defect in the goods. This is a higher standard than is required to reject the goods originally.

If the goods are nonconforming, the buyer may return them. The cost of transportation and the risk of loss remain with the seller.

6. The issue of who bears the risk of loss is decided largely based on whether the seller has completed her shipment obligations under the contract. When the seller's obligations are completed, the risk of damage or loss shifts to the buyer.

In a sale on approval the buyer may use the goods for a trial period before making a decision whether to accept them. The seller retains the risk of loss during this period.

In a sale or return contract, the buyer may return the goods that he is unable to resell. Under this type of contract, the buyer has the risk of damage or loss while the goods are in his possession or during the period they are being transported back to the seller.

If the parties want different results, they should provide for them in the contract.

QUESTIONS

1. What is a shipment contract?
2. What is a destination contract?
3. What are the consequences with respect to the risk of loss in shipment and destination contracts?
4. Who bears the risk of loss if there is a breach of the contract?
5. What is a bona fide purchaser?
6. What is the importance of being a bona fide purchaser?
7. What is the entrustment doctrine?
8. What are the reasons for the entrustment doctrine?
9. What is acceptance?
10. What are some different methods of accepting goods?
11. What is a warranty?

12. How may warranties be given?

13. What is an implied warranty of merchantability?

14. What is a warranty of fitness for a particular purpose?

15. What are some defenses to the assertion of a claim under the implied warranty of merchantability?

16. How may one disclaim the warranty of merchantability?

17. What are the consequences of disclaiming a warranty?

PROBLEMS

1. John goes to Cluck a Luck Chicken and orders a large chicken dinner. When he is eating his supper, he bites down on a chicken bone and chips a tooth. John brings an action against Cluck a Luck under the implied warranty of merchantability. Cluck a Luck defends on the grounds of reasonable expectations. Who will prevail?

2. Johnson brings his guitar to Gerry's Guitars for repair. Gerry takes the guitar and sells it to Tom. Gerry then skips town. Johnson brings a legal action to recover the guitar from Tom. Who will prevail?

3. Hanson sells 100 chairs to Sartore, who pays for them with a bad check. Sartore then sells them to Eanescco for value. Hanson brings an action against Eanescco to recover the chairs. Who will prevail?

4. Donald has a rare vase in his living room. A thief takes the vase and sells it to Joan, who knows nothing of the theft. Donald brings an action against Joan to recover the vase. Who will prevail?

5. Thompson goes to Burger Chuck and orders a special Group Burger dinner for 26, which would be sufficient to serve his fraternity. When the dinner arrives, it will serve only ten people. Thompson wants to bring a legal action against Burger Chuck. What do you suggest?

6. Mel goes to Grass City. He buys a lawn mower. Mel then uses the mower to cut the grass in front of the Tiny Tots School. The blade jumps out of the guard and cuts into Little Lucy, who was playing in the yard. Grass City argues that Little Lucy did not buy the mower and cannot prevail. Who will win?

7. Bert orders an item from Seas Beginning. They send the goods C.O.D. and Bert pays for the goods when they arrive. Bert later discovers a

defect in the goods. When he notifies the seller, they tell him it is too late to do anything because he has already paid for the goods. Who will prevail?

8. Rob orders some goods from Demi, who sends them to him on a sale on approval basis. The goods are damaged while they are in Rob's possession. Who will bear the risk of loss?

12 *Legal Remedies if the Contract Is Not Performed (UCC)*

SKILLS STUDENTS WILL LEARN

Students will learn the basic purpose of providing remedies for breach of contract under the UCC.

Students will learn the remedies available to the seller and to the buyer.

Students will learn that the parties may design their own remedies for problems relating to the performance of the contract.

Students will learn the doctrine of commercial impracticability, how it differs from the common law doctrine of impossibility, and how it affects the parties' duties to perform the contract.

Students will learn how a party may lose his rights under the contract as a matter of law based on the concepts of laches and under various statutes of limitations.

PURPOSE OF REMEDIES

The purpose of UCC remedies is to allow the parties to be placed in the same position they would have been in if the contract had been completed. This might mean that the parties receive money damages or that one party is required to perform the contract if money damages would not be sufficient to place the parties in the same position.

A breach of either a common law or a UCC contract is not a type of crime. The law does not want to punish people because they breached the contract, but it is useful to require that people carry out their contractual obligations.

SELLER REMEDIES

Student Skill Students will understand the remedies available to the seller if the buyer breaches the contract.

If the seller delivers conforming goods, the buyer's obligation is to pay the price. If the buyer breaches the contract by not paying the seller, the usual practice is for the seller to try to resell the goods.

Parties have a duty to mitigate the damages if another party breaches the contract. That is, the injured seller should attempt to reduce the damages created by the buyer's breach.

> EXAMPLE Mark has a contract with Herbert to deliver 1,000 video cassettes. He delivers conforming cassettes to Herbert but Herbert returns them without payment. Mark has a duty to reduce damages as much as possible. The contract price with Herbert was $10,000. Mark is able to resell the cassettes to Dick for $8,500. The measure of damages is $1,500.

The seller may also recover any expenses and consequential damages that resulted from the breach.

The seller may resell the goods at either a public or private sale. Section 2-706 provides that the sale must be made in a commercially reasonable manner.

If the sale is private, the seller must give the buyer reasonable notification of his intention to resell. The seller must also give the buyer reasonable notification of a public sale unless the goods are perishable or threaten to decline rapidly in value.

Someone who purchases goods at such a sale is treated as a good faith purchaser for value. As a result, the buyer will not have any claim against the purchaser of the goods subject to the contract.

The seller may sue for the price of the goods, if he cannot resell the goods that are the subject of the contract. Section 2-709, which covers this action, provides that the seller may recover the price, together with incidental damages, in either of the following circumstances:

- If the goods were conforming and accepted or if conforming goods were lost or damaged after a reasonable time, or after the risk of loss passed to the buyer.
- If the seller is unable to sell them after a reasonable time at a reasonable price.

The seller must hold the goods for the buyer and give the buyer credit for any amount received if the seller is later able to resell the goods.

The seller has remedies other than recovering damages. Among them are to withhold the delivery of the goods if the buyer informs the seller that he is not going to perform the contract. The seller also has the right to demand payment in cash if the buyer has become insolvent.

Under Section 2-705 of the code, the seller may also stop the goods in transit if the buyer refuses to perform the contract or becomes insolvent. The seller may only use this remedy if the goods are in the possession of a common carrier and the goods have not reached their destination. The seller must bear the cost to the carrier and any damages that might occur as a result of canceling the shipment.

The seller may cancel the contract if the buyer breaches. The seller's ability to pursue other remedies is not harmed by the cancellation of the contract.

The seller may also reclaim the goods if the buyer becomes insolvent. In order to do so, the seller must show that the buyer received the goods on credit while insolvent and that the seller demanded the return of the goods within ten days of delivery.

BUYER'S REMEDIES

Student Skill: Students will understand remedies available to the buyer of goods.

If a seller breaches the contract, the most common remedy is a suit for damages. Under Section 2-713, the proper measure of damages is the market price for the goods minus the contract price at the time of the breach. In addition, the buyer may recover any incidental damages.

Closely related to this is the concept of cover. This means that the buyer goes out into the market place and buys goods similar to those in the contract in order to mitigate damages. In this case, the measure of damages is the difference between the cover price and the contract price, plus any incidental costs associated with covering. The buyer must cover within a reasonable period of time.

DECREE OF SPECIFIC PERFORMANCE

Student Skill: Students will understand when the equitable remedy of a decree of specific performance will be available to the buyer.

Normally, decrees of specific performance will not be granted. However, if the goods are unique and the buyer is unable to cover, a court will grant a decree of specific performance to the buyer. The courts have construed the concept of unique strictly because they would rather award money damages than supervise decrees of specific performance.

EXAMPLE Jackson agrees to sell a 48" wide-screen television to Harrison. Jackson breaches the contract. While such a television is especially wide, it is not unique as required by the UCC. An order of specific performance will not be granted.

EXAMPLE James agrees to sell Johnson a television set suitable for installing in a major sports stadium. This is a unique good because it may only be used for the purpose of being a part of a stadium. The court will grant an order of specific performance because the buyer will not be able to obtain a reasonable substitute in the marketplace. As a result, money damages would be inadequate and equitable relief would be appropriate.

REVOCATION OF ACCEPTANCE

The buyer will have accepted the goods if she explicitly told the seller that she accepted the goods as conforming, waited beyond a reasonable time to reject the goods, or treated the goods as if she was the owner by selling or altering them.

The buyer has a reasonable time in which to inspect the goods to find defects. After acceptance, the buyer may discover other defects. The UCC provides that the buyer may revoke acceptance if she discovers a defect that sub-stantially impairs the value of the goods to the buyer.

This is a higher standard than that required when the buyer first inspects the goods. Initially, the buyer may reject the goods if they do not conform to the contract. The buyer must now find a defect that is more than a mere non-conformity.

> EXAMPLE Crash Motors has a contract to deliver a new automobile to Burke. He inspects the car when it is delivered and notices no substantial defect. However, he discovers a cracked engine block after a few weeks. He revokes his acceptance because the defect substantially impairs the value of the automobile. This would be permissible under the UCC.

In the above example, Burke could have rejected the automobile because it had relatively minor defects. However, he may only revoke his acceptance if he discovers a major defect.

KEEP GOODS AND ALTER CONSIDERATION

A common remedy for the buyer would be to keep the goods and adjust the price. The change in the amount of consideration would reflect the noncon-formity in the goods. This is a useful method of resolving problems between the buyer and the seller and would tend to keep the relationship going.

> EXAMPLE Frank delivers a shipment of 100 chairs to Ralph, who notices that some of the slats are missing from the backs of ten chairs. Ralph calls Frank and notifies him of the defect. The two of them talk and decide that Ralph will send the contract price of $5,000 minus the cost of $300 it will take to fix the chairs, for a total of $4,700. This allows Frank and Ralph to continue their relationship on an amicable basis.

The ability of the parties to adjust the price is consistent with the purpos-es of the UCC. Such a remedy allows the parties to work out their own prob-lems without the benefit of legal interventions, and to move on to the next transaction. This is one of the purposes of Article 2 of the UCC: It encourages the flow of commerce without unnecessary legal entanglements.

CONTRACTUAL REMEDIES OF PARTIES

The parties may also develop their own remedies for problems that may de-velop in the relationship. A common remedy is that of liquidated damages.

These provide agreed-upon amounts of money that will be exchanged if certain acts occur. Liquidated damages must be reasonable in order to be enforceable. If they appear to be a penalty, they will not be enforceable.

> EXAMPLE Charlie and Helen have a contract under which Charlie is to deliver 100 desks on August 1st. Because Charlie needs to obtain materials for making the desks, cash flow is very important to him. Late payments can substantially jeopardize his cash flow. Helen is aware of Charlie's concern. As a result, the parties insert the following clause in the contract:
>
> > "It is understood that the availability of cash is a major concern to the seller. As a result, both parties agree that the buyer will pay liquidated damages in the amount of an additional 2 percent per day for each day that the buyer is late with the payment of the price upon the seller's shipment of goods which conform to those specified in this contract."

The drafters of the contract may want to include a number of different remedies depending on changes in circumstances. The remedies can be tailored to the situation and may result in better solutions than resorting to legal action.

ANTICIPATORY REPUDIATION

One of the parties may discover that she is unable to perform the contract as anticipated. She could wait until the time for performance and then breach the contract. This is likely to result in legal action, which is very costly to the parties. In addition, such conduct is likely to damage their relationship severely.

A more useful course of action is to notify the other party that one does not plan to perform the obligations in the contract. This is called an anticipatory repudiation. However, such a course of action has the effect of impairing the contract for the other party. Under Section 2-610 of the UCC, the injured party may:

- wait for a commercially reasonable time for the performance of the repudiating party;
- resort to any of his legal remedies even though he indicated that he would wait until performance by the other party;
- suspend his own performance.

Under Section 2-611, a party may retract her repudiation by any reasonable method that indicates the party intends to perform, unless the other party had materially altered his position as a result of the prior repudiation or otherwise indicated that he believed the repudiation was final.

A party who allows retraction of the repudiation may demand commercially reasonable assurances of performance by the other party. If he does not receive the assurances within 30 days, he may treat it as a repudiation.

IMPRACTICABILITY OF PERFORMANCE

Under the common law, one was excused from performance if it had become impossible. Under the UCC, the standard is commercial impracticality. One still must show that there were unforeseen and external circumstances in order to reach the standard of commercial impracticability. However, the drafters intended that this standard be somewhat easier to reach than that of impossibility.

If a party claims impracticability of performance, he must reasonably notify the other party and allocate production and manufacture of goods to his current customers in a reasonable manner.

> EXAMPLE Mary has a contract to deliver 100 cartons of tomatoes to Nancy. Unfortunately, the first hurricane ever to hit the area wipes out nearly her entire tomato crop. Mary immediately notifies Nancy as well as her other customers. She tells Nancy that only 5 percent of her crop remains and that she is asserting the doctrine of impracticability. She further states that she will send Nancy five cartons in accordance with her plan to allocate 5 percent to every customer. Nancy may accept Mary's decision. However, Nancy may also cancel the contract and seek substitute performance from someone else.

STATUTE OF LIMITATIONS

One may not simply sit on one's rights to legal remedies either at common law or under the Uniform Commercial Code. At common law, the doctrine of laches prevented someone who waited too long to bring an action from recovering damages for breach of contract.

Under both the common law and the UCC, there are statutes of limitations that set time limits within which one may bring an action for breach of contract. Under the UCC, one must bring an action for a breach of a sales contract within four years of the date of the breach. The parties can agree on a shorter period of time, but not less than one year.

The parties may want to draft their own provisions regarding the time in which an action must be brought. Shorter time periods would encourage the parties to bring actions earlier in order to resolve them and to continue the relationship.

PARALEGAL'S "THINGS TO DO"

1. A party who does not perform his obligations under the contract has breached it. The law encourages the parties to perform the contract by imposing damages on a party who does not complete his duties under the contract.

> The usual remedy for a breach is to impose sufficient money damages to place the injured party in the position he would have been in if the contract was completed.

> The equitable remedy is to compel the party to perform the contractual obligations. This is a decree of specific performance.

> An additional remedy is restitution, which allows a party to recover benefits given to another.

> The paralegal should be familiar with all of the potential remedies that could benefit a client.

2. The paralegal may design remedies for the parties. The remedies will be enforceable as long as they are not grossly unfair to one of the parties.

3. Anticipatory repudiation is the notification by one party to the other that he will not perform his contractual obligations.

> It is useful to inform the other party if one is not going to perform. It establishes a more professional relationship than simply breaching the contract by not performing one's duties.

> The party who is injured by the failure of the other party to perform has a duty to mitigate (lessen) damages.

> One way of reducing damages is to seek to obtain performance from another. Cover means to buy goods from someone other than the original seller.

> The party who is injured by the anticipatory repudiation may cancel her own performance under the contract and may bring an action to recover damages immediately.

> The paralegal may also want to demand assurances of the other party that she will perform the contract before your client will render any more performance.

4. The drafter may also want to provide for the parties to take certain steps if performance by one or both parties becomes impossible or impracticable.

> The parties could allocate performance in any way that they believe to be appropriate under the circumstances.

5. The parties may also want to define the time period in which they may bring a legal action if one or both of the parties does not perform their contractual obligations.

QUESTIONS

1. What is the method of computing compensatory damages?
2. What is an anticipatory repudiation?
3. What are the consequences of an anticipatory repudiation?
4. When will the seller be able to recover the price from the buyer?
5. What does the concept of cover mean?
6. The party injured by the breach has a duty to do what?
7. How does one measure damages if the buyer covered?
8. What is a decree of specific performance?
9. When will a decree of specific performance be granted?
10. Give an example of goods made for a particular purpose.
11. Give some examples of a reasonable time in which to inspect goods.
12. What are liquidated damages?
13. What circumstances would constitute impracticability of performance?
14. What is the purpose of a statute of limitations as it relates to a contract for the sale of goods?

PROBLEMS

1. Donald has a contract to deliver 100 taxicabs to Cal's Cabs. Cal accepts the cars, but a week later discovers that the transmissions are broken. He calls Don, but is told that it is too late because he has already accepted the cars. Is Don correct?

2. Marcia has a contract with Barbara for the sale of 100 large chairs. The delivery date is October 1. On September 15th, Marcia calls Barbara and tells her that she will not be performing her contractual obligations. What should Barbara do?

3. Clarence has a contract to supply television sets to Harry. He sends the sets but they are stolen in transit by a group that specializes in the theft of televisions. Who bears the risk of the loss of the sets? Is there any way that the parties could have reduced the risk of loss?

4. Jill has a contract with John to supply him with 50 specialty commemorative plates for the Christmas holidays. The contract does not contain a specific delivery date. Jill wants to know when she should deliver the plates. What should she do?

5. Jim has a contract to deliver 100 wallets to Wes for $1,000. When Jim does not deliver the wallets, Wes finds another seller and buys the wallets for $1,475. How much should his damages be?

6. Doug has a contract to buy a guitar once owned by Elvis Presley from Sam. When Sam does not deliver the guitar, he tells Doug that "I'll give you money, but not the guitar." Does Doug have a remedy?

7. Deborah has several contracts to deliver widgets to a number of customers. A fire burns down her warehouse and she has only 9 percent of her supplies remaining. What should she do?

13 *Contracts By and With Agents*

Students will learn the three different types of authority that permit an agent to bind his principal to contracts with third parties. These include actual, implied and apparent authority.

Students will learn the principles involved in dealing with principals whose identity is not fully disclosed to the third party. Principals may be disclosed, partially disclosed, or undisclosed.

Students will learn that a third party has the obligation to understand the reasonable limits of an agent's authority. Certain transactions, such as the sale of a principal's business or real property, are beyond an agent's authority unless the agent has specific authorization to engage in these transactions.

Students will learn that an agent will be bound on any contract that she signs in her own capacity rather than as an agent. However, only the principal will be bound on the contract if the agent signs it in a capacity as an agent.

CONTRACTS BY AGENTS

Many contracts are agreed to by agents on behalf of their principals. In order to bind a principal, an agent must have received authority from the principal. There are different types of authority that an agent may be given. The most explicit is express authority. The principal tells the agent that she has authority to perform specific tasks.

> EXAMPLE Paul Principal informs Agnes Agent she is the new manager of his store in Springberg. Agnes now has the authority to manage the store and perform those activities necessary to manage the store. She now has explicit authority to manage the store for the benefit of her principal.

Implied authority stems from the express authority that the principal has given to the agent. This means that the agent has the authority to perform the usual activities necessary to carry out one's express authority.

> EXAMPLE Alice Agent has been given the express authority to manage Peter Principal's store. She has the implied authority to perform routine tasks such as buying and selling inventory and hiring employees. While the agent may engage in tasks that are reasonably related to the express authority, the agent may not engage in extraordinary activities such as selling the business or obtaining very large loans.

A businessperson is expected to know the reasonable limits of an agent's express or implied authority. If the third party is uncertain about whether the agent has the authority to engage in the transaction, she should ask the principal. The principal will not be bound by actions of the agent that were clearly outside of her authority.

A third type of authority results from the statements or conduct of the principal that would lead a reasonable person to believe that the agent had the authority to do a specific activity.

> EXAMPLE Aaron is Peter's agent. One day Peter is talking with Tony. He throws his arm around Aaron and says "I trust this man to do anything regarding my business." Tony could reasonably conclude from Peter's statement that Aaron had received a high degree of authority from Peter, and could engage in a wide range of transactions.

The key is what the principal did or said to the third party and not what the agent did or said. However, the third party must still act as a reasonable person would under the circumstances. That is, he should inquire into the agent's authority if a reasonably prudent person would do so.

EXAMPLE Frank tells his salesman, Sam, not to sell any automobiles on the lot for less than list price. Despite this, Sam sells a car listed at $25,000 to Joe for $22,000. Frank asks Joe to return the car but he refuses to do so. If the case is brought to court, Frank will lose. He has given Sam apparent authority. A reasonable third party could have believed that a salesperson had the authority to sell a car listed at $25,000 for $22,000. EXAMPLE Sally owns Sally's Car Lot. Tom is one of her salespeople. She tells him not to sell any vehicle for less than list price. Tom sells a $20,000 automobile to Herbert for $7,000. In this case, a reasonable person would have inquired before purchasing the automobile because of the substantial discount in price. There is no apparent authority. The third party may not take advantage of Tom's misuse of his position. Third parties engaged in business must be aware of the reasonable limitations of an agent's authority.

It is clear that one must be careful in the selection of one's agents and in the granting of authority to them. If one grants express authority to an agent to perform specific tasks, one may also grant additional authority to the agent that one did not intend.

The combination of express, implied, and apparent authority gives the agent a high degree of ability to bind the principal to contracts that she may not desire. One must select agents based on their judgment and experience. A principal should also give the agent careful instructions regarding the business activities in which the principal and the agent are engaged.

The paralegal may wish to consider placing the agreement between the principal and the agent into writing even if it is not legally required. In addition, instructions to the agent might also be placed into writing. Putting these matters into writing not only clarifies matters for the agent, but also tends to sharpen the thought process of the principal. Both parties are likely to benefit from the clarification of the expectations each has for the relationship.

DISCLOSURE OF PRINCIPAL

Student Skill: Students will understand the reasons that a principal's name may not be disclosed and the law relating to contracts with undisclosed principals.

In the vast majority of cases, it is clear that the agent is working on behalf of a principal. The agent agrees to the contract on behalf of the principal. If the contract is in writing, the agent will normally sign the contract as follows:

"Alan Aardvark, agent for Peter Principal."

When the agent signs a contract on behalf of a principal, it is clear that the agent is not personally liable on the contract. The principal will be held liable on the contract if the agent had the authority to agree to it.

> EXAMPLE Sam gives Joe the authority to manage his store. This authority includes the authority to buy and sell inventory. Joe agrees to buy 1,000 ashtrays for the store. He signs the contract: "Joe Agent, manager of Sam's Sundries and Supplies." It is clear that only Sam may be held liable on the contract agreed to by Joe.

More difficult cases occur when it is not clear who is the principal. In some cases, the principal may wish to keep his identity partially or fully undisclosed. The principal may be a wealthy or prominent individual who wishes to keep his identity a secret or believes the price of the real estate or other property will increase if his status as buyer becomes known.

As a result, the principal retains an agent to make purchases on his behalf. The agent makes a number of purchases on behalf of the principal, but signs her own name on all of the contracts. In these cases, the agent will be liable because she did not disclose that she was acting on someone's behalf.

The principal will also be liable on the contract because the agent had been given authority to agree to it on the principal's behalf. The third party will be bound to perform the contract even though the principal was undisclosed. If there had been no undisclosed principal, the other party had already agreed to the contract with the agent. Legally, it should not matter to the third party who performs it and to whom he renders performance.

> EXAMPLE Walter Wealthy wants to acquire land in the town of Springland. He retains Arthur Agent to purchase a number of pieces of property in the community. As a result of these instructions, Arthur signs a number of contracts to acquire real property in the community. Arthur simply signs his own name to the contract. He does not inform the other parties that he is acting on behalf of Mr. Wealthy. In this case, Mr. Wealthy is an undisclosed principal and Arthur is his agent. Both Arthur and Mr. Wealthy are liable on the contracts with the other parties. If they later discover that Mr. Wealthy is the principal, they may hold both Agent and Wealthy liable. The third parties will be held liable on the contract.

A third party might be able to rescind the contract if she asked the agent if there was an undisclosed principal. Failure to provide accurate information in this case would likely be construed as fraud. This would be grounds for rescinding the contract.

The contract between the agent and the undisclosed principal should be placed into writing in accordance with the statute of frauds. Agency agreements to acquire land must be written. In addition, one should carefully draft the agreement between the undisclosed principal and the agent. It should be clear that the principal will take over the agent's contracts with third parties.

Principals should be prepared to assume all of the obligations of the contract. In addition, the principal should review all of the agent's third party contracts before they are agreed upon. Furthermore, the agent should ensure that she has written authorization from the undisclosed principal. This will prevent any misunderstanding in the future.

Paralegals can provide value-added services to clients by providing additional services beyond merely drafting the contract. The paralegals could remind parties that they should ask if there are any undisclosed or partially disclosed principals. A useful summary to analyze the various possibilities appears below.

- •Agents will be liable for any contracts that they agree upon in their personal capacity. They will not be held liable for contracts that they agree to in their capacity as representatives for principals. Agents will also be held liable on contracts agreed to on behalf of an undisclosed principal. However, the agent will be relieved of her responsibilities by the undisclosed principal. The agent should ensure that her contract with the undisclosed principal will clearly accomplish this objective.

- •A principal will be liable for all authorized acts committed by an agent. A principal will not be held liable for an agent's unauthorized acts. However, the principal may have given authority to the agent in one of three ways. The authority may be express, implied, or apparent. These types of authority form a broad range of legal responsibility that could result in liability for the principal.

- •A principal may also ratify unauthorized actions and contracts of an agent. The principal must be aware of the facts in order to ratify the contract. The principal may ratify the contract by informing the other party that he ratifies the agent's unauthorized contract. The principal may also impliedly ratify by accepting the benefits of the contract or other actions of the agent.

- •A third party will be bound to all contracts to which he agrees. Third parties are expected to know the reasonable limits of an agent's authority. If they agree to contracts that are clearly beyond the agent's authority, the principal will not be bound by the contract. Third parties must ensure that the proper authority has been given or that the principal agrees to the contract.

WORKING AT THE LAW OFFICE

Third parties are expected to check the authority of the person with whom they are contracting. If the agent does not have sufficient authority, the principal will not be legally bound. The agent will be bound on the contract. It is extremely useful to ask the person with whom one is going to contract for as much information and authorization as possible.

PARALEGAL'S "THINGS TO DO"

1. If representing a client with an agent, ensure that the agent has the appropriate authority from the principal. Have clear instructions from the principal to the agent.

2. The principal and the agent should also have a written contract that delineates the responsibilities of the agent and the principal. Agency agreements for the sale of real estate must be in writing. Agency agreements that cannot be completed within one year must be in writing. Long-term employment contracts should be put into writing.

3. If the paralegal represents an agent, the agent should be reminded to sign the contract in a representative capacity only. It should be clear that the person is only acting as an agent when one looks at the contract.

4. If the agent agrees to an unauthorized contract, the principal must act within a reasonable time either to affirm or reject the contract. The principal may affirm or reject the contract expressly by informing the other party. If the principal waits beyond a reasonable time or accepts the contract benefits, he will have ratified the contract by implication.

5. If the paralegal represents another party dealing with an agent, the paralegal should check that the agent has the appropriate authority. When dealing with a corporate agent, one should obtain written authorization from the Board of Directors or other appropriate officers.

6. It is useful to ask a person if he is representing another party. This will allow your client to smoke out undisclosed principals.

QUESTIONS

1. What is authority?
2. What is express authority?

3. What is implied authority?

4. What is apparent authority?

5. How does a principal grant apparent authority?

6. What is a third party's responsibility with respect to an agent's authority to contract?

7. What is a disclosed principal?

8. What is an undisclosed principal?

9. What is the difference in terms of liability to the agent whether the principal is disclosed or undisclosed?

10. What are the differences between a disclosed and undisclosed principal relationship with respect to a third party?

PROBLEMS

1. Hugo Hugebucks is interested in acquiring a local restaurant in the area, but does not want people to know of his interest. What could he do?

2. Frank wants to name Sam as the general manager. However, he recognizes that Sam is new and wants to limit his authority. What could he do?

3. John sells small houses that are located on a large tract of land. The houses are listed for $100,000 each. He instructs all of his salespeople not to sell homes for less than that amount. Despite these instructions, one of his salespeople, Doris, sells one of the houses for $85,000 to Joe. John calls Joe and demands that he return the house. He argues that Doris had no authority to sell the house for less than $100,000. If a lawsuit is brought, who will prevail?

4. Jones gives Smith authority to manage his store. Smith decides to sell the store's parking lot to the next-door store owner, Jenkins. When Jones finds out he calls up Jenkins to cancel the transaction. Jenkins refuses. Who will prevail in a lawsuit?

5. Hanson is Watkins' agent. He has been given rather narrow authority. Despite this, he engages in a number of transactions that are outside of the scope of his authority. Among these are transactions with Dotson. Hanson decided that the transactions were in his interest even thought they were not authorized. He contacts Dotson and states that

he wants to ratify these transactions. Dotson says that he was informed that since Hanson had no authority, the transactions are invalid. Is Dotson correct?

6. Simpson wishes to hire an agent to manage his business. He is concerned about potential liability. What should he do?

7. Explain the differences between express, implied, and apparent authorities.

8. How does one grant implied authority?

9. How does one grant apparent authority?

10. Amantha is an agent for Paul, who is an undisclosed principal. Amantha signs a contract with Bob. Later, there is a dispute about the contract. What should Bob do with respect to enforcing the contract?

14 *Drafting the Contract*

Students will learn the basic principles of drafting a contract.

Students will learn which major terms should be included in the contract.

Students will learn how to craft their language and the importance of the relatively recent Plain English laws.

Students will learn how to interpret the language of contracts and how the courts interpret the language of contracts.

Students will learn how the major differences between the common law and the Uniform Commercial Code affect the drafting of contracts.

Students will learn how to draft certain clauses for different types of contracts.

DRAFTING THE BASIC CONTRACT

A person drafting a contract is usually acting on behalf of another. The person drafting the contract may be a lawyer or a paralegal acting on someone's behalf. In this case, she must be primarily concerned with protecting the interests of her client and must know what the client wants.

However, her most basic duty is to draft a contract that the law will enforce. This means that the contract should satisfy the basic elements of a contract. When drafting the contract, the drafter should ensure that the courts will find that a legally enforceable agreement existed.

Below are some suggestions for people who draft contracts.

1. Make an outline of the contract.

   (a) Names of the parties.

   (b) What is the purpose of the contract?

   (c) What is the role of each of the parties in the contract?

   (d) Define precisely the performance of each of the parties.

   (e) What must each party do in order to complete her contractual duties. When must it be done?

   (f) How will the parties resolve any disagreements?

   (g) Are there any conditions that are necessary to implement the contract? These events should be carefully and explicitly defined. Exact dates relating to these conditions should be defined in the contract.

   (h) The parties may want to provide for liquidated damages in the event of small or large breaches of the contract. If the parties can agree on the amount of damages ahead of time, it is more likely that the parties can maintain a working relationship.

   (i) If the date of performance is important, the drafter should insert a time is of the essence clause as well as a provision to calculate damages if performance is late.

2. Find a model form to use as a guide. Most law offices have form books that contain different forms of contracts that can be used in particular situations. These forms can be very useful because they reflect the accumulated wisdom of the people who wrote them and other members of the legal profession. These forms should be used as a guide only. They should not be followed blindly. In some cases, the language in the forms has become outdated and may be simplified. The forms may be adapted to fit the particular purpose. The drafter should examine the form carefully. Some clauses may not be applicable and may actually detract from achieving the contract's purpose.

3. Many states now require that consumer contracts be written in Plain English. The terms should be understandable by the average, reasonable person.

> Technical terms should be avoided. If one can simplify the language, one should do so. Use active verbs and try to personalize the contract as much as possible. Shorter paragraphs and white space also help promote readability.

> Many forms use terms such as "party of the first part." It will be clearer if one uses the actual names of the parties. Words such as "henceforth" and "heretofore" are not clear and should be deleted.

> Many of the old forms contain language that uses the masculine pronoun "he" almost exclusively. A good drafter will try to incorporate gender-neutral language and an equal amount of masculine and feminine pronouns.

> Check for spelling, grammatical, and typographical errors. Every document should be reviewed by several people to reduce the possibility that someone made an error or miscalculation.

4. Specific drafting suggestions:

   (a) Contractual duties and benefits are generally assignable from one party to another. If the parties want to forbid the assignment of the contract, they should specifically state this in the contract: "The rights and obligations in this contract may not be assigned or delegated without the consent of the other party."

   (b) "Time is of the essence with respect to the performance of this contract. Each party will be liable for consequential and compensatory damages for each day they are late with respect to its performance."

   (c) "Any disagreements with this contract will be submitted to Mary Wilson, Esq. for binding arbitration."

   (d) "All matters relating to this contract shall be governed by the laws of the State of New Jersey" (*forum clause*).

   (e) "If, for any reason, performance of either party becomes commercially impracticable, that party will notify the other party, and allocate performance in accordance with the standards of reasonableness and good faith."

   (f) "This contract represents all of the agreements and understandings of the parties."

   (g) Contracts for the sale of goods are governed by the Uniform Commercial Code, which provides clauses to fill in gaps that may have been left out by the parties. However, it is useful to specifically draft provisions with respect to particular terms. The contract must contain the quantity of goods that are to be sold and purchased. It is also useful to spell out the price, explicit warranties given by the seller to the buyer, and the delivery date.

(h) Employment contracts present special issues for the drafter. The contract should contain a description of the employee's duties, the salary, any provision for bonuses or other additional consideration, and clauses that relate to the consequences of terminating the employment before the end of the contract's term. This last provision might include such items as the continued payment of salary for the remainder of the term and coverage with medical and life insurance. A growing number of such agreements also make reference to provisions for outplacement services and other assistance.

SALE OF REAL ESTATE

A common law contract for the sale of real estate should contain a reasonable description of the land and buildings, the consideration of each party (particularly the price), the closing date, the names and signatures of each party, and other information that is relevant to the contract.

This additional information may include a description of any fixture or personal property that is part of the sale. A fixture is property that was personal, but has now become so permanently affixed to the real property that it has become part of the real property. For example, the parties may have agreed that a certain stove or cabinet will become part of the sale. If so, the contract should state it.

The parties to the contract may also want to make it subject to certain provisions. One condition of the sale of real estate may be that the buyer is able to obtain a mortgage from a reputable financial institution. If so, the contract should indicate the date by which the institution would grant the loan and accompanying mortgage agreement.

Certain parties may want to ensure that the various zoning laws have been researched and that they do not contradict the planned use by the buyer. The parties may also want to make reference to such items as property encroachments and utility or other easements that affect how the property is used.

While there are forms that outline many of these provisions, they are not a substitute for the good judgment of the drafter. She may wish to consult law texts and other manuals when putting together such a contract. A good rule of thumb is to look at the contract from the perspective of the other party in the event she wishes to avoid performance. Is there anything about the contract that would encourage or allow her to do so?

THE SERVICE CONTRACT

The common law also covers contracts dealing with services provided from one party to another. In a service contract, it is particularly important to specifically outline the exact nature of the services to be provided and the term of the services. Memories tend to fade and it is useful to describe the services of each party in exact detail.

The consideration for these services should also be specifically outlined in the contract. If there is a specific time schedule for payment, the drafter should also ensure that it is in the contract. If the stated services can not be completed within one year, the contract must be put into writing.

CONTRACTS FOR SALE OF GOODS

Contracts for the sale of goods fall under the Uniform Commercial Code. While the UCC contains a large number of gap-filling provisions for the parties, the drafter should still attempt to make the agreement as explicit as possible. Under the UCC, it is particularly important that the quantity term be included. This is the one term that must be included in writing in order to satisfy the statute of frauds.

The payment date or payment schedule should be explicitly included in the contract. Because it is not usually necessary to pay in exact accordance with the payment schedule, the drafter may wish to include a provision providing for liquidated damages if payments are not made promptly.

If the performance date is of special importance, one should include a time is of the essence clause that places the parties on notice that they will be held liable for consequential damages if delivery is late.

SPECIAL CONTRACTUAL PROVISIONS

Some contracts will require approval of the performance by an expert or by some other person. The contract's drafter should specify the details of this approval process. The drafter might want to reference manuals or other sources of information that could be utilized to review the expert's performance.

The contract might also include a schedule for partial payments. These could be made as approval is given for the completion of various portions of the work. This is particularly important in contracts calling for approval based on personal tastes, such as for portraits or personal clothing.

As an example, the contract might be written as follows:

> "Payment to Johnson for his services will be made after approval of the work is given by Dawson, who is Dotson's architect. The approval or disapproval shall be given in accordance with generally accepted architectural standards."

A contract relating to personal taste approval might read:

> "Ms. Harris will inspect the wedding gown made by Ms. Maker at three times as determined by the parties. In addition, Ms. Harris will inspect the gown two weeks (June 1) before her wedding. Ms. Harris will pay Ms. Maker a proportional sum of the total purchase price after she inspects and approves the work. The full payment will be due after the final inspection on June 1st. All approvals will be given in accordance with standards of reasonableness and good faith. Any disputes between the parties that cannot be resolved will be submitted to Ms. Florence Anderson for resolution."

DEFINITIONS

In certain contracts, definitions of particular terms may be very important. It is useful for the drafter to put definitions into Plain English if they are likely to be an important part of the contract.

If the term has a technical meaning, the drafter should seek to place it into easier to understand Plain English. Often, the process of redefining the term in understandable English forces the parties into a clearer understanding of the term. This can be beneficial to both parties.

RESTRICTIVE COVENANTS

In certain contracts, it would be useful to have clauses to prevent unfair competition. While these must be reasonable, they can be extremely important in certain circumstances. The purchaser of a business may need protection from unfair competition by the previous owner.

Some states have established guidelines as to what will be considered reasonable. The covenant must be reasonable as to both time and geographical scope. The paralegal should check applicable state statutory and case laws to ensure that the covenant is reasonable.

SIGNATURES AND DATE

The parties should sign the agreement and date it. This is particularly important in contracts for the sale of real estate.

If the contract involves a party who is acting as an agent, the signatures' blocks should provide for both the name of the agent and the name of the principal.

Certain contracts should be witnessed by other individuals. It may also be useful to have a notary public witness the contract as proof that the signatures and date were genuine.

INTERPRETING THE CONTRACT

The courts will try to find the clear meaning of the contract. They will interpret the words in a way that will normally make sense for a contract of that purpose. Certain contracts become rather standard in nature. Courts see them on a regular basis, and learn what is generally included in such contracts.

Terms that may seem technical to the average reader may become quite familiar to judges. Similarly, judges become familiar with clauses that are usually included in such contracts.

As a general rule, the courts will interpret language in a contract against the party who drafted the agreement. This means that the drafter must be especially careful in writing the contract. The drafter should use clear language that the parties and the court can understand.

The parol evidence rule provides that oral evidence that contradicts the written terms of the contract will not be admitted except under certain circumstances. This puts an added burden on the contract's drafter to get it right.

The drafter may want to send the contract to different people for their comments before placing it in final form. This will allow people to have input, help resolve problems, fill in missing terms, and clarify ambiguities.

KEY CHARACTERISTICS OF CONTRACTS

Common Law	Uniform Commercial Code
Applies to real estate and services.	Article 2 applies to goods (tangible, movable items).
Must have definite meeting of the minds. This means that the parties must reach agreement on all major terms. If not, there is no legally enforceable agreement. Key terms are price, quantity, subject matter, time, and place of performance.	The code provides gap-filling provisions that substitute for terms that the parties may have left out of the agreement. However, the parties should try to make the contract as specific as possible. Subject matter and quantity remain key terms.
Consideration is required for the contract and for any future modifications.	Must have consideration for original agreement, but not for future modifications.
Parties must have legal capacity.	Legal capacity required.
All contracts for sale of interests in real estate must be in writing. Future modifications must be in writing.	Contracts for sale of goods in excess of $500 must be in writing. Modifications need not be in writing below $500.
All common law contracts must be for a legal purpose.	Same.
Contracts for the sale of real estate, services that cannot be completed within one year, that answer for the debt of another, to pay the debt of an estate from one's own funds, and for the sale of securities must be evidenced by a writing.	Contract for the sale of goods of $500 or more must be evidenced by a writing.
Offers may be revoked at any time prior to acceptance by the offeree unless the offeree gives the offeror consideration.	A written firm offer from a merchant is irrevocable for up to three months even without consideration.
Any attempt to change the terms of the offer is called a counteroffer and terminates the offer.	A merchant must object to terms proposed by the offeree or may be bound by them.
A party must perform her obligations to receive the performance of the other party.	Same.

Impossibility based on unforeseeable, external standards will excuse performance.	Commercial impracticability based on similar standards will excuse performance. UCC standard is slightly lower.
Time is of essence clause should be included if time of performance is critical.	Same.
Basic remedy for nonperformance is compensatory damages, which are designed to place the injured party in the same position she would have been in if the contract had been performed.	Same.
A decree of specific performance will be granted in cases involving sale of real estate, but will not be granted in cases calling for services.	Decrees will be granted in cases involving unique goods or those specially made for buyer.

INTERNATIONAL CONTRACTS

International contracts need to be drafted with special care. There are risks associated with engaging in international transactions. These include the following:

1. Risk of not being paid. This risk is higher because one often does not know the buyer or his credit standing.

2. Risk of currency changes. The value of currency often fluctuates. In the international markets, this can cause a loss for the seller as the exchange rate changes.

3. Expropriation of the seller's assets may be made by a foreign government. This may take the form of either a 100 percent taking or less than a total taking.

4. The government of the foreign country may require that the seller allow foreign (domestic) citizens to be participants in one's business as a condition to doing business in the country.

5. The seller may be concerned with the choice of courts or legal forums in which to resolve disputes. A foreign court may not prove hospitable

for a businessperson from another country. Legal concepts may be quite different in other societies than under Anglo-American law.

The drafters of the seller's international contract should consider special clauses that would protect the seller from these risks. The contract may require that the buyer obtain a letter of credit from a major financial institution. This increases the likelihood that the seller will be paid.

The drafter could also require that the price be paid in United States currency. This reduces the risk of problems with currency changes that might effectively reduce the price to the seller.

The seller may be able to require the buyer to pay for expropriation insurance. Licensing agreements, partnerships, joint ventures, and other business agreements can reduce the risk of loss resulting from governmental action.

The drafter of the international sales contract should also include a clause that states the forum in which disputes will be resolved. It would be useful for the seller to have the disputes resolved in her own country.

QUESTIONS

1. What are some provisions (terms) that should be included in a contract for the sale of real estate?
2. Name some contracts that would be affected by the statute of frauds.
3. What are "Plain English" laws?
4. What are restrictive covenants?
5. How should restrictive covenants be drafted?
6. What is a "time is of the essence" clause?
7. What is a personal service contract?
8. How might you draft a personal service contract?

15 *Special Types of Contracts*

SKILLS STUDENT WILL LEARN

Students will learn the basic types of governmental contracts and their differences.

Students will learn the concepts of wills and trusts and how they may be used to assist one's family.

Students will learn how the basic concepts of contracts learned in earlier chapters may be applied in a variety of situations to include the attachment of security interests on real and personal property and contracts relating to a marriage.

GOVERNMENTAL CONTRACTS

Government contracts have special features of which paralegals need to be aware. This is because taxpayer dollars are involved. Certain types of contracts have evolved to meet specific governmental objectives. In addition, the bidding requirements are much stricter with respect to governmental contracts.

In order to protect the integrity of the bidding process, bids for governmental contracts must be placed into writing and must be submitted at specific times and in accordance with certain procedures relating to writings and time deadlines.

The bids must conform exactly with the specifications issued by the governmental agency. Any deviation from the requirements for a writing, time deadlines, or specifications relating to features or details of the product or service will be grounds for rejecting the bids.

Government contracts also tend to include a number of types based on the needs of the government. Cost plus contracts allow the successful bidder to obtain the costs of performing the contract plus a reasonable profit.

Governmental contracts may also be awarded to the low bidder. In some cases, contracts may only be awarded to the lowest bidder. This is designed to save taxpayers money. Unfortunately, this also makes it difficult for the bidder to earn a profit. This makes it imperative that the contract be drafted carefully by the paralegal. Careless drafting could result in reduced revenues, which might eliminate any profits for the contractor.

Some bids may be drafted so that only one contractor may meet the specifications of the bid. These are called single source contracts.

Contracts that ask for professional services may normally be granted without the need for competitive bids. This is based on the premise that professionals such as engineers, attorneys, and accountants should not be required to engage in competitive bidding because to do so might result in the dilution of the quality of the professional services.

Governmental contracts are different from agreements between private parties because the government is in the superior bargaining position. The paralegal must carefully check the agreements to protect her client's interests.

The government will have competent legal advice. As a result, attorneys and paralegals must be prepared adequately to represent the interests of their clients.

Governmental contracts also may contain special provisions that restrict assignments or subcontracting. The paralegal should review the contract to ensure that it does not overly restrict one's ability to perform the contract.

One advantage of working with the government is that one will eventually get paid. The paralegal should review these payment provisions carefully. Contractors often work on a close profit margin and small differences in the manner of payment may mean the difference between profit and loss.

SECURITY AGREEMENTS

A party may give a creditor a security interest in personal property. This is accomplished by a security agreement between the property owner and her creditor. In this case, the contract allows the creditor to seize the property if the debtor does not pay the debt.

The requirements for creation of a security interest include the following:

1. Ownership rights of the property by the debtor.
2. The creditor must grant value to the debtor. This usually takes the form of a loan or the extension of credit.
3. A security agreement between the two parties that grants a security interest to the creditor.

MORTGAGES ON REAL PROPERTY

Mortgages are agreements between a borrower and a lender given when the borrower purchases a house. The lender gives the borrower money and the borrower gives the lender the right to seize the house if the borrower does not pay off the loan.

The mortgage and the loan agreement that supports it are normally drafted by the lending institution. However, the lawyer or paralegal should carefully read the agreements to determine if the client's interests are protected by these agreements. These contracts tend to favor the financial institution.

The agreements are likely to contain agencies coupled with an interest. These agencies are different from others because the agent (the lender) has a specific financial interest in the agency. The agency allows the lender to seize the home. The mortgagor (the borrower, owner, and principal) must give the mortgagee (lender and agent) the right to sell the owner's house if he does not pay the loan.

The agreement for the sale of the real estate should also be carefully drafted. It should include:

1. A reasonable description of the land and buildings. This is normally set out in terms of metes and bounds, which are various reference points, as well as block and lot numbers that are contained on the tax maps in the locality.
2. The consideration exchanged by each party. This would clearly include the price that the buyer paid for the property.
3. The contract should include the closing date for the real estate transfer. This is the date at which the buyer gives the purchase price to the seller, and the ownership papers are given to the buyer by the seller.
4. The contract should include the signatures of the parties.

VALUE OF SECURITY INTERESTS

The security interest protects the secured party by giving him a priority interest over creditors. If the debtor defaults on the debt, the secured creditor will be able to seize the secured property and use it to pay off the debt.

A secured party who perfects her security interest will also have priority over a trustee in bankruptcy. The process of perfection is complicated. The security agreement and the documents relating to perfection must be carefully reviewed for accuracy by the paralegal.

Security agreements also require an agency coupled with an interest. In this case, the owner of the property is the principal and the agent is the secured party. In such a case, only the creditor agent can terminate the agency. This is usually done when the debt has been paid.

The security agreement should reasonably describe the personal property that is the subject of the security interest. It is permissible under the Uniform Commercial Code to list the assets as the current and future inventory of the debtor. This is called a floating lien. It allows the creditor to seize the current and future acquired inventory of a store or similar type of debtor.

> EXAMPLE Frank owns a used car dealership. He regularly borrows money from Bob Bigbucks. He gives a security interest in the automobiles on the lot. The security agreement also provides that Bob may seize automobiles that Frank may later acquire. The agreement also provides that Bob has the right to inspect the lot. In addition, their agreement provides that Frank must have an inventory on the lot of at least $30,000 in automobiles. This helps ensure that Bob will be able to seize sufficient assets to pay off the loan.

Security interests in personal property are generally perfected against other creditors by taking possession of the property or by filing notice of the security interest on the documents of title or in the appropriate state or county office. A security interest in real estate is generally filed in the appropriate county office where the land is located.

DRAFTING WILLS AND TRUSTS

Student Skill: The student will understand how to draft wills and trusts.

A will is a type of contract between the person writing it, prospective beneficiaries, and the state in which the parties reside. A will allows the person writing it to pass property to others after his death.

Because of the importance of a will, it must meet certain legal requirements in order to be valid. These legal requirements are similar to those necessary under the statute of frauds.

With certain very minor exceptions, a will must be in writing in order to be legally binding. It should contain provisions that indicate that the person is of sound mind and understands that he is making a will.

The will should be signed and witnessed by other individuals as required by state law. Many wills also contain an attestation clause, which states that the will has been signed by the maker in the presence of witnesses. The maker of the will should sign at the bottom of the will and should initial each page of the will. This indicates that the maker has read each page of the will and agrees with its provisions.

Drafting the Provisions

The provisions of the will should be drafted carefully and specifically. It is useful to avoid expressions such as "I give my property to be divided equally among my children or other individuals." Such clauses only tend to confuse the people involved with carrying out the will's provisions. It is difficult to decide what equal means. In addition, such clauses tend to create problems among the members of that class. Inevitably, there will be disputes among members as to who is entitled to which piece of property.

Real Property

The will or trust may contain provisions relating to disposing of both real and personal property.

Real estate that is held as a joint tenant with a right of survivorship may not be disposed of in a will. When a joint tenant dies, the real estate automatically belongs to the remaining joint tenant.

If the real estate is held either individually or as a tenant in common, it may be disposed of in the will. The provisions relating to the real estate must specifically state the location as well as precisely defining the dimensions of the piece of property that is being conveyed by the will.

A person who receives real property under a will generally receives the ownership rights of the will's maker unless she indicated otherwise. A number of possible rights to real estate are discussed below.

Fee simple is ownership of the property free of other claims to ownership. It represents the greatest amount of ownership rights one can claim in property.

A life estate is the right of a person to live upon the land for the remainder of one's life. It is common practice for a person to leave life estates to spouses or children. This allows them to live on the land and permits the land to be conveyed to other parties after their death.

Real estate may be owned by more than one person at the same time. Coownership may take several forms:

- A person may own the property as a joint tenant with a right of survivorship. This is a form of coownership in which the surviving joint tenant will receive all of the property when the other joint tenant dies. An attempt to transfer one's interest in such a tenancy in a will has no legal effect.

- A joint tenancy with a right of survivorship usually contains provisions prohibiting sale of one's interest in the joint tenancy. It is also useful to include provisions that specifically prohibit the attempted assignment or other disposition of the interest without the consent of the other party.

- A tenancy in common is different from a joint tenancy with rights of survivorship. In this case, the parties hold separate shares in the real estate. The parties may sell their share, assign it, or give it to someone else in their will unless provided otherwise in the original agreement between the parties. However, it is a good idea to prohibit the sale or assignment of the interest without the other party's consent.

Generally, coownership may not be a good idea. Often, the parties will disagree on what to do with the land or whether they should dispose of it. This can create difficult problems for the parties. Sometimes, the problems will make it difficult to utilize the land in a productive manner.

A tenancy by the entireties relates to real property owned by husband and wife. A tenancy by the entireties allows husbands and wives to own property jointly. This can have some advantages in terms of peace of mind and a sense of a common bond between the couple.

A lease is the right a tenant has to live on the land. A lease may be passed on to another in one's will because it is considered a property right unless the lease provides to the contrary. A lease, particularly a commercial one, may be a valuable asset. The rental fee may be lower than the market price. This difference, over a period of time, may amount to a significant value.

Personal Property and Trusts

Personal property is any property other than real property. It includes money, goods, copyrights, patents, and other personal property. One can leave personal property directly to beneficiaries or place it in a trust.

A trust is a legal mechanism that allows a person to transfer property to a trustee who will manage it on behalf of a beneficiary. One may place either real or personal property into a trust.

A trust established during one's lifetime is called an inter vivos or lifetime trust. A trust created in a will is called a testamentary trust. It takes effect upon the person's death.

The trust should name the trustee, the beneficiary, and the property that will go into the trust. One can also provide that property from the estate be poured over into an existing inter vivos trust. This can be a useful way of testing the skills of the trustee and the manner in which the trust functions prior to placing additional assets into the trust.

The trust's creator should also designate a person or institution that will receive the trust's assets after the death of the original beneficiary. This person or institution is called the remainderperson.

Use of trusts can have significant tax advantages for the family of the testator. While federal legislation has reduced many of these advantages, competent counsel can still utilize charitable trusts to obtain tax savings for the creator or the creator's family.

WORKING IN THE LAW OFFICE

Drafting wills and trusts as well as contracts relating to real estate is often the mainstay of many law offices. A paralegal should be aware of how to draft these agreements. Good work will also attract new clients, which will make the paralegal a very valuable asset to a law office.

MARRIAGE AND DIVORCE RELATED CONTRACTS

Student Skill: The student will understand some of the contractual provisions that could be part of marriage and divorce related contracts.

Legally, a marriage is an agreement between two people to share some or all of their property and responsibility for any children derived during that period. Historically, marriages have been used to cement political relationships or to consolidate property holdings. As a result, contracts related to marriage were particularly important. The statute of frauds recognized that importance by requiring that contracts in consideration of marriage be evidenced by some writing.

While prenuptial agreements usually deal with property, it is becoming more common for couples to draw up contracts relating to other aspects of the marriage. The following sections outline some of the provisions that might be included in a contract related to a marriage.

CONTRACTUAL PROVISIONS RELATED TO THE MARRIAGE

If one party to the marriage has more property than the other, it is useful to determine the status of the property that is brought into the marriage as well as the property that is acquired during the marriage. The parties should determine how this property will be distributed if the parties are divorced. The provisions related to the contract of marriage may be phrased in a number of ways.

The party with the most assets is likely to ask for some protection against demands from the other party either while the marriage exists or upon its dissolution. Some states have community property laws that provide that all of the assets acquired during the marriage are regarded as being owned 50 percent by each. Other states have similar laws that provide that each spouse has rights in property acquired during the marriage. In addition, many couples own property jointly, which means the property belongs to both of them.

In addition, laws that allow no-fault divorce tend to favor equitable division of property. If there are children involved, the custodian parent, usually the mother, will receive sufficient child support to take care of her and the children. As a result, the system tends to favor dividing up the property between the divorcing spouses.

A full discussion of matrimonial law is beyond the scope of this book. However, a paralegal may be asked to draft or review contractual provisions related to a marriage. These might include the following:

- The parties to this contract agree that each party will retain full ownership of property acquired before the marriage. Each party also agrees that neither will assert any claim on the property of the other acquired before the marriage.
- The parties also agree that the parties will dispose of the property acquired during the marriage in accordance with the following percentages: Husband—60 percent, wife—40 percent. The percentages are based on the earnings of the parties during the marriage.

- The parties agree that the following property belongs to the husband and was acquired before the marriage and is not subject to any claims of the wife. (Here list the husband's property acquired before the marriage.)

- The parties further agree that the following property belongs to the wife and was acquired before the marriage and is not subject to any claims of the husband. (Here list the wife's property acquired before the marriage.)

- The parties agree that each of them will bear responsibility for any children who are born of the marriage. The parties further agree that the parties will assume joint custody of any children and will provide equal support of the financial needs of such children until they reach adulthood.

- The parties agree that it is their intention to have two children.

- The parties further agree that (the wife) will stay home with the children for a period of six months after their birth.

- The parties intend to take two vacations per year for a total of four weeks.

- The husband agrees to be primarily responsible for the chores outside of the dwelling in which the parties reside.

- The wife agrees to be primarily responsible for the indoor chores of the dwelling in which both parties reside.

- The parties agree to share chores such as cooking, laundry, and shopping.

- The parties agree to pool their financial resources acquired during the marriage.

- The parties agree to own all real estate jointly with a right of survivorship.

The parties might want to outline any other specific agreement relating to the marriage. Although some people regard such specific marriage contracts as odd, they serve the purpose of clarifying each of the party's expectations before they enter the union. There are less likely to be problems if the parties have worked out any disagreements prior to living together.

While many people provide for guardians for their children in their wills, it might be useful to provide for the guardians in the marriage contract. The parties are less likely to postpone writing a marriage contract than writing a will.

DIVORCES

The final draft of a divorce agreement is a complicated matter and should be left to competent counsel. However, a paralegal may have the opportunity to write a first draft of the agreement or to review a final draft.

Below are some provisions that might be included in a divorce agreement:

- The parties agree that the house on 38 Elm Street in Springdale, New Jersey will belong to the wife upon the final effect of this divorce decree. In addition, the personal belongings in the house will also become the property of the wife.

- The parties further agree that the Cadillac owned by the couple will belong to the wife and the Buick will belong to the husband.

- The parties to this agreement also agree that the husband will contribute $1,000 per month to the wife to pay for her support for a period of five years.

- The parties agree that the husband will provide $1,000 per month to support their daughter, Mary, until she reaches the age of 21 or until she is married, whichever occurs first.

- The parties agree that if the wife remarries, the payments to her will be reduced to $500 per month.

- The parties agree that this agreement is reached without regard to fault and that any previous conduct of the parties is not relevant to the enforcement of this agreement.

- The parties agree that this agreement will be reviewed and is subject to the jurisdiction of the appropriate court.

- The parties agree that upon approval of the court of appropriate jurisdiction, this agreement will become effective.

- The parties agree that any proposals for modifying this agreement will be submitted to the appropriate court of jurisdiction. The parties agree that they will be bound by the court's decision.

- As an alternative to judicial determination, the parties agree to submit any dispute to an arbitrator selected by agreement of both parties from a list of three names submitted by the American Arbitration Association.

PARALEGAL'S "THINGS TO DO"

1. Paralegals should check to ensure that they understand what the will's creator wants to accomplish. This includes an understanding of who would be the testator's usual beneficiaries.

2. Paralegals should also check to ensure that all of the legal formalities required to have a valid will are satisfied. A law firm may be held liable for malpractice if it makes mistakes that relate to the legal validity of the will. It is important to double- or triple-check that all legal requirements have been satisfied.

3. Paralegals should also check the financial records and other documents of the person writing the will. They may discover undisclosed trust documents or other information that may impact on the will or the estate. Many law firms develop checklists when they write a will or administer an estate. These checklists are very useful for a lawyer and paralegal because they reduce the likelihood of mistakes and increase the chances that a thorough job will be performed. The checklists should answer the who, what, where, when, why, and how questions relating to the estate.

4. Paralegals may also want to consider the possibility of utilizing living or testamentary trusts as alternatives or additions to the provisions in the will.

5. A paralegal should review governmental contracts carefully to determine if his client's interests are adequately protected. It is particularly important to review, in detail, the provisions relating to payment for the services or the products provided to the government.

6. Security agreements allow a creditor to seize personal property to pay off loans owed to the creditor. They should be reviewed carefully to ensure that they permit the assets to be taken if the debtor defaults on the loan or credit.

7. Mortgage documents relating to real estate and underlying loan agreements are normally drafted by attorneys for the bank. As a result, they should be reviewed carefully by the paralegal working on behalf of a property owner.

QUESTIONS

1. What is the purpose of a will?
2. What are some of the legal requirements relating to wills?
3. What is a joint tenancy with a right of survivorship?
4. What are the legal consequences of a joint tenancy with a right of survivorship with respect to passing real estate under a will?
5. What is the difference between a tenancy in common and a joint tenancy with right of survivorship?
6. What is a living trust?
7. What is a testamentary trust?
8. How can a paralegal utilize testamentary trusts in estate planning?
9. What is a trustee?
10. What is a beneficiary of a trust?
11. Name some major differences between governmental contracts and other contracts.
12. Name some different types of governmental contracts.
13. What is a professional services governmental contract?
14. What is a security interest in personal property?
15. How does one create (attach) a security interest in personal property?
16. What is a security interest in real property (a mortgage)?
17. What are the purposes of security agreements in personal and real property?
18. How does one protect the security interest from other creditors?
19. What is a floating lien?
20. What is the purpose of a floating lien?
21. Why might one agree to a contract relating to one's marriage?
22. What provisions might one include in such a contract?

Cases

UNILATERAL/BILATERAL CONTRACTS

MARK REALTY, INC. v. ROGNESS
418 So. 2d 373 (1982)
District Court of Appeal of Florida

Facts. Rogness, who owned several pieces of real estate, entered into brokerage agreements with Mark Realty, Inc., which granted Mark Realty the exclusive right to sell the properties on behalf of Rogness for a stated period of time. Mark Realty was to be paid commissions upon the sale of the properties. The contract contained mutual promises made in exchange for each other. During the listing period, Rogness sold the properties himself and refused to pay Mark Realty commissions on the sales. Mark Realty sued for breach of contract, seeking the commissions. The trial court held in favor of Rogness and Realty appeals.

Opinion. Cowart, Judge. The most common recurring brokerage transaction is one in which the owner employs a broker to find a purchaser able and willing to buy, on terms stated in advance by the owner, and in which the owner promises to pay a specific commission for the service. Such a transaction as this is an offer by the owner of a unilateral contract, an offered promise to pay by the owner, creating in the broker a power of accepting the offer by actual rendition of the requested service. Here the only contemplated contract between the owner and broker is a unilateral contract—a promise to pay a commission for services rendered. Such an offer of a promise to pay a commission for service rendered is revocable by the owner by notice before the broker has rendered any part of the requested service.

On the other hand, the transaction between the owner and the broker can be a bilateral contract. An owner who puts his land in the hands of a broker for sale usually clearly promises to pay a commission, but the broker rarely promises in return that he will produce a purchaser, although he often promises, expressly or impliedly, that he will make certain efforts to do so. If the parties have made these mutual promises, the transaction no longer has the status of an unaccepted offer—there is an existing bilateral contract and neither party has a power of revocation. In this case, the broker promised to inspect the property, to list the property with a multiple listing service, to advertise the property in the local newspaper or other media, to furnish information to inquiring cooperating brokers and prospective purchases, to show the property, to make efforts to find a purchaser, to "make an earnest and continuous effort to sell," and to direct the concentrated efforts of his organization in bringing about a sale.

Not only are the agreements in this case enforceable bilateral contracts, but a reading of the contracts indicates that they granted the broker an "exclusive right of sale." In the instant case, the contract clearly provided that the brokerage commission would be paid "whether the purchaser be secured by you or me, or by any other person." Thus, the contract granted the broker an exclusive right of sale and the trial court erred in construing the agreement as an offer of a unilateral contract revocable at will at any time prior to performance.

Holding and Remedy. We hold that the contracts in question were bilateral contracts because they contained mutual promises made in exchange for each other by the contracting parties. The judgment of the trial court in favor of Rogness is *reversed*, and the case is remanded for further proceeding consistent with this opinion.

QUASI/IMPLIED CONTRACTS

NURSING CARE SERVICES, INC. v. DOBOS
380 So. 2d 516 (1980)
District Court of Appeal of Florida

Facts. Mary Dobos was admitted to Boca Raton Community Hospital with an aneurysm. Her condition was sufficiently serious to cause her doctor to order around-the-clock nursing care. The hospital implemented this order by calling upon Nursing Care Services, Inc. (Nursing Care), which provides individualized nursing services. Mrs. Dobos received two weeks of in-hospital care. Nursing Care billed Mrs. Dobos $3,475.90 for their services. Mrs. Dobos failed to pay. Plaintiff Nursing Care brought this action against Dobos to recover payment. The trial court denied recovery. Nursing Care appeals.

Opinion. Hurley, Judge. The law's concern that needless services not be foisted upon the unsuspecting has led to the formulation of the "officious intermeddler doctrine." It holds that where a person performs labor for another without the latter's request or implied consent, however beneficial such labor may be, he cannot recover therefore. A notable exception to this rule, however, is that of emergency aid:

> A person who has supplied things or services to another, although acting without the other's knowledge or consent, is entitled to restitution therefore from the other if he acted unofficially and with intent to charge therefore, and the things or services were necessary to prevent the other from suffering serious bodily harm or pain, and the person supplying them had no reason to know that the other would not consent to receiving them, if mentally competent, and it was impossible for the other to give consent or, because of extreme youth or mental impairment, the other's consent would have been immaterial.

In the case at bar it is unclear whether Mrs. Dobos, during the period of in-hospital care, understood or intended that compensation be paid. Her condition was grave. She had been placed in the hospital's intensive care unit and thereafter had attached to her body tubes and other medical equipment that necessitated special attention. She was alone, unable to cope and without family assistance. It is worthy of note that at no point during the litigation was there any question as to the propriety of the professional judgment that the patient required special nursing care. To the contrary, the record demonstrates that the in-hospital nursing care was essential to Mrs. Dobo's health and safety. Given these circumstances it would be unconscionable to deny the plaintiff recovery for services which fall squarely within the emergency aid exception.

Holding and Remedy. We find that there was an implied-in-law contract—a "quasi-contract"—between the parties. Accordingly, we remand the cause to the trial court with instructions to enter an amended final judgment for plaintiff Nursing Care Services, Inc., in the sum of $3,425.90 plus interest and court costs.

CHAPTER 2: OFFER AND ACCEPTANCE

TERMS OF AN OFFER

GOODWEST RUBBER CORPORATION v. MUNOZ
170 Cal. App. 3d 919, 216 Cal. Rptr.
604 (1985)

Facts. Munoz owned property which he leased to Goodwest Rubber Corporation (Goodwest) for five years. The lease granted Goodwest the option to buy the property at a fair market value. Goodwest sought to exercise the option to purchase the property and tendered $80,000 to Munoz. When Munoz rejected this offer, Goodwest filed suit seeking specific performance of the option agreement. The trial court held for Munoz. Goodwest appeals.

Opinion. Rickles, Justice. We are presented with a single issue for review: Was a price designation of "fair market value" definite enough to support an action for specific performance? This precise issue has not been resolved in California. However, text writers and courts in other jurisdictions are in general agreement that "fair market value," "reasonable value," or "current market value" are sufficiently certain price terms to support specific performance of an option. We see no need to reach a different result in this instance.

The modern trend of the law is to favor the enforcement of contract, to lean against their unenforceability because of uncertainty, and to carry out the intention of the parties if this can feasibly be done. Neither law nor equity requires that every term and condition of an agreement be set forth in the contract. Option agreements have generally been held or recognized to be sufficiently definite as to price to justify their enforcement if either a specific price is provided in the agreement or a practicable mode is provided for the court to determine price without any expression by the parties themselves. "Fair market value" is a well established means of property valuation and is a common task performed by courts on a daily basis. Specifying "fair market value" as the price to be paid when exercising the option to purchase does not require future agreement of the buyer and seller.

Holding and Remedy. The term "fair market value" is a proper substitute for a specific price and will support an action for specific performance. The judgment of the trial court is reversed.

ACCEPTANCE/MAILBOX RULE

SOLDAU v. ORGANON, INC.
860 F.2d 355 (1988)
United States Court of Appeals, Ninth Circuit

Facts. Soldau was discharged by his employer, Organon, Inc. He received a letter from Organon offering to pay him double the normal severance pay in exchange for a release by Soldau of all claims against Organon regarding the discharge. Soldau signed and dated the release and deposited it in a mailbox outside of a post office. When he returned home, he had received a check from Organon for the increased severance pay. Soldau returned to the post office, persuaded a postal employee to open the mailbox, and retrieved the release. He cashed the severance paycheck and brought this action against Organon, alleging a violation of the federal Age

Discrimination in Employment Act. The U.S. District Court granted summary judgment for Organon. Soldau appeals.

Opinion. Per Curiam. The district court was clearly correct under California law. Under federal as well as California law, Soldau's acceptance was effective when it was mailed. The so-called "mailbox" or "effective when mailed" rule was adopted and followed as federal common law by the Supreme Court prior to Erie R.R. Co. v. Tomkins. We could not change the rule, and there is no reason to believe the Supreme Court would be inclined to do so. It is almost universally accepted in the common law world. It is enshrined in the Restatement (Second) of Contracts, Section 63 (a), and endorsed by the major contract treatises. Commentators are also virtually unanimous in approving the "effective when mailed" rule, pointing to the long history of the rule; its importance in creating certainty for contracting parties; and its essential soundness, on balance, as a means of allocating the risk during the period between the making of the offer and the communication of the acceptance or rejection to the offeror.

Holding and Remedy. Since Soldau's contractual obligation to release Organon in return for Organon's obligation to make the enhanced severance payment arose when Soldau deposited his acceptance in the post office mailbox, his subsequent withdrawal of the acceptance was ineffectual. The judgment of the district court in favor of Organon, Inc., is *affirmed.*

CHAPTER 3: CONTRACTS REQUIRING A WRITING

EXCEPTIONS TO STATUTE OF FRAUDS

SHEPHERD v. MOZZETTI
545 A.2d 621 (1988)
Supreme Court of Delaware

Facts. Adolfo Mozzetti owned a construction company. He orally promised his son, Remo, that if Remo would manage the family business for their mutual benefit and would take care of him for the rest of his life, he would leave the family home to Remo. Section 2714 of the Delaware Code requires contracts for the transfer of land to be in writing. Section 2715 of the Delaware Code requires testamentary transfers of real property to be in writing. Remo performed as requested—he managed the family business and took care of his father until the father died. When the father died, his will devised the family home to his daughter, Lucia M. Shepard. Remo brought this action to enforce his father's oral promise that the will should be upheld. The Court of Chancery entered judgment in favor of Remo and ordered specific performance. The daughter appeals.

Opinion. Per Curiam. A written will executed with the formalities required by Delaware law is a document of great dignity and not to be deviated from lightly. However, in law there are few absolutes without exceptions, and the Statute of Frauds is but one example. One well-rooted exception to the absolute command of the general Statute of Frauds controlling contracts is the equitably derived principle that a partly performed oral contract may be enforced by an order for specific performance upon proof by clear and convincing evidence of actual part performance.

Thus, a court of equity may decree specific performance of an oral land contract, notwithstanding Section 2714, when there is evidence of actual part performance of the oral contract. The exception is applied to prevent the Statute of Frauds from working an injustice. Thus, we must affirm the chancellor's ruling that actual part performance by the son upon his deceased father's oral promise to devise the family home to him obviates the bar of Section 2715.

There is substantial evidence of record to support the factual findings of the chancellor. It is clear from the record that the son met his burden of establishing by clear and convincing evidence the existence of an oral promise by the father to devise the family home to his son in return for the son's promise to continue to mange the family business and to care for the father for the rest of his life. Moreover, the record equally supports the chancellor's finding that the performance by the son of his duties under the oral contract amounted to legal consideration. Given the fact that the chancellor's factual findings also appear to be the product of an orderly and logical deductive reasoning process, this court declines to disturb these rulings.

Holding and Remedy. We hold that the part performance exception to the Statute of Frauds applies in this case. The judgment of the Court of Chancery in favor of the son, Remo Mozzetti, is *affirmed.*

CHAPTER 4: THE DOCTRINE OF CONSIDERATION

PROMISES

ALDEN v. PRESLEY
637 S.W. 2d 862 (1982)
Supreme Court of Tennessee

Facts. Elvis Presley became engaged to Ginger Alden. He was generous with the Alden family, paying for landscaping the lawn, installing a swimming pool, and making other gifts. When his fiancee's mother, Jo Laverne Alden, sought to divorce her husband, Presley promised to pay off the remaining mortgage indebtedness on the Alden home, which Mrs. Alden was to receive in the divorce settlement. On August 16, 1977, Presley died suddenly, leaving the mortgage unpaid. When the legal representative of Presley's estate refused to pay the mortgage, Mrs. Alden brought an action to enforce Presley's promise. The trial court denied recovery. Mrs. Alden appeals.

Opinion. Fones, Justice. The mortgage indebtedness was in the sum of $39,587.66, and it is this amount which is the subject of the present suit, all the other gifts and promises to plaintiff having been fulfilled.

In the instant case, the trial court held decedent did make a promise unsupported by consideration to plaintiff, that no gift was consummated for failure of delivery, that plaintiff suffered no detriment as she "would be much better off after her association with Elvis A. Presley than if he had never made any promise to Jo Laverne Alden." The court of appeals concurred in the finding that there was no gift for failure of delivery, holding that delivery is not complete unless complete dominion and control of the gift is surrendered by the donor and acquired by the donee.

Holding and Remedy. We concur in the reasoning of the trial court and court of appeals' findings that decedent did not make a gift promise of the money.

PAST CONSIDERATION

DEMENTAS v. ESTATE OF TALLAS
764 P.2d 628 (1988)
Court of Appeals of Utah

Facts. Jack Tallas emigrated to the United States from Greece in 1914. He lived in Salt Lake City for nearly 70 years, during which time he achieved considerable success in business, primarily as an insurance agent and landlord. Over a period of 14 years, Peter Dementas, who as a close personal friend of Tallas, rendered services to Tallas, including picking up his mail, driving him to the grocery store, and assisting with the management of his rental properties.

On December 18, 1982, Tallas met with Dementas and dictated a memorandum to him, in Greek, stating that he owed Dementas $50,000 for his help over the years and indicated in the memorandum he would change his will to make Dementas an heir for this amount. Tallas signed the document. Tallas died on February 4, 1983, without changing his will to include Dementas as an heir. He left a substantial estate. Dementas filed a claim for $50,000 with Tallas's estate. When the estate denied the claim, Dementas brought this action to enforce the contract. The trial court dismisses Dementas's claim. Dementas appeals.

Opinion. Orne, Judge. The burden of proving consideration is on the party seeking to recover on the contract. If plaintiff fails to show there is consideration to support the contract, that party has failed to meet its burden and the contract will be held invalid by the court. A generally accepted definition of consideration is that a legal detriment has been bargained for and exchanged for a promise. The mere fact that one man promises something to another creates no legal duty and makes no legal remedy available in case of nonperformance. A performance or a returned promise must be bargained for.

Even though the testimony showed that Dementas rendered at least some services for Tallas, the subsequent promise by Tallas to pay $50,000 for services already performed by Dementas is not a promise supported by legal consideration. Events which occur prior to the making of the promise and not with the purpose of inducing the promise in exchange are viewed as "past consideration" and are the legal equivalent of no consideration. This is so because the promisor is making his promise because those events occurred, but he is not making his promise in order to get them. There is no bargaining, no saying that if you do this for me I will do that for you. A benefit conferred or detriment incurred in the past is not adequate consideration for a present bargain.

This rule can surely work unfair results and has accordingly been criticized. We acknowledge, as have other courts in disregarding contracts for lack of consideration, that appellant will probably remain convinced he should be paid. Nevertheless, he failed to meet his burden of proof, and this court will not find a contract where one has not been proved to exist. **Holding and Remedy**. We hold that the promise is unenforceable because it is only supported by past consideration, which is not legal consideration. The judgment appealed from is *affirmed*.

RELIANCE AS CONSIDERATION

LAMPLEY v. CELEBRITY HOMES, INC.
Colorado Court of Appeals, Division II 594
P.2d 605 (1979)

Linda Lampley, plaintiff, began work at Celebrity Homes in Denver in May of 1975. On July 29 of that year Celebrity announced the initiation of a profit-sharing plan. Under that plan all employees were to receive bonuses if a certain "profit goal" were reached for the 1975 fiscal year — i.e., April 1, 1975 to March 31, 1976.

Plaintiff's employment was terminated in January of 1976. At the end of March 1976, the company announced that the profit goal had been reached, and it made its first distribution of profits in May 1976. When plaintiff was excluded from this distribution, she brought this suit for the share allegedly due her.

In the trial court Celebrity argued that its promise to pay the bonus was a mere "gratuity" on its part, on the ground that there was no consideration on the employee's part to support its promise. The trial court rejected this contention and entered judgment for plaintiff. Celebrity appealed.

Decision. The trial court was correct in ruling that consideration existed on plaintiff's part. First, defendant's plan stated that its objective was to bring about "teamwork in our day-to-day operation," and also "better performance for our customers...and fairer treatment of our customers, subcontractors and suppliers...." Thus the plan was an inducement to Celebrity's employees to perform more efficient and faithful service. Such result would be of obvious benefit to Celebrity, and thus it did receive consideration from the employees.

Secondly, plaintiff was employed for an indefinite term originally; that is, she was under no obligation to work until a fixed future date at the time that the profit-sharing promise was made to her in July. Thus it can be inferred that she was induced by that promise to remain on the job until the following January. By so remaining as a result of the promise, plaintiff incurred a detriment that also supported Celebrity's promise.

PROMISSORY ESTOPPEL

HOFFMAN v. RED OWL STORES, INC.
Supreme Court of Wisconsin, 133 N.W. 2d 267 (1965)

In 1960 Hoffman, plaintiff, hoped to establish a Red Owl franchised grocery store in Wautoma, Wisconsin. During that year he and the divisional manager of Red Owl, Lukowitz, had numerous conversations in which general plans for Hoffman's becoming a franchisee were discussed. Early in 1961 Lukowitz advised Hoffman to buy a small grocery in order to gain experience in the grocery business before operating a Red Owl franchise in a larger community.

Acting on this suggestion, Hoffman bought a small grocery in Wautoma. Three months later Red Owl representatives found that the store was operating at a profit, at which time Hoffman told Lukowitz that he could raise $18,000 to invest in a franchise. Lukowitz then advised Hoffman to sell the store, assuring him that the company would find a larger store for him to operate elsewhere, and that he would "be operating a Red Owl store in a new location by fall."

Relying on this promise, Hoffman sold the grocery and soon thereafter bought a lot in Chilton, Wisconsin (a site which the company had selected for a new store), making a $1,000 down payment on the lot. Hoffman then rented a home for his family in Chilton and, after being assured by Lukowitz that "everything was all set," made a second $1,000 payment on the lot.

In September 1961, Lukowitz told Hoffman that the only "hitch" in the plan was that he (Hoffman) would have to sell a bakery building he owned in Wautoma and that the proceeds of that sale would have to make up a part of the $18,000 he was to invest, thereby reducing the amount he would have to borrow. Hoffman sold the building for $10,000, incurring a loss thereon of $2,000.

About this time, Red Owl prepared a "Proposed Financing for an Agency Store" plan that required Hoffman to invest $24,100 rather than the original $18,000. After Hoffman came up with $24,100 by virtue of several new loans, Red Owl told him that another $2,000 would be necessary.

Hoffman refused to go along with this demand, negotiations were terminated, and the new store was never built. When Hoffman and his wife brought suit to recover damages for breach of contract, Red Owl defended on the ground that its promises were not supported by consideration on Hoffman's part (in view of the facts that no formal financing plan was ever agreed to by Hoffman and no franchise agreement obligations were undertaken by him). Hoffman contended that liability should nonetheless be imposed on the basis of promissory estoppel; the trial court agreed, entering judgment in his favor. Red Owl appealed.

Decision. The judgment for Hoffman is affirmed. The purpose of the doctrine of promissory estoppel is to permit a promise to enforce a promise, even though consideration is lacking on the promisee's part, if a substantial injustice would otherwise result. In this case several promises were made by the defendant company to Hoffman, the promisee, and in each instance he took definite and substantial actions on the basis of these promises. Specifically, these actions consisted of the sale of his grocery, the purchase of a lot in Chilton, the renting of a home in Chilton, and the sale of his bakery building. As a result of these actions, Hoffman would obviously suffer great injustice if he were not awarded damages from the defendant company based on its refusal to live up to the promises made to him.

CHAPTER 5: LEGAL CAPACITY

RECOVERY BY MINOR

HOGUE ET AL. v. WILKINSON
Court of Civil Appeals of Texas
291 S.W. 2d 750 (1956)

In November 1953, Gordon Wilkinson, an eighteen-year-old, purchased a pair of chinchillas from Hogue and McCoy, the defendants, for $1,150. In December 1953 he purchased a second pair for $700. (At all times involved in this action the age of majority under Texas law was twenty-one.)

The chinchillas were delivered to Wilkinson soon after the contracts were made, and by December 1954 he had paid the total consideration of $1,850. By that time the number of chinchillas had increased to eight, the original pair having produced four offspring.

In March 1955, Wilkinson, still a minor, went to defendants' place of business and disaffirmed both contracts. At that time he offered to return the six chinchillas that were then living and demanded the return of the $1,850. (Between December 1954 and March 1955 one of the $700 pair and one of the young had died.)

Defendants would not accept the chinchillas and refused to return the money. Wilkinson then brought suit in April of 1955 asking for the return of the $1,850. (By that time, only two chinchillas were living.)

At the trial, the defendants contended that the inability of the plaintiff to return all eight of the chinchillas barred this action, particularly in view of the evidence that the deaths of the chinchillas resulted from the plaintiff's negligence. The court, acting without a jury, rejected this contention and entered a summary judgment for the plaintiff. Defendants appealed.

Decision. The court was correct in permitting the minor, Wilkinson, to recover all his payments. Under Texas case law the only obligation of minors who wish to recover payments is to return the consideration if they are able. In this case, by returning the surviving chinchillas, Wilkinson met the requirement. The fact that he was unable to return all the chinchillas he had owned at one time (because his negligence caused some of them to die) does not take away his right of recovery. Under the case law of this state, mere negligence on the part of the minor—as distinguished from fraud—does not prevent recovery.

NECESSITIES OF LIFE

GASTONIA PERSONNEL CORPORATION v. ROGERS
Supreme Court of North Carolina
172 S.E. 2d 19 (1970)

Rogers was a minor who was studying civil engineering in a North Carolina college. When his wife became pregnant he had to quit school and go to work. In order to get suitable employment, Rogers signed a contract with an employment agency, Gastonia Personnel Corporation, the plaintiff. Under the terms of this agreement Rogers agreed to pay plaintiff a fee of $295 if it produced a "lead" that resulted in a job for him.

Soon thereafter one of plaintiff's personnel counselors put Rogers in touch with a Charlotte firm which hired him as a draftsman. Rogers subsequently disaffirmed the contract with plaintiff on the ground of minority, and refused to pay its fee. Plaintiff then brought suit to recover the $295 or, in the alternative, the reasonable value of its services. Plaintiff's primary contention was that its services constituted a necessity under the circumstances of the case. The trial court ruled as a matter of law that the services were not a necessity, and dismissed the action. Plaintiff appealed.

Decision. The trial court was wrong in ruling as a matter of law that plaintiff's services were not a necessity. Today, "necessaries" includes not only food, clothing, and shelter, but also such articles of property and services that are reasonably necessary to enable the minor to earn the money required to provide the necessities of life for himself and those who are legally dependent upon him.

Here, plaintiff was married, a high school graduate close to obtaining a college degree, and capable of holding a draftsman's job. To hold, as a matter of law, that such a person cannot obligate himself to pay for services rendered in obtaining employment suitable to his ability and education (by which he could provide the necessities of life for himself, wife and children), would place him and other minors under a serious economic handicap. Accordingly, the case is remanded to the trial court for the purpose of determining the reasonable value of plaintiff's services.

CHAPTER 6: CONTRACTS AND THIRD PARTIES

BENEFICIARIES TO CONTRACTS

BAIN v. GILLISPIE
357 N.W. 2D 47 (1984)
Court of Appeals of Iowa

Facts. James C. Bain, a college basketball referee, had a contract with the Big 10 Basketball Conference (Big 10) to referee various basketball games of universities belonging to the conference. During a game that took place on March 6, 1982, Bain called a foul on a University of Iowa player that permitted free throws by a Purdue University player. That player scored the point that gave Purdue a last-minute victory and eliminated Iowa from the championship of the Big 10. Some fans of the University of Iowa blamed Bain for the team's loss, asserting that the foul call was clearly in error.

John and Karen Gillispie operated a novelty store in Iowa City known as "Hawkeye John's Trading Post," which sold University of Iowa sports memorabilia. The Gillispies filed a complaint against Bain, alleging that his refereeing constituted negligence and a breach of his contract with the Big 10, and that such negligence destroyed a potential market for their Hawkeye memorabilia touting Iowa as a Big 10 champion. The Gillispies sought $175,000 compensatory damages plus exemplary damages from Bain. The trial court granted Bain's motion for summary judgment. The Gillispies appeal.

Opinion. Snell, Presiding Judge. The trial court found that there was no issue of material fact on the Gillispies' claim that they were beneficiaries under Bain's contract with the Big 10. Because the Gillispies would not be privy to the contract, they must be direct beneficiaries to maintain a cause of action, and not merely incidental beneficiaries.

A direct beneficiary is either a donee beneficiary or a creditor beneficiary. The Gillispies make no claim that they are creditor beneficiaries of Bain, the Big 10 Athletic Conference, or the University of Iowa. The real test is said to be whether the contracting parties intended that a third person should receive a benefit that might be enforced in the courts. It is clear that the purpose of any promise that Bain might have made was not to confer a gift on the Gillispies. Likewise, the Big 10 did not owe any duty to the Gillispies such that they would have been donee beneficiaries. If a contract did exist between Bain and the Big 10, the Gillispies can be considered nothing more than incidental beneficiaries and as such are unable to maintain a cause of action. Consequently, there is no genuine issue for trial that could result in the Gillispies obtaining a judgment under a contract theory of recovery.

Holding and Remedy. We hold that the Gillispies are not intended beneficiaries of the contract between Bain and the Big 10 Basketball Conference, but were merely incidental beneficiaries. Therefore, they cannot maintain this lawsuit for an alleged breach of that contract. The judgment of the trial court in favor of Bain on this issue is *affirmed.*

PERSONAL SERVICE CONTRACTS

SCHUPACH v. MCDONALD'S SYSTEM, INC.
Supreme Court of Nebraska
264 N.W. 2d 827 (1978)

McDonald's, defendant, is the corporation that grants all McDonald fast-food restaurant franchises. In 1959 defendant granted a franchise to a Mr. Copeland, giving him the right to own and operate McDonald's first store in the Omaha-Council Bluffs area. A few days later, in conformity with the negotiations leading up to the granting of the franchise, McDonald's sent a letter to Copeland giving him a "Right of First Refusal" i.e., the right to be given first chance at owning any new stores that might be subsequently established in the area. In the next few years Copeland exercised this right and opened five additional stores in Omaha. In 1964 Copeland sold and assigned all of his franchises to Schupach, plaintiff, with McDonald's consent.

When defendant granted a franchise in the Omaha-Council Bluffs area in 1974 to a third party without first offering it to Schupach, he brought this action for damages resulting from establishment of the new franchise, and for injunction restraining defendant from granting new franchises in this manner.

A number of issues were raised in this litigation. Defendant contended, among other things, that the right it gave to Copeland was personal in nature, and thus was not transferable without its consent. Plaintiff alleged, on the other hand, that the right was not personal in nature, or, in the alternative, that its transfer was, in fact, agreed to by defendant.

On these issues the trial court ruled that the right was personal in nature. It also ruled, however, after analyzing voluminous correspondence between the parties, that defendant had consented to the transfer. It entered judgment for plaintiff, and defendant appealed.

Decision. The trial court was clearly correct in finding that the right was personal in nature, and thus could not be assigned without McDonald's permission. This finding was based on testimony of Mr. Ray Kroc, founder of McDonalds, that the people who were granted franchises were selected with great care, were people who had a great deal of pride, and who would create "an image of cleanliness, and image where parents would be glad to have their children come" as patrons or employees. The evidence overwhelmingly established the fact that the Right of First Refusal was personal in nature, and was separately a grant independent of the terms of the franchise itself.

CHAPTER 7: LEGALITY OF CONTRACTS

LICENSING STATUTES

BREMMEYER v. PETER KIEWIT SONS COMPANY
Supreme Court of Washington
585 P.2d 1174 (1978)

The State of Washington awarded Peter Kiewit a prime contract to construct several miles of Interstate 90. The highway right-of-way was overgrown, and needed to have the trees and debris cleared before construction could begin. For this purpose, Peter Kiewit subcontracted the necessary clearing operation to Bremmeyer. Under the subcontract, Bremmeyer agreed to pay Peter Kiewit $35,000 for the right to fall, yard, load, haul and sell to a mill all the merchantable timber within the right-of-way. (Bremmeyer was to keep the proceeds of the sale as his compensation.)

Bremmeyer paid the $35,000 and began clearing the right-of-way, but before he had finished the job the state terminated Peter Kiewit's prime contract. Peter Kiewit, in turn, canceled Bremmeyer's subcontract. Peter Kiewit received $1,729,050 from the state for "cancellation costs," but it offered to pay Bremmeyer only $38. Bremmeyer brought this action for breach of contract.

In defense, Peter Kiewit's primary argument was that a state statute, RCW 18.27, required contractors to be registered with the state, and that Bremmeyer's failure to register barred his recovery. The trial court, citing a 1973 Washington State case, agreed with this contention and summarily dismissed the action. Bremmeyer appealed.

Decision. Bremmeyer is entitled to maintain this suit even though he has not registered with the state. The 1973 case is no longer controlling for two reasons. First, there were strong dissenting opinions when it was decided in this court, and it should be reviewed for that reason alone. More importantly, after the 1973 case was decided the Washington state legislature amended RCW 18.27 by adding this section:

> It is the purpose of this chapter to afford protection to the public from unreliable, fraudulent, financially irresponsible, or incompetent contractors. (Emphasis supplied by the court.)

It is thus clear that the purpose of the statute is to provide protection to members of the general public against suits by unregistered contractors, rather than to provide protection to prime contractors (such as Peter Kiewit) against suits by unregistered subcontractors. The judgment of the lower court is, therefore, reversed and the case is remanded to it for further proceedings.

COVENANTS NOT TO COMPETE

BECKMAN v. COX BROADCASTING CORPORATION
296 S.E.2d 566 (1982)
Supreme Court of Georgia

Facts. From 1962 until June 30, 1982, John Beckman was employed by Cox Broadcasting Corporation (Cox) as a meteorologist and television personality on Cox's affiliate WSB-TV in Atlanta, Georgia. During the term of his employment with Cox, WSB-TV spent over $1 million promoting Beckman's name, voice, and image as an individual television personality and as a member of the WSB-TV "Action News" Team. Beckman is one of the most recognized television personalities in the Atlanta area. Beckman's employment contract with Cox includes the following covenant not to compete:

> Employee shall not, for a period of one hundred eighty (180) days after the end of the Term of Employment, allow his/her voice or image to be broadcast "on air" by any commercial television station whose broadcast transmission tower is located within a radius of thirty-five (35) miles from Company's offices at 1601 West Peachtree Street, N.E., Atlanta, Georgia, unless such broadcast is part of a nationally broadcast program.

In April 1981, Beckman entered into a five-year employment contract with WXIA-TV, a competitor of Cox, to commence working for WXIA as a meteorologist and television personality when his contract with Cox expired on July 1, 1982. Cox was made aware of Beckman's plans in July 1981 and undertook an extensive campaign to promote Beckman's replacement, including advertisements featuring both Beckman and his replacement and gradually phasing out Beckman on WSB-TV. On June 12, 1982, Beckman filed suit for declaratory judgment that the covenant not to compete with Cox should not be enforced against him. The trial court held in favor of Cox. Beckman appeals.

Opinion. Gregory, Justice. A covenant not to compete, being in partial restraint of trade, is not favored in the law, and will be upheld only when strictly limited in time, territorial effect, the capacity in which the employee is prohibited from competing and when it is otherwise reasonable. In determining whether a covenant is reasonably limited with regard to these factors, the court must balance the interest the employer seeks to protect against the impact the covenant will have on the employee, factoring in the effect of the covenant on the public's interest in promoting competition and the freedom of individuals to contract.

In this case it is not disputed that WSB-TV has invested substantial sums in promoting Beckman's image as part of its "Action News" team, and thus, as part of the image of the station itself. The evidence supports the trial court's finding that WSB-TV has a significant interest in the image of its television station that it has created, in large measure, by promoting those individuals who appear on behalf of the station, whether as newscasters, sports announcers, meteorologists, or television personalities. This interest is entitled to protection. We further agree with the trial court that WSB-TV would be greatly harmed by Beckman's appearance on a competing station prior to the completion of WSB-TV's transition plan.

Beckman urges that the "television personality of Johnny Beckman" belongs solely to him and that he is entitled to take this image, which he maintains he has developed by his own skills and resources, to any competing station without interference from WSB-TV. It is true that an employee's aptitude, skill, dexterity, manual and mental ability, and other subjective knowledge obtained in the course of employment, are not property of the employer that the employer can, in absence of a contractual right, prohibit the employee from taking with him at the termination of employment. We agree that Beckman is entitled to take the "image and personality of Johnny Beckman" to WXIA-TV. However, the record supports the trial court's determination that throughout Beckman's career the resources of WSB-TV have been used to bolster and promote the image of Beckman as a part of the image of WSB-TV. As such we conclude that for a limited time and in a narrowly restricted area, WSB-TV is entitled to prevent Beckman from using the popularity and recognition he gained as a result of WSB-TV's investment in the creation of his image so that WSB-TV may protect its interest in its own image by implementing its transition plan.

Holding and Remedy. We agree with the trial court and hold that the covenant not to compete in this case is reasonable in scope, time, and territory. The judgment of the lower court in favor of Cox Broadcasting Corporation is *affirmed.*

CHAPTER 8: ENDING THE CONTRACT AND REMEDIES

STANDARD OF PERFORMANCE

MORIN BUILDING PRODUCTS COMPANY, INC. v. BAYSTONE CONSTRUCTION, INC.
717 F.2d 413 (1983)
United States Court of Appeals, Seventh Circuit

Facts. General Motors Corporation (General Motors) hired Baystone Construction, Inc. (Baystone), to build an addition to a Chevrolet plant in Muncie, Indiana. Baystone, in turn, hired Morin Building Products Company (Morin) to supply and erect the aluminum walls for the addition. The contract required that the exterior siding of the walls be of "aluminum with a mill finish and stucco embossed surface texture to match finish and texture of existing metal siding." The contract also included a satisfaction clause that provided

> That all work shall be done subject to the final approval of the Architect or Owner's (General Motors) authorized agent, and his decision in matters relating to artistic effect shall be final, if within the terms of the Contract Documents.

> Should any dispute arise as to the quality or fitness of materials or workmanship, the decision as to acceptability shall rest strictly with the Owner, based on the requirements that all work done or materials furnished shall be first class in every respect. What is usual or customary in erecting other buildings shall in no wise enter into any consideration or decision.

Morin put up the walls. The exterior siding did not give the impression of having a uniform finish when viewed in bright sunlight from an acute angle and General Motors' representative rejected it. Baystone removed Morin's siding and hired another subcontractor to replace it. General Motors approved the replacement siding. When Baystone refused to pay Morin the $23,000 balance owing on the contract, Morin brought suit against Baystone to recover this amount. The trial court held in favor of Morin. Baystone appeals.

Opinion. Posner, Circuit Judge. Some cases hold that if the contract provides that the seller's performance must be to the buyer's satisfaction, his rejection—however unreasonable—of the seller's performance is not a breach of the contract unless the rejection is in bad faith. But most cases conform to the position stated in Section 228 of the Restatement (Second) of Contracts:

> If it is practicable to determine whether a reasonable person in the position of the obligor would be satisfied, an interpretation is preferred under which the condition occurs if such a reasonable person in the position of the obligor would be satisfied.

Indiana courts adapt the Restatement position as the law of Indiana. We do not understand the majority position to be paternalistic, and paternalism would be out of place in a case such as this, where the subcontractor is a substantial multistate enterprise. The requirement is not read into every contract, because it is not always a reliable guide to the parties' intentions. The reasonable person standard is employed when the contract involves commercial quality, operative fitness, or mechanical utility that other knowledgeable persons can judge.

We have to decide which category the contract between Baystone and Morin belongs in. The building for which the aluminum siding was intended was a factory—not usually intended to be a thing of beauty. That aesthetic considerations of function and cost is suggested by the fact that the contract specified mill-finish aluminum, which is unpainted. When in doubt on a difficult issue, it is only prudent to defer to the view of the district judge. The circumstances suggest that the parties probably did not intend to subject Morin's rights to aesthetic whim.

Holding and Remedy. We hold that the objective reasonable person standard, and not the subjective aesthetic standard, governs the satisfaction clause in this case. The judgment of the trial court in favor of Morin Building Products Company, Inc., is *affirmed.*

FAILURE TO PERFORM

LA GASE POOL CONSTRUCTION CO. v. CITY OF FORT LAUDERDALE
District Court of Appeals, Fourth District
288 So.2d 273 (1974)

The LaGase Company, plaintiff, made a contract with the City of Fort Lauderdale under which it was to repair and renovate one of the city's swimming pools for a specified price. One night, when the job was almost completed, vandals damaged the pool so badly that most of the work had to be redone.

When the city refused to pay more than the contract price, plaintiff brought this action to recover compensation for the additional work. The trial court held that it was plaintiff's responsibility to redo the work, and entered judgment for defendant. Plaintiff appealed.

Decision. The trial court was correct in ruling that plaintiff was not entitled to recover for the additional work. In the case of contracts to repair existing structures, the general rule is that total destruction of the structure, without fault of either the contractor or owner, excuses performance by the contractor and entitles him to recover the value of the work done. The reason for this rule is that the contract has an implied condition that the structure will remain in existence so that the contractor can render performance. Destruction of the structure makes this performance impossible.

But where the building or structure to be repaired is not totally destroyed, and the contractor's work is damaged so that it must be redone, performance is still possible. It is thus the contractor's responsibility to redo the work so as to complete the original repair contract. Any loss or damage to his work during the process of repairs which can be rectified is his responsibility. The reason for allowing recovery without full performance in the case of total destruction is because, in that situation, the destruction of the structure constitutes a legal impossibility, while in the partial destruction situation, the structure remains and simply requires a duplication of the repair work.

SUBSTANTIAL PERFORMANCE

BUTLOVICH & SONS v. STATE BANK OF ST. CHARLES
Appellate Court of Illinois, Second District
379 N.E.2d 837 (1978)

This was essentially an action by a contractor, Butlovich, against a home owner, Grane, in which the contractor was seeking the balance due on a construction contract. The primary issue was whether the contractor had substantially performed the contract. (The State Bank of St. Charles was named a co-defendant only because it held a mortgage on Grane's home, and its interest would be affected if the contractor won a judgment which Grane was unable to pay.)

Butlovich contracted to do certain construction work on a home owned by Grane in Oak Brook, Illinois, for $19,290. The work involved enlargement of the existing basement, construction of a new room over that basement, and the laying of a new garage floor and patio. After the work was completed Grane refused to pay the balance due, $9,290, alleging that there were a number of defects in the work. The major allegations were that plaintiff (a) failed to install water stops; (b) failed to install reinforcing wire in one concrete floor; and (c) built the main floor of the addition at a level approximately nine inches lower than the plans called for.

The trial judge, viewing plaintiff's performance in its totality, ruled that he had substantially performed the contract despite the defects, and entered judgment for plaintiff. Defendants appealed.

Decision. The trial court was wrong in ruling that plaintiff had substantially performed the contract, for several reasons. First, the court should not have accepted plaintiff's argument that the contract did not call for the installation of water stops. In fact, a part of the contract entitled "Supplemental Conditions" contained a drawing in which water stops clearly appeared. Second, plaintiff's testimony that he was not aware that reinforcing wire was called for in the basement floor should not have been accepted by the court in view of the fact that specifications did call for the wire.

Because these two material deviations from the terms of the contract were, therefore, not excused, and because the evidence was undisputed that the main floor was, in fact, 8 7/8 inches lower than the plans called for, it is clear that plaintiff did not substantially perform the contract. Accordingly, judgment is reversed and the case remanded to the trial court for further proceedings.

SUBSTANTIAL PERFORMANCE

W.E. ERICKSON CONSTRUCTION, INC. v. CONGRESS-KENILWORTH CORPORATION
503 N.E.2d 233 (1986)
Supreme Court of Illinois

Facts. The Congress-Kenilworth Corporation (Congress) hired W.E. Erickson Construction, Inc. (Erickson), a general contractor, to construct "Thunder Mountain Rapids," a concrete waterslide in Creswood, Illinois. The total cost of the slide was not to exceed $535,000. Construction of the water slide began on April 15, 1981, and the slide was completed on July 3, 1981, the day before the projected opening date. After construction, cracks appeared in the concrete flumes of the slide. The cracks did not interfere with the operation of the slide, but the defects did need to be repaired at a substantial cost. Erickson billed Congress $550,000 for full performance of the contract. To date, Congress had paid Erickson $150,000. When Congress refused to pay Erickson for full performance, Erickson sued Congress for breach of contract to recover the full contract price. The trial court awarded Erickson $352,000, less the $150,000 already paid to Erickson, for a judgment of $202,000. The appellate court affirmed. An appeal was taken.

Opinion. Clark, Chief Justice. In its brief, Congress argues that the appellate court erred in finding that Erickson had substantially performed. The question of whether there has been substantial performance of the terms and conditions of a contract sufficient to justify a judgment in favor of the builder for the contract price is always a question of fact. A purchaser who receives substantial performance of a building contract must pay the price bargained for, less an offset for defects in what he received as compared to what strict performance would have given him.

We agree with the appellate court that the trial court did find that Erickson substantially performed under the contract and that the trial court's finding is not against the manifest weight of the evidence. The trial court found that the defects in the slide were not severe enough to support a finding that Erickson performed in a wholly unworkmanlike manner. As we stated earlier, substantial performance means performance in all the essential elements necessary to accomplish the purpose of the contract. In this instance, the purpose of the contract was to build a concrete waterslide for recreational purposes. According to the record, the slide was completed on time and has served the purpose for which it was intended since its opening. While there was conflicting testimony presented as to whether the cracks in the concrete flumes of the slide were beyond acceptable limits, it was clear from the evidence that the cracks have not interfered with the operation of the structure in its intended use. We therefore conclude that the trial court's finding of substantial performance is not against the manifest weight of the evidence.

Holding and Remedy. We find that Erickson had substantially performed the contract. Accordingly, the decision of the appellate court is *affirmed.*

IMPOSSIBILITY OF PERFORMANCE

PARKER v. ARTHUR MURRAY, INC.
295 N.E.2d 487 (1973)
Appellate Court of Illinois

Facts. In November 1959, Ryland S. Parker went to the Arthur Murray Studies in Oak Park, Illinois, to redeem a certificate entitling him to three free dancing lessons. At that time he was a 37-year old college-educated bachelor who lived alone in a one-room attic apartment in Berwyn, Illinois. During the free lessons the instructor told Parker that he had "exceptional potential to be a fine and accomplished dancer" and generally encouraged further participation. Parker thereupon signed a contract for more lessons. Parker attended lessons regularly and was praised and encouraged by his instructor despite his lack of progress. Contract extensions and a new contract for additional instructional hours were executed, which Parker prepaid. Each written contract contained bold-type words, "NON-CANCELABLE CONTRACT" and "NON-CANCELABLE NEGOTIABLE CONTRACT." Some of the agreements also contained the bold-type statement, "UNDERSTAND THAT NO REFUNDS WILL BE MADE UNDER THE TERMS OF THIS CONTRACT."

On September 24, 1961, Parker was severely injured in an automobile accident, rendering him incapable of continuing his dancing lessons. At that time he had contracted for a total of 2,734 hours of dance lessons, for which he had prepaid $24,812. When Arthur Murray refused to refund any of the money, Parker brought suit to rescind the outstanding contracts. The trial court held in favor of Parker and ordered Arthur Murray to return the prepaid contract payment. Arthur Murray appeals.

Opinion. Stamos, Presiding Justice. Plaintiff was granted rescission on the ground of impossibility of performance. In Illinois, impossibility of performance was recognized as a ground for rescission in *Davies v. Arthur Murray, Inc.** Defendants do not deny that the doctrine of impossibility of

*260 N.E.2d 240 (Ill.App. 1970).

performance is generally applicable to the case at bar. Rather they assert that certain contract provisions bring the case within the Restatement's limitation that the doctrine is inapplicable if "the contract indicates a contrary intention." It is contended that such bold-type phrases as "NON-CANCE-LABLE CONTRACT," "NON-CANCELABLE NEGOTIABLE CONTRACT," and "I UNDERSTAND THAT NO REFUNDS WILL BE MADE UNDER THE TERMS OF THIS CONTRACT" manifested the parties' mutual intent to waive their respective rights to involve the doctrine of impossibility.

This is a construction that we find unacceptable. Courts engage in the construction and interpretation of contracts with the sole aim of determining the intention of the parties. We need rely on no construction aids to conclude that plaintiff never contemplated that by signing a contract with such terms as "NON-CANCELABLE" and "NO REFUNDS," he was waiving a remedy expressly recognized by Illinois courts. Were we also to refer to established tenets of contractual construction, this conclusion would be equally compelled. An ambiguous contract will be construed most strongly against the party who drafted it. Exception or reservations in a contract will, in case of doubt or ambiguity, be construed least favorably to the party claiming the benefit of the exceptions or reservations. Although neither party to a contract should be relieved from performance on the ground that good business judgment was lacking, a court will not place upon language a ridiculous construction. We conclude that plaintiff did not waive his right to assert the doctrine of impossibility.

Defendants have also contended, albeit indirectly, that plaintiff failed to establish the existence of an incapacitating disability. Plaintiff in the case of bar produced both lay witnesses and expert medical testimony corroborating the severity and permanency of his injuries. That testimony need not be recited; suffice it to say that overwhelming evidence supported plaintiff's contention that he was incapable of continuing his lessons.

Holding and Remedy. We hold that impossibility excused Parker's performance of the personal service contracts and they can therefore be rescinded by him. The judgment of the trial court in favor of Parker and ordering Arthur Murray to return prepaid contracts payments to Parker is *affirmed.*

CHAPTER 9: SALE OF GOODS (UCC)

OFFER AND ACCEPTANCE (UCC)

PERDUE FARMS, INC. v. MOTTS, INC., OF MISSISSIPPI
25 UCC Rep.Serv 9 (1978)
United States District Court, N.D. Mississippi

Facts. Perdue Farms, Inc. (Perdue), sells dressed poultry under the brand name "Perdue Roasters." On October 30, 1975, Motts, Inc., of Mississippi (Motts) entered into an oral contract with Perdue to purchase roasters from Perdue. Motts was to pick the roasters up at Perdue's Maryland plant. Motts entered into a contract to resell the roasters to Dairyland, Inc. Motts sent a confirmation letter ("Confirmation of Purchase No. 3384") to Perdue confirming their oral agreement. Perdue received the confirmation and did not object to it. When Motts' truck arrived at Perdue's Maryland plant to pick up the roasters, Perdue informed Motts' drivers that the roasters would not be loaded unless complete payment was made before delivery. Under previous contracts between the parties, payment was due seven days after delivery. Perdue informed Motts that the roasters would not be sold to Motts on credit. Perdue then sold the roasters directly to Dairyland, Inc. Motts sued Perdue for breach of contract. Perdue filed a motion for summary judgment.

ISSUE: Did Motts' letter to Perdue constitute a written confirmation of a prior oral agreement that satisfied the UCC's Statute of Frauds?

Opinion. Smith, District Judge. Defendant Perdue contends that the contract does not satisfy the Statute of Frauds found in Mississippi's version of UCC 2-201(2). UC. 2-201(2) is a new provision to the Statute of Frauds. It was drafted to correct an unfair condition that developed under other Statutes of Frauds when one contracting party sent a letter to the other contracting party to confirm an oral contract made by them. The party sending the confirmatory letter often could not invoke the Statute of Frauds as a defense because he had signed a writing that satisfied the statute. The party receiving the confirmatory writing had not signed the confirmatory writing. If the contract proved to be advantageous for the receiving party, he was able to enforce it against the sending merchant. But if the contract was not to the receiving party's advantage, he could refuse to perform, assert the Statute of Frauds as a defense, and prevent the sending party from enforcing the oral contract. UCC 2-201(2) attempts to remove this inequity and thereby encourage the sending of writings to confirm oral contracts.

UCC 2-201(2) contains several prerequisites that must be met before a merchant can invoke the subsection to satisfy the Statute of Frauds. The merchant sending the writing must show that (1) Both parties are merchants. (2) The writing was in confirmation of the contract and sufficient against the sender. (3) The writing was received by the other merchant within a reasonable time after the contract was made. (4) The merchant receiving the writing had reason to know of its content. (5) The merchant receiving the writing did not give written notice of objection within ten days after the date of receipt.

Number 3384 is a preprinted form containing blank spaces where information pertaining to each purchase may be inserted. Printed at the top of the form in large capital letters are the words "CONFIRMATION OF PURCHASE." The last sentence on the front of No. 3384 reads: "The terms and conditions of the reverse side of this Confirmation are an integral part of this order." Printed on the reverse side are various terms including certain responsibilities of the buyer and the seller. On the front of the form, certain blank spaces have been filled in to provide the following information. The form is "confirming to Perdue Farms," the buyer is Motts, Inc., the seller is Perdue Farms, the date of the form is October 30, 1975, the items being purchased are fresh roasters, 1500 boxes are purchased, the unit price is $0.50, per cwt., delivery is by "pick-up," and it is signed by B.J. Crawford. The court finds that No. 3384 satisfies the requirements of UCC 2-201 (2) so that Perdue is denied the Statute of Frauds as a defense thereby making No. 3384 "sufficient against the sender."

Holding and Remedy. The court holds that Confirmation of Purchase No. 3384 qualifies as a confirmatory writing under UCC 2-210 (2). Perdue Farms' motion for summary judgment is *denied.*

APPLICABLE LAW

BONEBRAKE v. COX
U.S. Court of Appeals, Eighth Circuit
499 F.2d 951 (1974)

Donald and Claude Cox owned a bowling alley called Tamarack Bowl in Missouri Valley, Iowa. It was gutted by fire in February 1968. They decided to rebuild and, on April 17, 1968, entered into a written contract with Simek, who agreed to sell and install the necessary equipment. Specifically, the contract called for Simek to sell and deliver quantities of bowling balls, lockers, storage racks, and shoes. It also required him to install the lockers and racks and to lay land beds (which involved laying "foundation materials" and sub-floors). All of this was to be done for a lump sum of $20,000.

Before delivery and installation were complete and with less than half the purchase price paid, Simek died. The Coxes obtained equipment elsewhere and hired others to finish the installation. Frances Bonebrake, adminstratrix of Simek's estate, sued the Coxes in federal district court to recover the balance of the contract price. The Coxes countersued for their damages. The trial court held for plaintiff Bonebrake on the claim for the unpaid contract price and denied defendants' counterclaim. Judgment was in the sum of $28,000.

At issue in the case was whether certain provisions of the UCC should apply with respect to performance and damages. The trial court had held the UCC to be inapplicable, ruling that no "sale of goods" was involved. It reached this conclusion on the ground that substantial amounts of labor were involved in addition to the sale of goods. Defendant appealed.

Decision. The trial court was found to be wrong. Thus the judgment was reversed and the case was remanded for further proceedings.

Article 2 of the UCC applies to "transactions in goods." Sec. 2-105 of the code essentially defines goods as all movable things at the time the contract is made or at the time title is to pass. On that basis the bowling balls, shoes, lockers, and racks were clearly goods. So, too, were the materials ultimately to be used in laying the foundation and subfloors.

The fact that the contract also obligated Simek to perform labor did not prevent it from being a contract for the sale of goods. In a mixed contract calling for the sale of goods as well as the rendition of services, the test is whether the rendition of the services is incidental to the sale or whether it is the major part of the contract. Here the services were merely incidental to Simek's basic obligation to sell goods, and the provisions of the UCC therefore should have been applied by the trial court.

CHAPTER 10: PERFORMANCE, TERMINATION, AND BREACH

COMMERCIAL IMPRACTICABILITY

EASTERN AIRLINES, INC., v. GULF OIL CO.
U.S. District Court, So. Dist. of Florida
415 F. Supp. 429 (1975)

For a number of years Gulf Oil Co. had been a major supplier of the jet fuel used by Eastern Airlines to operate its fleets. The most recent contract between the two was made in 1972, and obligated Gulf to supply Eastern's fuel requirements at certain specified cities.

Since jet fuel is refined from crude oil, the cost of producing the fuel is directly affected by the price of crude. Although the price of crude oil produced in the U.S. was regulated by the federal government, this price had been increasing and was expected by Gulf and Eastern to continue rising. In addition, the percentage of oil imported into this country from foreign sources had been growing. The price of imported oil could not be regulated by the U.S. government and, therefore, was subject to market fluctuations. Because of these factors, Gulf and Eastern included in their 1972 contract a clause which permitted Gulf to charge higher prices on future deliveries of jet fuel to Eastern as the price of crude oil increased. However, this "escalator" clause in their contract permitted a rise in the jet fuel price only insofar as the government-regulated price of U.S.-produced oil increased.

After Gulf and Eastern made their agreement, the federal government partially decontrolled the price of domestically produced oil. In other words, the government removed the ceiling on the price of a portion of the oil produced in this country, thus permitting this price to rise to the world market level. Shortly thereafter, the foreign oil cartel, OPEC (Organization of Petroleum Exporting Countries), increased the price of its oil about 400 percent. This, of course, also caused the price of the unregulated portion of U.S. produced oil to rise. The escalator clause in the Gulf-Eastern contract only permitted jet fuel price increases in accordance with increases in the government regulated price of domestic oil. Gulf ultimately found this clause to be quite inadequate to cover its increased costs of production.

In March 1974, Gulf demanded that Eastern pay more for jet fuel than the escalator clause permitted, or Gulf would shut off Eastern's supply of fuel. Eastern refused to pay more and sued Gulf for breach of contract. Gulf defended on the ground that performance of the contract had become "commercially impracticable" and that it should therefore be excused from the contract as provided in UC. Sec. 2-615. The federal district court ruled as follows.

Decision. The judgment was for plaintiff, Eastern, and the court issued a decree of specific performance requiring Gulf to live up to the contract. A seller will not be excused from performing a contract simply because its costs have increased, even if the increase has been substantial. In this case, Gulf never really proved what its cost were because all the cost data it produced in court included intracompany profits on transfers between its different divisions. Gulf continued to be an extremely profitable company, so the crude oil price increases evidently were not hurting it as badly as it claimed. Finally, the dramatic increase in the price of imported oil, and the U.S. government's partial decontrol of the domestic oil price, were reasonably foreseeable events. A firm in the oil business, like Gulf, should reasonably have anticipated them.

ANTICIPATORY REPUDIATION

OLOFFSON v. COOMER
Appellate Court of Illinois
296 N.E. 2d 871 (1973)

Oloffson, plaintiff, was a grain dealer; Coomer, defendant, was a farmer. In April 1970 Coomer agreed to sell forty thousand bushels of corn to Oloffson at $1.1225 per bushel, delivery to be in October and December. On June 3, Coomer informed Oloffson that he was not going to plant corn because the season had been too wet. He told Oloffson to arrange elsewhere to obtain the corn if Oloffson had already obligated himself to delivery to any third party. The market price for a bushel of corn on June 3 was $1.16. Oloffson asked Coomer in September about delivery of the corn, and Coomer repeated that he would not be able to deliver. Oloffson persisted, however, and mailed Coomer confirmations of their April agreement, which Coomer ignored. Oloffson's attorney then requested that Coomer perform, and Coomer also ignored this request. When no corn was delivered on the scheduled delivery dates, Oloffson covered his obligation to his own buyer by purchasing twenty thousand bushels at $1.35 per bushel and twenty thousand bushels at $1.49 per bushel.

Oloffson sued Coomer to recover damages for breach of contract. He contended that his damages should be the difference between the contract price of the corn ($1.1225 per bushel) and the price he paid for the 40,000 bushels in October ($1.35 per bushel for 20,000 bushels and $1.49 per bushel for 20,000 bushels). The trial court granted Oloffson only $1,500 damages, the difference between the contract price of the corn ($1.1225 per bushel) and the market price of corn on June 3 ($1.16 per bushel) multiplied by 40,000 bushels. Oloffson appealed.

Decision. Judgment for $1,500 was affirmed. Oloffson's choices upon Coomer's anticipatory repudiation were to pursue his remedies immediately or to await performance for a reasonable time (Sec. 2-610 of the UCC). Since the repudiation was so definite and the market price of the corn was rising, it was unreasonable to wait for performance any time at all after June 3. Thus, Oloffson should have purchased the corn immediately on June 3, rather than waiting until later to do so. Accordingly, the measure of damages applied by the trial court was correct.

CHAPTER 11: UNIFORM COMMERCIAL CODE (TITLE, RISK OF LOSS, WARRANTIES)

EXPRESS WARRANTIES

COMMUNITY TELEVISION SERVICES, INC. v. DRESSER INDUSTRIES, INC.
U.S. Court of Appeals, 8th Circuit
586 F.2d 637 (1978)

In 1965, two television stations in South Dakota created a separate corporation, Community Television Services, Inc. (Community), for the purpose of constructing and operating a 2,000 foot tower that would broadcast signals for both stations. Community contracted with Dresser Industries, Inc. (Dresser), who designed, manufactured, and erected the tower for a price of $385,000. The tower was completed in 1969 and Community used it until 1975. During this time, Community regularly inspected and properly maintained the tower. On January 10 and 11, 1975, a severe winter blizzard occurred in the area where the tower was located. During the early morning hours of January 11, as the storm reached its height with wind speeds of up to 80 miles per hour near the top of the tower, the structure collapsed.

Dresser denied responsibility and Community sued in federal district court for breach of an express warranty. Dresser, the defendant, contended that there was no such breach because the tower did conform to the technical specifications in the sale contract. These specifications required the tower to be capable of withstanding wind-exerted pressure of 60 pounds per square foot on the flat surfaces of the tower. Under ordinary circumstances a wind velocity of 120 miles per hour would be required to exert such pressure. Expert testimony at the trial established that the tower did in fact meet these specifications. During the storm, however, ice had collected on the tower, increasing the area of its flat surfaces. This increased the pressure exerted by the wind. Thus, the 80 mile-per-hour wind during the storm had exerted more pressure on the tower than ordinarily would be the case.

Community, the plaintiff, contended that statements in Dresser's advertising catalog had expanded the scope of the express warranty. These statements indicated that Dresser's towers would withstand the maximum wind speeds and ice loads which were likely to occur wherever the towers were erected. A storm like the one that toppled the tower can be expected occasionally in South Dakota. Community asserted that these advertising claims were part of its contract with Dresser. Thus, according to Community, the tower was expressly warranted to be capable of withstanding reasonably foreseeable South Dakota weather conditions.

The verdict and judgment in the trial court were in favor of Community for damages of $1,274,631.60, and Dresser appealed.

Decision. The judgment for plaintiff, Community, was affirmed. The advertising claims made by Dresser prior to the making of the contract with Community were "part of the basis of the bargain." These claims expanded the scope of the express warranty beyond the technical specifications in the contract. Since storms as severe as the one that blew over the tower did occur occasionally in South Dakota, the tower should have been able to withstand the wind and ice.

WARRANTY OF MERCHANTABILITY

BURRUS v. ITEK CORP.
Appellate Court of Illinois
360 N.E. 2d 1168 (1977)

Sherman Burrus is a job printer doing business in East Peoria, Illinois, under the name of Metropolitan Printers. His business, in which he had been engaged since 1961, primarily involved the printing of letterheads, envelopes, brochures, and cards. In 1970 Burrus purchased a printing press from Itek Corp. for about $7,000. From the time the press was delivered to Burrus's place of business difficulties were encountered almost continuously. Although Itek's representatives had worked for several days in an effect to install the press and get it operating properly, it never did function satisfactorily.

Burrus' specific complaints were that the press did not feed properly, had paper jam-ups, failed to register properly (which is a process where one symbol is printed on top of another identical symbol without any visible overlap on the printed surface), streaked or smeared the printed surface, was not timed properly, produced crooked printing, and was slow in printing. Burrus and his employees spent many hours in an unsuccessful effort to correct the deficiencies of the press and get it to work properly. One witness, a former employee of Burrus, testified that out of an eight-hour working day the press performed satisfactorily not more than two hours. About sixty days after buying the press, Burrus asked Itek to replace it. Mr. Nessel, a salesman for Itek, recommended to his company that the press be replaced, but Itek refused. Burrus, plaintiff, then sued Itek, defendant, for breach of the implied warranty of merchantability. The trial court held for plaintiff, and defendant appealed.

Decision. The judgment for plaintiff was affirmed. To be merchantable, goods must be fit for the ordinary purposes for which such goods are used. This press did not satisfactorily perform the normal functions of such machines, and therefore was not merchantable. The evidence established that the defects in the press were not caused by improper maintenance—it began malfunctioning immediately after delivery. There was nothing to indicate that the press had been operated by incompetent individuals. In fact, one of plaintiff's employees who had operated the press was an instructor in the printing department of a local college. This operator experienced the same problems with the press as others had.

CHAPTER 12: LEGAL REMEDIES IF THE CONTRACT IS NOT PERFORMED (UCC)

REVOCATION OF ACCEPTANCE

CONTE v. DWAN LINCOLN-MERCURY, INC.
Supreme Court of Connecticut
374 A.2d 144 (1976)

On March 25, 1970, Conte purchased a 1970 Lincoln Continental from Dwan, who was an authorized Lincoln Continental dealer under a franchise agreement with the manufacturer, Ford Motor Co. The following day, after being notified that the car was ready, Conte went to pick it up but refused to do so because it was dirty and a door was out of alignment. The next day Conte did take possession of the car, a warranty booklet, and other printed material inside the vehicle. The written sale agreement made by Conte and Dwan included a provision that there were no warranties applicable to the automobile, except the most recent printed Ford Motor Co. warranties, "and they shall be expressly in lieu of any other express or implied warranty, condition or guarantee on the new vehicle, chassis or any part thereof, including any implied warranty of merchantability or fitness...." The basic Ford warranty provided that with respect to each 1970 passenger automobile, the dealer would repair or replace any part, except tires, that was found to be defective in factory materials or workmanship in normal use within twelve months from the date of original retail delivery.

The day after Conte took delivery of the automobile he noticed that the motor and transmission were leaking oil and that the cigarette lighter and windshield wiper did not work. The next morning the car was brought in to Dwan, the windshield wiper was fixed and the plaintiff was told that he should make a list of his problems and Dwan would take care of them. Within a week, the electric windows did not operate and paint blistered on the vehicle. Between the time that Conte took delivery in March 1970, until May 3, 1971, Dwan had attempted to repair the car eight times as shown by Dwan's records. Between October 25, 1970, and May 1971, it became undriveable five times on the road and was towed to Dwan for repairs. At one time when the car was driven, Conte received an electrical shock. Subsequently, an alternator was replaced and a fan belt repaired. Soon after he purchased the automobile and until May 1971, Conte corresponded directly with Ford about his problems. On October 27, 1971, Conte met with a representative of Ford and was assured, in the presence of Dwan's service manager, that his automobile would be repaired to his satisfaction. The last repair order for the automobile was May 3, 1971, when, two weeks after an alternator was replaced, the automobile had to be towed and a fan belt repaired. Upon being informed that the car had been repaired, Conte told Dwan to keep it because it was dangerous and he wanted his money back or another automobile. After that, Conte never picked up his car.

Conte, plaintiff, then filed suit against Dwan, defendant. Conte contended that the clause limiting his remedy to repair or replacement of defective parts had "failed of its essential purpose" and should be ignored by the court. He asked the court to permit him to revoke his acceptance and get his money back. The trial court ruled in plaintiff's favor and defendant appealed.
Decision. The judgment for plaintiff was affirmed. The seller had numerous opportunities to repair the automobile, but after fourteen months it still did not operate satisfactorily. Therefore, the clause in the sales contract limiting the buyer's remedies to repair or replacement of defective parts had "failed of its essential purpose." The court ignored the clause and the remedies provided in the UCC were available to the buyer. Plaintiff was permitted to revoke his acceptance and get his money back because (1) the defects in the car had "substantially impaired its value" to the buyer and (2) the revocation was made within a reasonable time. Regarding the second point, the court ruled that fourteen months was reasonable because throughout this period of time the plaintiff had been assured by defendant that the car would be repaired satisfactorily. If it had not been for these assurances, plaintiff surely would have given up on the car much earlier.

MONEY DAMAGES

NATIONAL CONTROLS, INC. v.
COMMODORE BUSINESS MACHINES, INC.
163 Cal.App.3d 622, 209 Cal. Rptr. 636 (1985)
Court of Appeal of California

Facts. National Controls, Inc. (NCI), manufactures electronic weighing and measuring devices. Among its products is the model 3221 electronic scale that is designed to interface with cash registers at check-out stands. On March 31, 1981, Commodore Business Machines, Inc. (Commodore), placed an order to purchase 900 scales from NCI, 50 to be delivered in May, 150 in June, 300 in July, and 400 in August. Commodore accepted only the first 50 scales and did not accept or pay for the remaining 850 units. Thereafter, NCI sold all of the 850 units to National Semiconductor. NCI sued Commodore to recover the profits it lost because Commodore did not purchase the scales. The trial court held in favor of NCI and awarded it $280,000 in lost profits. Commodore appeals.

Opinion. Scott, Associate Justice. Damages caused by a buyer's breach or repudiation of a sales contract are usually measured by the difference between the resale price of the goods and contract price, as provided in UCC 2-706. When it is not appropriate to use this difference to measure the seller's loss (as when the goods have not been resold in a commercially reasonable manner), the seller's measure of damages is the difference between the market and the contract prices as provided in UCC 2-708(1). Ordinarily, this measure will result in recovery equal to the value of the seller's bargain. However, under certain circumstances this formula is also not adequate means to ascertain that value, and the seller may recover his loss of expected profits on the contract under UCC 2-708(2).

When buyers have repudiated a fixed price contract to purchase goods, several courts elsewhere have construed UCC 2-708(2) to permit the award of lost profits under the contract to the seller who establishes that he is a "lost volume seller," that is, one who proves that even though he resold the contract goods, that sale to the third party would have been made regardless of the buyer's breach. The lost volume seller must establish that had the breaching buyer performed, the seller would have realized profits from two sales. Commodore accurately points out that the lost volume seller rule has been criticized by some commentators. Nevertheless, that criticism has not resulted in any revision of the section.

In this case, the evidence was undisputed that in 1980 and 1981, NCI's manufacturing plant was operating at approximately 40% capacity. The production of the 900 units did not tax that capacity, and the plant could have more than doubled its output of 3221s and still have stayed within its capacity. That evidence was sufficient to support the court's findings that NCI had the capacity to supply both Commodore and National

Semiconductor and that had there been no breach by Commodore, NCI would have had the benefit of both the original contract and the resale contract. Accordingly, the trial court correctly determined that NCI was a lost volume seller, that the usual "contract price minus market price" rule set forth in UCC 2-708(1) was inadequate to put NCI in as good a position as performance would have done, and that NCI was therefore entitled to its lost profits on the contract with Commodore, without any setoff for profits on the resale to National Semiconductor.

Holding and Remedy. We hold that Commodore breached the sales contract to purchase 850 electronic scales from NCI, and that NCI was a lost volume seller. Therefore, NCI is entitled to recover its lost profits on the contract with Commodore, without any setoff for profits on the resale of the scales to National Semiconductor. The judgment on the trial court in favor of NCI is *affirmed.*

MONEY DAMAGES

UNIVERSAL BUILDERS CORPORATION v. UNITED METHODIST CONVALESCENT HOMES OF CONNECTICUT, INC. AND J.H. HOGAN, INC.
508 A.2d 819 (1986)
Appellate Court of Connecticut

Facts. J.H. Hogan, Inc. (Hogan), is a general contractor. Hogan contracted to build several buildings on property owned by United Methodist Convalescent Homes of Connecticut, Inc. (United Methodist). Hogan entered into a sales contract with Universal Builders Corporation (Universal) whereby Universal would supply roof trusses and gables to Hogan for the United Methodist building project. Hogan placed an initial order for 58 trusses in late February 1983. Universal delivered the trusses in the middle of March 1983. Hogan placed a second order for 102 trusses during the second week of April 1983. Universal delivered the trusses during the last week of May 1983. Hogan's employees placed several more orders for trusses. None were delivered by Universal. On June 28, 1983, Hogan sent a letter to Universal that stated:

> For the past seven weeks, we have attempted to have your firm deliver wood trusses under our order number 1805.6.2. Your continued excuses and delays have severely handicapped us in expediting this project. Unless a minimum of 200 trusses are delivered by July 5, 1983, you may consider your order canceled.

Universal failed to deliver additional trusses to Hogan. Hogan purchased the necessary trusses from another supplier. Hogan sued Universal to recover $16,779 as damages, the amount it had to pay in excess of the contract price to obtain substitute trusses. The trial court held in favor of Hogan. Universal appeals.

Opinion. Spallone, Judge. UCC 2-711 provides in part that upon a seller's failure to make delivery as required or upon his repudiation of the agreement, the buyer may cancel the sales contract and whether or not he has done so may in addition to recovering so much of the price as has been paid may "cover". A buyer covers by making a good faith and without unreasonable delay reasonable purchase of or contract to purchase goods in substitution for those due from the seller. When a buyer chooses to cover, he may recover from the seller the difference between his cost to cover and the contract price as well as any incidental and consequential damages. Expenses saved in consequence of the seller's breach are subtracted from the buyer's recovery.

The trial court concluded that Hogan proved by a fair preponderance of the evidence that the trusses it purchased in substitution for those that Universal was obligated to supply under the parties' agreement totaled $16,779 above the contract price. There is no evidence produced from which the court could conclude that Hogan's cover was made in bad faith or with unreasonable delay. To the contrary, the court concluded that Hogan obtained the substitute, albeit slightly different, materials promptly on the open market in order to break the bottleneck in the construction schedule, and to end Hogan's frustration with Universal. The record amply supports these conclusions. We conclude that the measure of damages employed by the trial court was proper.

Holding and Remedy. We hold that Universal breached the sales contract and that Hogan properly covered by purchasing substitute goods from another supplier. We hold that Hogan can recover as damages the $16,779 it paid in excess of the contract price to obtain these substitute goods. The judgment of the trial court in favor of Hogan is *affirmed.*

CHAPTER 13: CONTRACTS BY AND WITH AGENTS

AUTHORITY OF AGENT

INDUSTRIAL MOLDED PLASTIC PRODUCTS INC. v. J. GROSS & SON, INC.
Superior Court of Pennsylvania, 398 A.2d 695 (1979)

Industrial Molded Plastic Products (Industrial) is in the business of manufacturing custom injection molded plastics by specification for various manufacturers. Industrial also manufactures various "fill-in" items during slack periods, such as electronic parts, industrial components, mirror clips, and plastic clothing clips. J. Gross & Sons (Gross) is a wholesaler to the retail clothing industry, selling mostly sewing thread, but also other items such as zippers, snaps, and clips.

Sometime in the fall of 1970, Mr. Stanley Waxman (Gross' president and sole stockholder) and his son Peter (a 22-year-old salesman for Gross) appeared at the office of Industrial's president, Mr. Judson T. Ulansey. They suggested to him that they might be able to market Industrial's plastic clothing clips in the retail clothing industry where they had an established sales force. At this initial meeting, there was no discussion of Peter Waxman's authority or lack thereof in the company.

After this meeting, Stanley authorized Peter to purchase a "trial" amount of clips (not further specified) to test the market, but neither this authorization nor its limitation was communicated to Ulansey. All subsequent negotiations were between Ulansey and Peter Waxman only. Deceiving both his father and Ulansey, Peter held himself out as vice-president of Gross, and on December 10, 1970, signed an agreement obligating Gross to purchase from Industrial five million plastic clothing clips during the calendar year of 1971, at a price of $7.50 per thousand units, delivery at Industrial's plant in Blooming Glen, Pennsylvania. Before the execution of this agreement, Ulansey telephoned Stanley Waxman, who told Ulansey that Peter could act on behalf of Gross. There was no discussion of the specific terms of the agreement, such as the quantity purchased.

Industrial immediately began production of the five million clips during "fill-in" time. As they were manufactured, they were warehoused in Industrial's plant as specified in the contract. In February, 1971, Peter Waxman picked up and paid for 772,000 clips. Stanley Waxman, who had to sign Gross' check for payment, thought that this was the "trial amount" he had authorized Peter to buy. These were the only clips which Gross ever took into its possession. On numerous occasions during the year Ulansey urged Peter to pick up more of the clips, which were taking up more and more storage space at Industrial's plant as they were being manufactured. Peter told Ulansey that he was having difficulty selling the clips and that Gross had no warehousing capacity for the inventory that was being accumulated. At no time, however, did Peter repudiate the contract or request Industrial to halt production. By the end of 1971, production was completed and Industrial was warehousing 4,228,000 clips at its plant.

On January 19, 1972, Industrial sent Gross an invoice for the remaining clips of $31,506.45. However, Gross did not honor the invoice or pick up any more of the clips. Ulansey wrote to Stanley Waxman on February 7, 1972, requesting him to pick up the clips. Receiving no response, Ulansey wrote to Stanley Waxman again on February 23, 1972, threatening legal action if shipping instructions were not received by March 1, 1972. Finally, on March 30, 1972, Peter Waxman responded with a letter to Ulansey, which stated that Gross' failure to move the clips was due to a substantial decline in the clothing industry in 1971 and competition with new lower cost methods of hanging and shipping clothes. The letter asked for Industrial's patience and predicated that it would take at least the rest of the year to market the clips successfully. At this point Industrial sued. Stanley Waxman learned of the five million clip contract for the first time when informed by his lawyer of the impending lawsuit. At this time, Peter began an extended (four-year) leave of absence from Gross.

The trial court ruled in favor of Industrial, the plaintiff, but awarded damages of only $2,400. Both parties appealed, plaintiff claiming that it should be entitled to the entire contract price of over $31,000, and defendant claiming that it should not be liable at all.

Decision. The judgment for plaintiff was affirmed, but the appellate court ruled that plaintiff should receive the entire contract price of over $31,000. The defendant company was liable to plaintiff under the doctrine of apparent authority. Stanley Waxman's actions made it appear that his son Peter had the authority to do what he did, and plaintiff was misled by his appearance of authority.

AGENT/INDEPENDENT CONTRACTOR

SINGLETON v. INTERNATIONAL DAIRY QUEEN, INC.
Superior Court of Delaware, 332 A.2d 160 (1975)

Christine Singleton, nine years old, went to the local Dairy Queen store in Newark, Delaware. After purchasing ice cream, she started to leave. As she attempted to open the door, not by touching the glass but by pushing on a metal crossbar designed for the purpose, the bottom part of the door glass cracked and fell outward. Because of her forward motion, Christine fell through the door and onto the broken glass, suffering severe lacerations and other injuries.

In Christine's behalf, her father sued W.R. Hesseltine, the owner of the local Dairy Queen franchise, and International Dairy Queen, Inc., the franchisor. The franchisor ("Dairy Queen") filed a motion for summary judgment prior to trial, claiming that the documentary evidence established as a matter of law that Hesseltine was an independent contractor. In other words, Dairy Queen asserted that there was no issue of fact as to its liability and that it should be dismissed from the case, because even if plaintiff proved that the franchisee had been negligent in not maintaining a safe premises (which almost certainly would be the case), Dairy Queen could not be held liable for that tort.

Decision. The court denied Dairy Queen's motion for summary judgment. The case against both the franchisor (Dairy Queen) and the franchisee (Hesseltine) should go to trial. For several reasons, a fact issue existed as to whether there was a master–servant or employer–independent contractor relationship between Dairy Queen and Hesseltine. First, a recent remodeling of the franchisee's store had been done according to Dairy Queen's detailed plans, as Dairy Queen required. Second, the franchise agreement gave Dairy Queen the right to control most of the details of

Hesseltine's business. For example, the agreement permitted Dairy Queen to regulate the formula for the ice cream "mix"; approve the uniforms of employees; dictate the amounts of portions served to customers; dictate what items can be sold; require equipment and supplies to be purchased from "authorized" suppliers; closely regulate how Dairy Queen's trademark is used on containers and in advertisements; inspect the premises at any time; and terminate the franchise if Hesseltine failed to live up to any of the contract's provisions. In another clause of the franchise agreement, Dairy Queen renounced any responsibility for Hesseltine's business operations. However, this clause was at odds with the control rights reserved by Dairy Queen elsewhere in the agreement. In addition, Hesseltine had testified in his pretrial deposition that Dairy Queen did actually control his day-to-day operations. Third, because of Dairy Queen's requirements as to the use of its name on the building and in advertising, there was a fact question as to whether Hesseltine was an "apparent servant" of Dairy Queen. In other words, Dairy Queen may have made itself liable by leading the public to believe that the franchise was its servant and subject to its control, regardless of whether the franchisee was an actual servant.

Glossary

acceptance. The indication by an offeree that he is willing to be a party to a contract based on the offer communicated by the offeror. Under the Uniform Commercial Code, acceptance also means that the buyer has taken the goods as being in conformity with the terms of the contract.

accord. An agreement that is often referred to as an accord and satisfaction, which means that the parties have substituted one type of performance for another or that one party has taken a lesser amount as settlement of her claim.

adhesion contract. A contract prepared by one party that is unfair and one-sided and often presented to the other party on a "take it or leave it" basis.

agent. A person who works for a principal. An agent may agree to contracts on behalf of a principal based on actual, implied, or apparent authority.

anticipatory breach (anticipatory repudiation). The notification by one party to another that she will not be performing the obligations under the contract. The other party may immediately bring an action to recover her legal remedies.

arbitration. A process by which the parties submit a dispute to a neutral third party for resolution. The parties may submit to binding arbitration, under which they agree to be bound by the arbitrator's ruling, or to non-binding arbitration, under which they do not agree to be bound.

assignee. A person to whom a right is assigned. Often, the person receives the rights and obligations of a contract.

assignment. The transfer of the rights and obligations under a contract from one party to another.

assignor. The person who transfers his rights and obligations under a contract to another person. The assignor remains liable to perform the contract if the assignee does not.

authority. The power that a principal gives to an agent to agree to a contract on the principal's behalf.

bailee.   The person who receives property that is temporarily given from one party to another.

bailment. The temporary relinquishment of property from one party to another.

bailor. The party who temporarily gives up personal property to another with the intention of having it returned to him.

beneficiary. A person who the parties intend to benefit from a contract. This might be a named beneficiary in an insurance policy or a creditor beneficiary in another contract.

bid. A type of offer that is often associated with auctions or construction contracts under which a person solicits this type of offer from a number of people.

bilateral. A type of contract under which the offeror asks for a promise in return for another promise. The offeree accomplishes this by accepting the offer made by the offeror. Each party's promise supplies consideration for the contract.

Black Letter law. A well established law and may be relied upon by the parties.

boilerplate. Commonly used language in a contact. Often, it is language that is part of a preprinted form retained by an attorney.

breach. The failure of a party to perform her obligations under the contract.

bulk sale. The sale of a large percentage of one's inventory. The buyer and seller must give notice to the creditors of this acquisition.

buyer. One who makes a purchase.

capacity. One's legal ability to enter a contract. An adult over the age of 18 is presumed to have legal capacity and be capable of understanding the contract and its essential terms.

cause of action. Circumstances that allow a party to obtain relief from a court. This is normally achieved by bringing a suit in court.

closing date. The date at which the parties complete the details relating to the purchase and sale of a real estate contract.

common carrier. A person or organization that is paid to transport items from one location to another. A common carrier is treated as a professional bailee and will be responsible if the property is damaged or lost during transit.

common law. The law that is derived from precedents as a result of court decisions.

compensatory damages. The amount of money necessary to place a party injured by a breach in the same position he would have been in if the contract had been completed.

complaint. The initial pleading in a lawsuit that alleges that one has a remedy because of the conduct of the defendant.

condition. An event that will affect the parties' obligations to carry out their obligations under the contract.

consideration. The exchange of values or substantial detriments that is necessary to create a contract.

counteroffer. A response to an offer that attempts to change the terms of the offer. At common law, such an attempt is treated the same as a rejection of the offer and there is no contract. Neither party has obligations or remedies.

covenant not to compete. A clause in a contract that restricts one party's legal right to compete. This restriction must be reasonable in terms of time and geographical area. If it is not, it will be struck down as invalid. Normally, such covenants may be broader if they protect a new owner of a business rather than an employer.

cover. The purchase of substitute goods by the buyer as a result of the breach of the contract by the seller's failure to deliver conforming goods.

damages. The amount of money a person will recover to compensate her for injuries resulting from a breach of contract or other wrongful acts.

defendant. The person or organization against whom a legal action is brought.

delegation. The transfer of one's duties under a contract. The person transferring the duties is the delegator and the person receiving them is the delegatee. When the delegatee performs the duties, the delegator should obtain the benefits and transfer them to the delegatee.

detriment. The giving up of something of value such as a legal right. Incurring a significant detriment will constitute consideration for contractual purposes.

disaffirm. The rejection of one's duties under a contract. This is sometimes asserted by a minor who refuses to perform a contract.

discharge. The release of one's obligations under a contract by the other party.

divisible contract. A contract that is capable of being divided into separate parts.

document of title. A document that is some evidence of ownership of goods. Ownership would include the right to dispose of or sell the goods.

donee. A person to whom a gift is made. Also, a person who the parties intend to be a beneficiary of a contract (donee beneficiary).

duress. Use of force or threatened use of force to compel to do or to prevent a person from doing a particular act.

election of remedies. The requirement that one must choose a particular remedy as opposed to another when bringing a lawsuit.

equitable relief. A remedy that is available in equity. For example, a decree of specific performance (as opposed to money damages) is equitable relief.

estoppel. The legal principle that states that a person must keep a promise if the other party relied on the promise to his detriment.

exculpatory clause. A clause that attempts to exclude other parties from recovering from one's own negligent conduct. Such clauses are usually declared void as being against public policy.

executed contract. A contract that has been fully completed.

executory contract. A contract that has not been fully completed.

express contract. A contract in which the terms are explicitly defined by the parties.

express warranty. An explicit guarantee given by the seller to the buyer.

fiduciary relationship. A relationship in which one party owes the highest duty of loyalty to another. A trustee, a guardian of children, and an executor are considered fiduciaries.

firm offer. A written offer given by a merchant to an offeree that states that it will be held open for a specific period of time.

fraud. The deliberate or reckless misrepresentation about a material fact from one party to another with the intention of deceiving the other party.

gift. The transfer of property from one party to another without the exchange of consideration. The person making the gift is the donor and the person receiving the gift is the donee.

goods. Under the Uniform Commercial Code, these are tangible, movable items that are normally sold in the marketplace.

implied contract. A contract that must be inferred from the conduct of the parties rather than from an explicit agreement.

implied warranty. A warranty that is not given expressly by the parties, but is implied as a matter of law. The warranty of merchantability associated with the sale of goods is an implied warranty.

impracticability. An excuse for not performing a contract under the Uniform Commercial Code. It is caused by external circumstances that were unforeseen by the parties and make performance commercially unreasonable.

incidental beneficiary. A person who would benefit from a contract, but may not enforce it because the parties did not intend to allow him to do so.

idemnify. To compensate someone for a loss.

injunction. A court order that compels a person to stop performing certain acts. It is often issued to prevent a person from violating a personal service contract.

installment. A partial payment of a total amount due.

installment contract. A contract that requires delivery of goods in separate lots.

insurable interest. An economic interest in property or a life such that one would suffer a loss if either the property or life was harmed or destroyed.

irrevocable. Not capable of being canceled by the party who made the instrument.

irrevocable offer. Under the Uniform Commercial Code, a merchant may create an irrevocable offer for up to three months by placing it into writing. The offer will be irrevocable by the offeror even if the offeree provided no consideration.

lease. An agreement between the owner of property (the landlord) and the person who will take possession of it for a period of time (the tenant). The person leasing the property is called the lessor and the tenant is called the lessee.

legal remedy. A remedy available for a breach of contract or tort through the law.

letter of credit. An instrument issued by a bank that states that it will pay the bills of its customers. It is a way of substituting the bank's credit for its customer's. A letter of credit is particularly useful in international transactions as a way of protecting the seller of goods.

limited warranty. A guarantee (warranty) limited in time or with respect to specific defects.

liquidated damages. Amounts of money agreed upon by the parties in the event of a breach of their contract. If the amounts are reasonable, they will be upheld by the courts. If not, they will be struck down as an improper penalty.

mailbox rule. The legal principle that an acceptance of an offer is effective when it is mailed (dispatched). This means that the contract will be effective from the moment that the acceptance is dispatched.

merchant. A person who regularly deals in goods of that kind. The law requires greater duties of a merchant than of a casual seller, to include a duty that the goods sold be fit for normal use (warranty of merchantability).

minor. Someone who has not yet reached the age necessary to contract (age 18). A minor may disaffirm the contract before reaching 18 and for a reasonable time thereafter.

misrepresentation. A statement that is untrue about a material fact. The statement may have been deliberate or innocent.

mistake. An error about a particular fact. A mistake by both parties to a contract (bilateral mistake) will allow either party to rescind the contract. A one-party (unilateral) mistake will allow the party who made the mistake to rescind the contract if the other party knew or should have known of the mistake.

mitigation of damages. The legal principle that a person injured by a breach of contract has the legal duty to take reasonable steps to reduce the amount of loss to as little as possible.

motion. A request to the court.

mutual consent. The meeting of the minds of the parties to a contract.

mutual (bilateral) mistake. A condition that occurs when both parties to the contract make the same mistake.

necessities. Those items that are reasonably necessary for a minor to live. Contracts for necessities will be binding on a minor.

negligence. The failure to act as a reasonable person would act under the circumstances. The concept of negligence also implies that one has a duty to the other person or people involved.

no arrival, no sale. Means that if the goods do not arrive at their destination, there has been no sale and the purchaser does not owe the purchase price to the seller.

nominal damages. Very small amounts of money awarded to someone who is injured by a breach of contract. Nominal damages are awarded when the actual injury to the party is small.

novation. The substitution of another person for one of the original parties to the contract. The new party will take over the duties and rights of the original party to the contract and that party will be released from her obligations.

obligor. The person who owes an obligation. A person who makes a promise.

offer. An invitation to make a contract by asking the other party to accept the offer.

offeree. A person to whom an offer is made.

offeror. A person who makes an offer.

option contract. An offer that the offeror agrees to keep open for a period of time.

parol evidence rule. A rule of evidence that states that oral evidence will not be admitted to contradict the written terms of a contract.

performance. The completion of the terms of a contract.

plain meaning. The legal principle that language in a contract will be given its usual or common meaning.

plaintiff. A person who brings a lawsuit.

pleadings. Formal statements in court that set forth each party's side of the case.

precedent. A ruling of court (especially a higher court) relating to a specific legal case that will serve as a guide to future courts on law suits relating to similar facts.

principal. A person who hires an agent to do work on her behalf. The agent may be given broad or narrow authority.

promisee. A person to whom a promise is made.

promisor. A person who makes a promise.

promissory estoppel. The legal doctrine that one must complete a promise if one knew that the promisee would rely on the promise to her substantial detriment.

puffing. The exaggeration about a fact or situation by a salesperson. It is not regarded as fraud because it represents an opinion.

punitive damages. Money damages that will be awarded in order to punish a defendant who has committed an action that is considered wrongful.

quasi contract. A contract that the court will impose on a party in order to prevent that person's unjust enrichment at the expense of another person.

ratification. The act of giving approval to a prior act. The act could be a contract agreed to during one's minority or the act of another person.

reformation. A court order that changes the terms of the contract. It will be issued if a party can prove that the contract's terms do not reflect the true intention of the parties.

rejection. Words or actions that indicate that a person does not accept an offer.

release. A discharge of a claim or obligation by one of the parties.

rescission. The act of canceling a contract.

restitution. The legal remedy of restoring the parties to the position they were in before a contract or wrongful act.

revocable. Capable of being withdrawn or nullified.

revocation. The act of canceling or nullifying.

sale. The act of transferring property to another in exchange for payment.

satisfaction. The discharge of an obligation or debt. The completion of one's obligation under a contract.

seller. A person who transfers.

specific performance. A court order that compels a person to perform a specific act. Court decrees of specific performance will be granted in cases involving the sale of real estate and items that are unique.

statutes of frauds. Laws that have been enacted in every state that require certain types of contracts to be evidenced by a writing. They are designed to help reduce the possibility of fraud.

statutes of limitations. Statutes that require that a claim relating to a breach of contract or a tortious act must be brought within a certain period of time.

strict liability. Liability that the law will impose regardless of whether there was fault or negligence.

substantial performance. Performance of a contract, while not complete, was done in good faith and with minor deviations.

surety. A person or organization who guarantees the debt of another. The surety is primarily liable for the debt.

temporary restraining orders (TROs). Temporary injunctive relief that is granted by a court in order to prevent immediate harm.

term of art. Technical words or terms that have a specific meaning in a profession or trade.

third-party beneficiary. A person who the parties intended would benefit from a contract.

title. Evidence of ownership of property. A document that evidences ownership.

tort. A wrongful act that causes damage to a person or to one's property.

treble damages. Three times the actual damages. Treble damages are often imposed in cases involving fraud or other wrongful conduct.

unconditional. Without any conditions. Absolute or without regard to other events.

unconscionable. With respect to contracts, one whose terms are so unfair that they would shock the conscience of the court. Often, an unconscionable contract results from grossly unequal bargaining positions.

undue influence. The improper use of one's position of power to obtain benefits for oneself.

Uniform Commercial Code. Laws that govern contracts for the sale of tangible, movable items (goods). Other articles in the Code govern the sale of securities, secured transactions, and other contractual relationships.

unilateral. One-sided or relating to one party.

unilateral contract. A contract that is created when one party performs the act requested by the other party in consideration for the completion of a promise.

unilateral mistake. An error by one of the parties to the contract.

unjust enrichment. The legal doctrine that one may not retain assets that one has wrongfully obtained at the expense of another.

unliquidated claim. A claim whose existence and amount are not agreed upon by the parties.

usage of trade. Any practice or course of dealing that is commonly accepted in the trade, industry, or profession.

usury. The charging of interest payments at amounts above the interest rate allowed by state law.

valid. Effective in law.

value. Something of worth.

venue. The location at which a trial is held.

void. Without any legal effect.

voidable. Capable of being rendered void. Subject to being disaffirmed.

waiver. The relinquishment of a right or claim.

warranty. A guarantee regarding a fact given by one party to another.

warranty of merchantability. Every merchant warrants that the goods sold will be fit for the purposes sold, and for which they are normally used.

warranty of title. Sellers guarantee that they have good title (ownership) of the items sold. They will be held responsible if there are problems with the title and the buyer must defend it.

will. The document of a person that disposes of property owned at his death.

Index